Light ON THE PATH

Light on the Path

A Christian Perspective on College Success

Second Edition

John A. Beck

Marmy A. Clason

THOMSON

™

WADSWORTH

Australia · Brazil · Canada · Mexico · Singapore · Spain · United Kingdom · United States

Light on the Path

A Christian Perspective on College Success

Second Edition

Beck · Clason

Publisher: Lyn Uhl
Acquisitions Editor: Annie Todd
Development Editor: Maggie Barbieri
Editorial Assistant: Dan DeBonis
Associate Technology Project Manager: Marla Nasser
Managing Marketing Manager: Mandee Eckersley
Marketing Manager: Kirsten Stoller
Marketing Assistant: Kate Remsberg
Associate Content Project Manager: Jessica Rasile
Manufacturing Manager: Marcia Locke
Senior Art Director: Cate Rickard Barr
Production Service/Compositor: Lachina Publishing Services, Inc.
Cover Designer: Maria Ilardi
Cover Image: © Martin Ruegner/Getty Images
Cover/Text Printer: Edwards Brothers

Library of Congress Catalog Card Number: 2007931350

Thomson Higher Education
25 Thomson Place
Boston, MA 02210-1202
USA

For more information about our products, contact us at: **Thomson Learning Academic Resource Center 1-800-423-0563**

For permission to use material from this text or product, submit a request online at **http:/www.thomsonrights.com**

Any additional questions about permissions can be submitted by e-mail to **thomsonrights@thomson.com**

ISBN-13: 978-1-4130-3368-7
ISBN-10: 1-4130-3368-7

Dedicated to the success of Aaron, Peter, Jonathan,
Jared, Jacob, and Hannah.

Dedicated to the happiness of Bernie, Barb, Tom, Steve, Annette, Jim,
and Sue, who know that endurance is the basis of success.

Surely goodness and love will follow me all the days of my life,
And I will dwell in the house of the LORD forever.

(Psalm 23:6)

Table of Contents

5 Pursuing Careful Thought 65

9 Saying It Just Right: Writing and Speaking Successfully

Preface

Your word is a lamp to my feet and a light for my path.

Psalm 119:105

College students who are starting down the pathway of college life get well-meaning advice from a variety of people, including family members, friends, and campus professionals. This textbook presumes that these students will also benefit from the advice, direction, and encouragement offered in God's Word. This book's authors are persuaded by the Apostle Paul's declaration: "For everything that was written in the past was written to teach us, so that through endurance and the encouragement of the Scriptures we might have hope." (Rom 15:4) The Bible portrays itself as a light that can dispel the shadows of confusion and the darkness of doubt falling on the path of life. The authors take that claim seriously, affirming with the words of the inspired poet, "Your word is a lamp to my feet and a light for my path." (Ps 119:105) Consequently, this first-year orientation textbook proposes to add the Bible's beacon of light to the traditional direction and encouragement offered to first-year college students.

We know that the new students arriving on a Christian campus come in all shapes and sizes. Some students have just graduated from high school; others are returning to college after a time in the work world. Some students have family members who had previously attended college; others are the first in their family to go. Some students who attend a Christian school are Christians; others are not. No matter in what category you find yourself, you will face a variety of challenges as you enter college. Those challenges can threaten both your sense of well-being and your ability to be successful. That is why we believe that students who are making this transition deserve spiritual, emotional, and intellectual support from the institution as they make the transition. And we believe that such support and encouragement can be delivered most effectively within a semester-long orientation course. This book is designed to function in just such a class.

Of course, it is possible to orient new students to college life in such a class without using the Bible. Most first-year orientation textbooks propose to do just that. But from the perspective of many Christian schools, the absence of the Bible's voice comes with a steep price. First of all, it means that the contribution of the Bible on traditional first-year topics such as time management, motivation, and stress management is unclaimed. Consider the story of Mary and Martha. When these women display different priorities in their time management plans, Jesus speaks about a plan of action designed to establish priorities and reduce stress (Luke 10:38–42). Within the pages of this book, those contributions of the Bible to first-year success will be brought to the reader.

Second, the secular textbook also leaves topics important to the Christian school unaddressed. How does the Bible fit into the life of the well-educated person? How does the voice of the Bible shape the conversations we have in history classes, science classes, and art classes? What do we do when the voice of the Bible and the voice of science stand in apparent conflict? In contrast to other textbooks, this one honors those questions and others like them, exploring ways in which the Bible contributes to higher education.

Third, because of differing world views, the presentation of certain topics in the secular textbook may conflict with the ethical and moral position of the school. For example, the approach to alcohol, sexuality, and relationships advocated in other textbooks may violate the school's code of ethical conduct. This book honors the Bible as a source of moral planning.

And finally, many first-year textbooks give very little attention to the spiritual development that the Christian college or university sees as critical to the development of its students. By contrast, this book encourages the use of Bible reading, spiritual reflection, prayer, and worship as part of the process that leads to greater happiness and success during college.

Although Christian colleges and universities can use a secular textbook for their first-year orientation courses, it is more desirable to have a book in greater harmony with the culture of the school. That is why we present a first-year orientation textbook that addresses the unique needs of evangelical Christian schools of higher learning. Each chapter offers the following features: the Bible's contribution to college success, review questions, meaningful exercises, Web resources, a Spiritual Reflection Journal, and the encouragement to pray. The heart of each chapter presents the attitudes and behaviors that lead to greater success and happiness as a college student. This summary includes not only the material traditionally found in first-year textbooks but also biblical illustrations and references where appropriate. By design, the message of the Bible shines through the pages of this book and onto the path being walked by the reader.

Ideas that are not reviewed and practiced are quickly forgotten. That is why each chapter includes exercises that may be used both in and outside class. These exercises provide opportunities to reflect on the chapter topic and to practice new learning habits that foster success.

Times of change are also times for spiritual growth. Consequently, each chapter also offers opportunities for Bible reading, spiritual reflection, and prayer. In connection with the chapter topic, we encourage the spiritual formation of our readers by offering biblical texts that may be used for personal meditation. That meditation leads to insights that may be kept in the Spiritual Reflection Journal. And because prayer has traditionally been a source of empowerment for Christians, each chapter includes encouragement to pray during the college week. The close of each chapter contains a suggested prayer list that may be used as a starting point.

Because Christian schools are rooted in various denominations and belief systems, this book takes care not to preach from just one pulpit. We wish to respect the fact that the schools wishing to adopt such a textbook espouse a variety of beliefs that use the Bible as their foundation. Given that reality, this book takes a more biblical than doctrinal approach. The authors have identified biblical texts that they believe contribute to the topic of each chapter. Those texts are presented with a minimum of interpretive suggestion so that they can be interpreted within the classroom.

New to the Second Edition:

- Recognizing the important insights that successful upper-class students bring to the first-year classroom, we have included their words in a feature called Student Voice.
- The world view discussion in Chapter Two has been revised and expanded.
- The learning style discussion in Chapter Four has been revised and expanded.
- Chapter Nine has been revised and expanded to better address the use of the Internet and electronic databases for college research.
- Each chapter now contains more Web resource suggestions.
- Each chapter closes with a set of review questions.

And the entire book has been edited to improve the visual appearance of each page.

Our Gratitude and Thanks . . .

First and foremost, we thank the students who have used this book and the students who will use it in the future. In the end, we are convinced that happiness and success are very attainable for the students reading this book. We know that each of you, no matter what your background, will be able to design a personal success plan from the pages ahead that includes direction and encouragement offered in the Bible. We will pray for you and look forward to hearing of the ways that the Lord has blessed you during this time of transition.

Second, we are grateful for the thoughtful feedback from our reviewers of the first and second editions. This manuscript has passed through the hands of many reviewers whose comments and suggestions have clearly improved the final product. We wish to thank the following individuals for their meaningful contributions.

Reviewers of the First Edition:

Rosalind Alderman, St. Mary's College
Maria Avalos, Texas Lutheran University
Leslie Bailey, St. Martin's College
Jeff Gundy, Bluffton College

Janice Heerspink, Calvin College
Tonya Holman, Greenville College
Amy Janzen, Oklahoma Christian University
Pamela Johnston, Texas Lutheran University
David Marley, Vanguard University
Charles W. Mattis, Abilene Christian University
Brian McKinney, Quachita Baptist University
Barbara N. Sherman, Liberty University
Mary Todd, Concordia University
John Yeats, Messiah College

Reviewers of the Second Edition:

Charles Bethel, Appalachian Bible College
Barbara Howard, Central Bible College
Rebecca Kuhn, Cedarville University
Charles W. Mattis, Abilene Christian University
Barbara N. Sherman, Liberty University
Mike Tenneson, Evangel University

And finally, we wish to thank the students who shared with us some invaluable lessons and insights in the new Student Voice feature. We also wish to thank the faculty from each of these schools for helping us find such insightful individuals.

Chapter 1: Hannah Duncan, Trinity College
Chapter 2: Emily Smith, Oklahoma Christian University
Chapter 3: Samuel Cocar, Trinity College
Chapter 4: Hilary Hurst, Brigham Young University
Chapter 5: Anne Rasschaert, Bethel College
Chapter 6: Maher Saab, Abilene Christian University
Chapter 7: Nyanna Potter, Oklahoma Christian University
Chapter 8: Kevin Sheridan, Cardinal Stritch University
Chapter 9: Jennifer Brantsen, Trinity College
Chapter 10: Eric Mallet, Abilene Christian University
Chapter 11: Alexis Glover, Liberty University
Chapter 12: Lauren Burge, Abilene Christian University
Chapter 13: Peter Beck, Concordia University

Putting Light on the Path 1

Your word is a lamp to my feet and a light for my path.

Psalm 119:105

- **What challenges will I face in my first year of college?**

- **How can God's Word and this course help me this semester?**

- **How can I set effective goals for myself?**

- **What can I do when I am not feeling motivated?**

Congratulations! You are now a college student. Whether you are the first in your family to go to college or the fifth, whether you have just finished high school or are returning to school many years after high school graduation, your letter of acceptance signals a wonderful achievement and distinguishes you as a person of great intellectual promise. Your choice to pursue a more advanced education places you among many of the great leaders in history and among the renowned leaders in the Bible. Moses pursued advanced learning in the Egyptian royal court as a member of the royal family (Acts 7:22). Solomon pursued advanced learning and became a distinguished author of proverbs and songs as well as a famous instructor who taught about the animal and plant kingdoms (1 Kgs 4:29–34). Daniel left home and pursued his education in the royal household of Babylon (Dan 1). Paul left his home and traveled to Jerusalem to seek higher education from the best rabbinic scholars of his day (Acts 22:3). And Jesus himself pursued higher education as he sat among the leading teachers of the Temple in Jerusalem listening carefully to what they had to say and pursuing them with questions (Luke 2:46). The God who created us with the ability to think clearly honors the practice of maturing our minds. For centuries, great leaders such as those named here have done just that by stepping through the doorway of higher education that lies immediately ahead of you.

Advantages of a College Education

You are not alone in your quest. According to the National Center for Education Statistics, more and more hopeful first-year students are stepping onto college campuses each year. A little more than a century ago, only about 2 percent of Americans continued on after high school to earn a college degree. Today more than 65 percent of high school graduates are accepted as first-year students. So what is the attraction? Your walk across the stage to receive your college diploma will create advantages for you in a variety of ways. Compared to those who have not earned a college degree, college graduates know themselves better, have a stronger sense of well-being, and have the ability to compete for careers open only to college graduates. They are more effective thinkers and more confident about themselves. College graduates have more mobility in their careers, have the potential to earn up to a million dollars more in income during their lives, and are uniquely poised to make meaningful changes that will positively shape their society and the church in which they become leaders.

Challenges for First-Year Students

To acquire all of the benefits of being a college graduate, you must first successfully negotiate the transition between your former life and your college life. No two first-year students will have exactly the same experience. But one thing is for sure: your life this year will be different from your life last year.

That kind of change can be exciting, but it will also introduce challenges into your life. If you were in high school last year, you will find that college is a very different experience. Here you will enjoy more freedom and more free time to manage. College classes meet less frequently, but are more difficult. In those classes, you will complete more reading and produce more writing than you did in your high school classes. And while every college class will cover more material, you will be tested less frequently. This means each exam will count more toward the final grade and measure your ability with significantly more information than a high school exam.

If you are returning to college after years in the workplace, you will also experience changes. You may sense a loss of freedom as college claims time that you had otherwise dedicated to family or recreation. As you look around the classroom at the younger faces that surround you, you may feel anxiety about returning to a school setting after years away from textbooks and term papers. And time away from work may create financial stresses that weigh on you and those who live in your home.

Everyone coming to college will be working through the process of making new friends and editing old relationships. All that change can precipitate the dark feelings of displacement anxiety. Your appetite may be off, your sleep patterns unsatisfying, and your stress levels off the chart. It is no wonder that as many as 40 percent of those who begin college as a first-year student never walk across the stage to receive their college diploma. Success is simply not something that should be taken for granted.

Hannah Duncan

Major: English/Communication
Hometown: Cooperstown, North Dakota
School: Trinity College

When I decided to attend a college that was 750 miles from home, I was as nervous about that as I was uncertain. It was a bit like venturing on a safari with a trusted guide; I had no idea where I was going, but I knew God held a map. At first, suburban life felt claustrophobic compared to my small home-town. Yet at the same time I was lonely and struggling with the awkwardness of new relationships. My faith was pivotal in my first uncomfortable week at college because I knew I could always depend on Jesus, who guides me in both North Dakota and suburban Chicago.

Suggestions for Adult Students

If high school graduation is a very distant memory for you, you may feel overwhelmed by your return to school life. While you may feel disadvantaged by your time away from classes, books, and term papers, you have gained valuable experience during that time that will help you negotiate the waters ahead. Consider implementing the following suggestions offered by older college students who found happiness and success in their return to school.

Maintain a strong relationship with your family.

Become involved in campus activities beyond the classroom.

Ask for help when you need it.

See your life experience as a real advantage you have over younger students.

Be ready to give up some activities and free time you had enjoyed.

Plan your finances carefully.

You Can Do It!

But here is the good news. You can do it! You can do it if you take this transition in your life seriously and develop a plan that will lead to success. This book is designed to help you do just that. It is different from most other college success books because it takes into account the advice and encouragement offered in God's Word. You undoubtedly have received well-meaning advice from family and friends that is a product of their experience. Here the authors will provide you with advice and encouragement developed over years of working with first-year students while adding insights they have gained directly from the Bible. As Moses, Solomon, Daniel, Paul, and Jesus pursued higher learning in their own contexts, they did so with an awareness that God's Word can make a critical contribution to that learning process. That is why this book has the title *Light on the Path*. It reflects the view of the inspired poet who wrote, "Your word is a lamp to my feet and a light for my path." (Ps 119:105)

There Is Help in This Book

The illumination this book provides will take place in a variety of areas that contribute to the success and happiness of your first year in college. Here are some of the topics discussed in the chapters ahead. It has been argued that higher education and belief in the Bible are incompatible. In Chapter Two, we will assert that just the opposite is the case. Not only will the Christian faith support you in your transition to college life, it will also enhance your understanding of the world in which you live. Chapter Three will discuss the critical issue of time management. Time is a great gift from God, and no skill as a college student may be as critical to your success as the ability to manage your time efficiently. The authors believe that everyone who reads this book is a unique creation of God and that everyone will have his or her own distinctive ways of learning. Chapter Four invites you to explore your personal learning style and discover ways to become a more effective learner by taking advantage of the unique person you are. While your former education focused on facts and data, your new learning experience will focus more on developing effective thinking. Chapter Five will help you define effective thinking and discuss ways to use your college experience in order to develop yourself as an effective thinker. Subsequent chapters will address a wide variety of fundamental study skills that you will use every semester: taking notes, reading textbooks, taking exams, writing college papers, and giving presentations. This textbook will help you evaluate the current condition of your study skills and help you discover ways to improve them.

Your success as a college student is more than just intellectual development and study skills. It also involves making difficult decisions about many things, including your relationships and your health. Chapters Ten through Twelve make a point of pursuing your habits in these critical arenas of life. The final chapter will help you learn more about the vocation you have chosen and help you think about and even reconsider your choice of major. Believe it or not, you can be doing things right now that will help you acquire an entry-level position in your field or acceptance into your chosen graduate school.

There Is Help in God's Word

In each of the areas discussed in this book, your success as a college student will be enhanced through the advice and direction that God offers you in his Word. We will challenge you to reflect on that divine advice while we challenge you to grow in your relationship with the Lord. Every chapter will invite you to read the Bible and reflect on its message in a spiritual reflection journal. We will also encourage you to open your heart to the Lord in prayer, starting with the prayer suggestion lists that accompany each chapter.

Because we do not know the exact plans that God has for you in your life, we cannot promise that you will be successful in your current quest. But we can assure you that by listening carefully to the advice offered in this book and through the Bible, you will come to a place of greater peace and happiness with your life. "For everything that was written in the past was written to teach us, so that through endurance and the encouragement of the Scriptures we might have hope." (Rom 15:4)

A Word of Encouragement

There will be days ahead when you feel as if you will not make it. Take heart; the first days of your college life will be different from those that lie ahead. As you grow more accustomed to your new environment and routine, things will naturally get better. There was a time in David's life when he was feeling some of the anxiety and uncertainty you are feeling right now. Samuel, the prophet, had anointed him as the new king of Israel and the Lord had given him a great victory over the giant Goliath. But following those momentous events, he was driven from the royal court and pursued by King Saul, who was dead set on ending David's life. At just this time of uncertainty, the author of 1 Samuel has this to say about David: "In everything he did he had great success, because the LORD was with him." (1 Sam 18:14) Read that passage again, write it down, and put it in a place where you will see it regularly for the next week. God's Word reveals a reality that David was not feeling at that moment in time. Realize that God is present with you at this very moment, ready to support your success as you take the next steps in your life.

Plan to Succeed

As comforting as the presence of God is in our lives, the Bible does not advocate complacency. Success is no accident and should not be left to chance. The old axiom is true: failing to plan can amount to planning to fail. While it is important to honor the power and will of God in our lives, it is also prudent to consider the Parable of the Talents (Matt 25:14–30). God expects us to think ahead and to use the abilities he has given us wisely. While we do not control everything that will happen in our lives, it is critical to take ownership of our future to the degree that this is possible. In regard to your success as a first-year college student, that means developing a success plan for yourself. This plan should address the four areas that contribute the most to your success: spiritual health, academic habits, physical health, and the well-being of your relationships.

Spiritual Health

We have placed spiritual health first because we believe that it has the most to offer you during this time of transition. Give careful attention to the time you set aside for reading your Bible and speaking to God in prayer. Successful people in the Bible are closely associated with both of those habits. As Joshua was beginning a new chapter in his life as the leader of Israel, God gave him this invitation: "Do not let this Book of the Law depart from your mouth; meditate on it day and night, so that you may be careful to do everything written in it. Then you will be prosperous and successful." (Josh 1:8) The Bible holds up the young man Samuel as a model who humbly called out to the Lord, "Speak, for your servant is listening." (1 Sam 3:10) And it celebrates the passion of the Berean Christians: "Now the Bereans were of more noble character than the Thessalonians, for they received the message with great eagerness and examined the Scriptures every day to see if what Paul said was true." (Acts 17:11) Through the reading of your Bible, the Lord wants you to enjoy both a more successful time on this earth and a certain eternity. "These are written that you may believe that Jesus is the Christ, the Son of God, and that by believing you may have life in his name." (John 20:31)

Your spiritual well-being will be enhanced not only by your time spent with God's Word but also by your time spent in prayer. Successful living is closely linked to speaking with God as well as listening to him. The unnamed servant of Abraham was sent to find a wife for Isaac. Read Genesis 24 and see how closely the success of his important mission was linked to prayer. It is living testimony to the fact that a believer's prayer is powerful and effective (James 5:16). And it is a living example of the invitation Jesus extends: "Ask and it will be given to you; seek and you will find; knock and the door will be opened to you." (Matt 7:7) Your day as a college student will be filled with more demands on your time than you can imagine. Time spent in reading your Bible and time spent in prayer can easily take a backseat to the pressing demands of your schedule. Now is the time to design a weekly habit that sets aside time for both.

Academic Habits

Your success plan also needs to take stock of your academic habits. Certainly you have been successful in your previous academic work or you would not be reading this book as a new college student. But many new students make a mistake in two fundamental areas: they fail to go to class and they fail to complete their assignments. The power of those two habits is much greater than their simple appearance suggests. Go to class and do your assignments. Once you have committed yourself to these two fundamentals of academic growth, strive to keep an open mind as you engage old topics in new ways. If you are accustomed to thinking of school as the place where you are merely given the answers to the questions someone else has asked, be ready to find that college is more about designing your own questions and entertaining the value of various answers. Do not be frightened by ambiguity. Let the tension of the questions drive you to think beyond the old borders that blocked broader thinking so that you can see and explore life in new and refreshing ways. And on the way, be prepared to sharpen your reading, writing, time management, and exam preparation skills. Most college students find that their old study habits and attitudes will not yield the same results they did in high school. Be ready to edit not only how you think but how you work as well.

Physical Health

Your plan for success will also take into account the way in which you manage your physical health. Although a college education transforms your mind, your mind cannot live successfully or work effectively in a body that is in disrepair. Check your eating habits, your sleeping habits, and your exercise habits to see if you are providing a good home for your mind. Where you find a need for improvement, let your first-year success plan reflect the changes necessary to keep you thriving physically.

Relationships

Finally, let your success plan take into account the various levels of relationships that surround you. In the story of creation, God announced that it was not good for Adam to be alone (Gen 2:18). The same is true for you. In coming to college, you may have placed some distance between yourself and people who have been very important to you. It will be critical for you to find new relationships on campus with students in your residence hall, on your athletic team, or in the campus organizations you join. You will also have to make decisions about your former relationships. Which relationships will you maintain and which will receive a diminishing amount of your time and attention? How will you maintain the relationships you wish to keep while seeing those people less frequently?

   As you can see, you have plenty to do. Because success is no accident, today is an excellent day for you to make goals related to the four areas mentioned here. What can you begin to do today that will enhance your spiritual health, your academic health, your physical health, and the well-being of your relationships?

Effective Goal Setting

If you believe that you will become a more successful student by creating a success plan, then you are ready to think about how to set goals that are effective. Passion and activity are wonderful, but undirected passion and activity may be more harmful than doing nothing at all. In this portion of the chapter, we invite you to think about a series of steps that will help harness your energy and direct it more effectively. That process has four steps: writing intention statements, turning intention statements into goal statements, developing an action plan around each goal statement, and implementing the action plan.

Get Started with Some Daily Goals

If setting goals is new to you, it will be helpful for you to experiment with some daily goals. This will allow you to get a feel for the process as well as some early satisfaction as you accomplish those goals. Identify three things that you will commit to doing every day for the next two weeks. Write them down, post them in a prominent place, and act on them. You will find great satisfaction in accomplishing even basic things such as:

Exercising for twenty minutes each day

Eating at least one serving of fruit and one serving of vegetables each day

Watching only two hours of TV per day

Saying out loud two positive things that happened today

Write Intention Statements

The first step in the process of effective goal setting invites you to think freely about both the long-term dreams and the short-term wishes you hold at the moment. Take a packet of self-sticking notes, turn off the distractions in your life, and free your mind to explore the future. On each slip of paper, begin a sentence with "I intend to . . . ," and then complete the sentence with whatever comes to mind. Express your wishes and passions freely. Note that intention statements can range far and wide across the various dimensions of your life.

Examples of Intention Statements

"I intend to read my Bible."
"I intend to go to every class unless I am ill."
"I intend to get my bike fixed this week."
"I intend to become an accountant."
"I intend to introduce myself to one new person every week this month."

Once you have finished, paste your notes on the desk or wall in front of you. Now play with the positions of the notes. Group them according to topics, rank them in importance, or organize them by level of difficulty. In brainstorming about your intentions, you have made an important step toward success. For the mere act of reflecting and writing down your intentions places you among those who are more likely to accomplish what they desire in life.

Turn Your Intention Statements into Goal Statements

Although writing down your intentions is helpful, they are just the raw materials you will use in creating goal statements. Goals are more than wishes, and this is the time to separate one from the other. This step will force you to identify the intention statements that are most important to you and sharpen your thinking on them. Select several intention statements that you wish to act on and get ready to turn them into goal statements. Well-written goal statements have five characteristics. You can recall them by memorizing the acronym *SMART.*

S stands for SPECIFIC. Transform your intention statement into a goal statement by making it more clear and specific. For example, the intention statement "I intend to read my Bible" becomes more clear and specific when it is reworded this way: *"I will read my Bible every day during my lunch hour."* Be sure to avoid using words such as *try, think, hope,* or *should* when composing your goal statements. They are less powerful and communicate less commitment to your plan.

M stands for MEASURED. When possible, it is helpful to assign measurable values to your intention statement. This allows you to measure your progress toward the goal's achievement more precisely. For example, "I will read *five chapters* of my Bible every day during my lunch hour."

A stands for ACCEPTED. Others may support your intentions, but you are the one who needs to own the goal. Make sure that your goal springs from the very core of your passions and desires. Then announce that passion by changing the statement from the hopeful "I intend to . . ." to the more powerful "I will. . . ." "*I will* read five chapters of my Bible every day during my lunch hour *because I want to hear God speaking to me every day."*

R stands for REALISTIC. Accomplishing a goal typically means changing old habits and attitudes. But the change cannot be so great that it threatens your relationships, your physical well-being, or your mental health. Reach high, but do so in a responsible way. This may mean editing your goal to reflect the realities of your life. Perhaps reading five chapters of your Bible every day during your lunch break is unrealistic. So the goal statement changes to this: "I will read my Bible *for thirty minutes* every day during my lunch hour because I want to hear God speaking to me every day."

T stands for TIMED. Each goal you set can have a built-in time limit. When the time limit expires, you will have the chance to inspect your progress toward accomplishing the goal. At the end of the time period you designate, you can confirm the accomplishment of your goal or consider editing the goal to make accomplishing it more likely in the next period of time you set. "I will read my Bible for thirty minutes every day during my lunch hour *during September* because I want to hear God speaking to me every day."

Develop an Action Plan

Even well-written goals may not be accomplished unless they are part of a carefully designed action plan. An action plan identifies the specific tasks or steps you will take to accomplish the goal. The formation of this plan demands that you take into account challenges that will arise in acting on the goal and ways to defeat those challenges.

For example, consider the goal statement we formulated earlier: "I will read my Bible for thirty minutes every day during my lunch hour during September because I want to hear God speaking to me every day." As you consider this goal, you recall that you had previously made a commitment like this to yourself but had failed to follow through, and you are concerned that your old habits will get in the way. You can meet this challenge in a number of ways. Perhaps you could find an accountability partner with whom you could share this goal. Or you could create a chart for yourself on which you mark the days on which you honor the goal in your daily schedule.

Once you have brainstormed the possible challenges and possible solutions, you are ready to write down your action plan in connection with that goal. It may look something like this.

My Action Plan

Goal: "I will read my Bible for thirty minutes every day during my lunch hour during September because I want to hear God speaking to me every day."

To accomplish this goal I will:

Find an accountability partner with whom to read my Bible

Make a chart for the month of September on which I note the days
I accomplish this goal

Implement the Action Plan

Writing out your goal and associated action plan puts you on the road to accomplishment. All that is left is implementing the plan. Consider posting the goal and action plan in a prominent place, such as on your bedroom door or bathroom mirror, so that you are reminded of it every day.

Remember to remain flexible. Goals are designed to be guides, not brutal taskmasters. There will be days or weeks when circumstances do not permit you to take the steps you had planned to take. That does not mean that your goal is bad or that you are a failure. It just means that life is neither regular nor perfect. A prudent amount of flexibility will help you accomplish your goals more regularly and make the process much more rewarding.

And Then There Is Motivation

Did we just say the magic word? Have your present circumstances left you feeling less than excited about moving forward with your college life? Then it is time to consider motivation. This connects nicely with the notion of setting goals because a necessary, even circular relationship exists between accomplishing goals and motivation. Motivation is the inner drive that moves us to act on the goals we set as well as the catalyst for making goals in the first place.

But what if you do not feel motivated? The first step is to realize that in saying that you are unmotivated, you are not describing the way you were

Criticism and the Motivation Crash

You will definitely experience criticism as a college student. It will come your way in the form of grades on your exams, comments on your papers, and instructors' critiques of answers you give during class discussion. Such criticism is designed to help you become a more effective thinker and communicator, but if you internalize it and feel it as a personal attack, criticism can crash your motivation. Although it is important for you to experience all the constructive criticism offered for your improvement, it is also important that you keep that criticism in its place. A lower grade on an exam is not a sign that you are a bad person who will not succeed in college, but a signal that you need to rethink your approach to exam preparation for that class. The real danger is not in being criticized but in ignoring its value. Let the criticism you experience in college come in, but not in so far that it crashes your motivation.

created but your attitude toward a particular responsibility or task. We have heard students express their lack of motivation for attending classes that meet before 10:00 in the morning, but have seen the same students jump out of bed well before daylight to begin a spring break vacation. Motivation is an attitude toward a specific task or responsibility.

If you are feeling unmotivated about college, determine the source of that attitude. Perhaps you feel put off by the behaviors closely associated with college life: attending class, reading, writing, and speaking. But realize that each of those behaviors has an intimate connection with your future professional life. It begins with responsible attendance; your employer will expect you to show up every day and be on time for work. You are practicing that behavior when you are regular and punctual in your class attendance. College professors will ask you to write and will evaluate your writing skills. Your future career will likely require you to write reports and memos that are both clear and free of grammatical errors. College professors will ask you to read and be ready to evaluate what you have read. In the same way, your future employer will ask you to read and evaluate reports as well as follow written instructions. Listening and speaking are also skills that you will apply in your future vocation, whether it be listening to presentations at meetings or giving oral reports. College gives you the chance to practice and hone these fundamental work skills.

Perhaps your lack of motivation lies elsewhere. Maybe you are feeling unmotivated about attending college in general or are feeling little passion for completing a paper for your composition class—"Why am I doing this anyway?" First of all, honor the question. It is very difficult to pursue a goal, particularly one as challenging as college graduation, without stopping to reflect on what motivates us to achieve that goal. As human beings, we are motivated to engage in a task by a complex set of stimulants.

Still Feeling Unmotivated?

Are you still feeling unmotivated? The following questions address the things that can quickly rob you of your passion for a task. Answer the following questions honestly to learn more about where your motivation challenges may lie.

1. Can you focus? If you lack motivation or are having trouble completing important tasks, you may be having trouble keeping your focus because of external distractions. For example, noise from your roommates or children may prevent you from attending to your task.

2. Are you able? Completion of a goal assumes that you have the ability to perform certain tasks. If you lack information or the ability to perform the task, it can rob you of your motivation. For example, if you lack the ability to conduct effective library research, you may become very unmotivated to complete a term paper.

3. Are you satisfied? To remain motivated for a task you must expect to feel satisfied on its completion. For example, you are unlikely to feel motivated to complete a major course of study if it is your parents, and not you, who will feel satisfied when you graduate.

Sources of Motivation

Sense of pride
Need for money
Desire for accomplishment
Religious or moral conviction
Desire for power
Need for respect
Fear of failure
Fear of disappointing others
Fear of personal pain
Sense of loyalty
Spirit of adventure
Need for prestige
Need for acceptance

Both of the authors of this book enjoy scuba diving. What motivated us to pursue this form of recreation despite the risks and personal cost? The answer is found in the illustration on the next page. At the center lies the topic and streaming from it lie the factors that motivated us.

Your decision to attend college and your letter of acceptance have started you down an exciting and prosperous path. This class, this book, and your Bible will combine to put light on the path you are walking. They will both encourage you during your transition and direct your steps to greater success. Now is the time to plan for success by setting goals and acting on them. And now is the time to check your motivation, remembering that motivation is an attitude. When you are feeling unmotivated you can explore the cause of that attitude and work to repair it.

Motivated to Scuba Dive

Exercises for **Success**

Review Questions

1. How does the following statement apply to you as a new college student? "Success is no accident."

2. Compare and contrast the nature and purpose of intention statements and goal statements.

3. List three things you can do if you are feeling a lack of motivation as a college student.

First-Year Student Fears

Below you will find some of the most common concerns expressed by students entering college and space to add concerns of your own that are not listed. Place a check next to all of those that apply to you at this moment, adding to the list as necessary. Then identify the five fears that are the strongest within you.

_____ I will not have enough money to do all the things I want to do.

_____ I will not be able to manage my time for study, sleep, and so on.

_____ I will have difficulty making new friends.

_____ I will have trouble relating to my parents.

_____ I will get depressed and it will affect my grades.

_____ I will get poor grades.

_____ I will feel that I do not belong.

_____ I will disappoint my parents and family with the grades I get.

_____ I will have trouble getting along with my roommate.

_____ I will get lost on campus.

_____ I will have difficulty finding a major that I really like.

_____ I will sleep when I should be in class or doing homework.

_____ I will become homesick.

_____ I will not be able to develop proper study habits.

_____ I will have trouble understanding the professors.

_____ I will be viewed by others as an inferior person.

_____ I will cheat in class to get good grades.

_____ I will have to work too much.

_____ I will not find anyone who will help me here.

_____ I will have to interrupt my college education to participate in a military deployment.

_____

_____

_____

When you have completed the exercise on your own, compare your results with those of your roommates and classmates. You may be surprised to learn that the feelings of other first-year students are very similar to your own.

Success and Survival Plan

If you went hiking in the Rocky Mountains during the late fall and became lost, survival experts note that your ability to survive would depend on your willingness and ability to complete three basic tasks: stay hydrated, stay warm, and stay put. More than a few hapless hikers have put themselves at great risk by not following these basic rules. This illustration makes it clear that survival and success is an intentional process.

The same could be said of your first year in college. Now is the time to plan a strategy that will allow for success and survival in the four areas discussed in the chapter. Take out a blank sheet of paper and divide it into four areas labeled "Spiritual Strategy," "Academic Strategy," "Health Strategy," and "Relationship Strategy." Set aside some quiet time and brainstorm what you would like to do in each of these four areas during the next two months to improve your chances for success. After you have collected five or more ideas in each area of the page, pick two items from each category that you will try for the next two months. This is the beginning of your success and survival plan.

Goal Setting and Implementation

This chapter has described a method for setting and implementing effective goals. Now it is time for you to give the method a trial run.

Step One Write down your intention statements. Take a packet of self-sticking notes and complete the sentence "I intend to . . ." Write down as many intentions as you can in ten minutes. Then spend another fifteen minutes editing and organizing those notes on the desk or wall in front of you.

Step Two Turn your intentions into goal statements. Intention statements become goal statements when you change the words "I intend to" to "I will." Take three of the intention statements and edit them according to the SMART criteria discussed earlier in this chapter.

Step Three Develop an action plan. On a blank sheet of paper, write each edited goal statement and brainstorm all the challenges that may stand in the way of your accomplishing that goal. Then identify resources and strategies you can put into play in order to accomplish the goal noted on the top of the page. Your time in this part of the process may lead you to edit the goal slightly. Write the edited goal at the top of another piece of blank paper. Then in two or three sentences describe the action plan you will follow in completing the stated goal.

Implement Your Action Plan You will not know if you like it until you have tried it. Select at least one of the goals and its associated action plan you developed and pursue the goal for the time you have designated. In time, you may elect to edit the process as described earlier. Until then, stick with this outline and you will find that you are charting a course toward successful accomplishment of those things that are important to you.

Picture Your Motivation

Select one of the goals on which you worked earlier and think carefully about what would motivate you to complete it. Consult the list of possible motivating factors listed earlier in the chapter, but do not hesitate to add to that list in your quest to find what will motivate you to pursue your goal. Take a piece of blank paper and draw an oval in the middle of the page. Place the goal in the oval and then surround that shape with arrows that point to the factors that will motivate you to act.

SPIRITUAL REFLECTION JOURNAL

You are experiencing a significant amount of change in your life, and with that change comes worry. Take a few moments now to write about the things that concern you most deeply as you make this new beginning. After you have written your concerns down, read Psalm 46 and Matthew 6:25–34. Describe the ways in which these two Bible passages speak to your worries and concerns.

Time in Prayer

In your personal time in prayer or in connection with others in your class, take time to pray for the following people and needs:

- For family members back home who are supporting you

- For members of your class who are feeling homesick

- For the instructors of your classes

- For your ability to design an effective success strategy

- For a good night's rest

On the Web

The Internet can be a helpful resource as you look for ideas to make yourself a happier and more successful student. Visit the College Success page offered by Thomson Wadsworth for Web links that will help you grow further on this topic. Go to http://www.success .wadsworth.com/ and click on Resource Web Links.

In particular, we recommend the following:

http://www.sc.edu/fye/

http://www.topachievement.com/articles.html

http://www.mygoals.com/content/college-goals .html

http://www.goal-setting-college.com/

http://webhome.idirect.com/~readon/procrast.html

http://www.alma.edu/community/student_life/the_ center/academic/reading/procrastination/

http://www.edinboro.edu/cwis/acaff/suppserv_ archive/tips/CAT5.html

Turning the Light on Higher Education 2

The fear of the LORD is the beginning of knowledge.

Proverbs 1:7

- **What role does college play in our culture?**
- **What makes the Christian college unique?**
- **How can I best design my academic course of study?**
- **How can I most effectively use my academic advisor?**

The first few days and weeks of college life may leave you feeling overwhelmed. So much is new and different that you may ask when things will feel normal again. Two things will move you closer to that goal: more practice and more knowledge. The first time you rode your bike, you did not do it as well as you do it now. The first time you wrote a high school term paper, you did not write as well as you do now. Practice may not make you perfect, but it goes a long way toward improving your skills and your comfort with any given task. The same is true of going to college. Your first semester will be very different from the other semesters because you are doing everything for the first time. There will be your first college test, your first college roommate, and your first time registering for classes. With practice, each of those "firsts" will become easier, even second nature.

Apart from time and practice, there is another way to ease the challenges that attend the first year of college. The more you know about a new experience, the less threatening it will be to you. This chapter sheds light on the unique type of education that is offered on a Christian college campus. We believe that the more you know about higher education, the more comfortable you will be as a college student. Toward that end, this chapter will discuss the general purposes of higher education within American culture. It will describe the philosophical foundations that are used within Christian higher education to determine both what is studied and how your school defines what is true and cherished. This chapter will then help you become acquainted with the general structure of an academic program so that you can better understand the road that lies ahead and be able to answer questions such as the following: What courses should I take next semester? What academic policies can impact those decisions? How can I register for those classes? How can I most effectively use the academic advisor assigned to me?

The Purpose of Higher Education

As you join the ranks of college students this fall, you are entering an institution that has been around for centuries. Over the years, millions of men and women have preceded you, leaving home for college with exactly the same intentions you have. They hoped that the time and money invested in a college education would pay off by leading to a career of their choosing, a career that would both provide a comfortable income and allow them to make a real difference in the world. It is what people did centuries ago to get the best and most influential careers, and they still do so today.

Because people in such careers are expected to know more, to think better, and to communicate effectively, the college experience includes two complementary types of courses whose purpose is to deliver that kind of person to the work world. The future will always build on the past, so students will meet a variety of liberal arts courses that peruse the building blocks of the human experience. Among the liberal arts courses you may take are those addressing history, literature, art, philosophy, math, the social sciences, and the natural sciences. Such classes are further designed to advance each student's general thinking skills and to mature their writing and speaking skills. By contrast, vocational courses are career specific and designed to introduce students to the practical knowledge they need to begin their professional lives. Examples would include courses in accounting, an introduction to nursing class, or a student teaching practicum. Through a combination of both liberal arts and vocational courses, your time in college will prepare you to take your place in the work world.

But one more important purpose lies behind the college experience that is critical to the growth of our society. College students are taught to question and critique what they study, not merely accept what they hear. They will learn historical details, but also learn to question and critique the way history has been recorded and interpreted. They will learn scientific theory, but also learn to question and critique that theory and its application. Through this type of critical thinking, college graduates will step into society not just as participants but as leaders who will edit the status quo. Yes, college will prepare you for a career. But it will also make you a key player in our world, making changes that will enhance both your profession and your society.

World View and Higher Education

As your college experience prepares you to think more effectively and function more efficiently in your chosen career, subtle but critical decisions are made both about what to teach and how to put a value on what is taught. Those judgments will be grounded on what is called a *world view*. An accepted definition of *world view* and even the way it is spelled (*world view* versus *worldview*) are still seeking common ground. But for our purposes, we will define *world view* as the fundamental presuppositions held by individuals or institutions that allow them to interpret and make sense of their world. It is the filter that allows us to determine what we will regard as true and cherished. Although it may not have been obvious to you before, the conscious decision of your school to conduct your education with the Christian world view as its foundation is the most powerful difference between it and other secular colleges and universities. So we will spend a bit of time surveying the world view options that have influenced higher education in general before speaking in greater detail about the world view that lies behind Christian higher education.[1]

Christian Theism

For centuries, Western society and the colleges within those societies shared a common world view. Christian theism dominated the stage. It affirmed without question the existence of God and the authority of the Bible. It affirmed that God had spoken to mortals in the Bible and that the discovery of absolute truth was not only possible but available to the readers of God's Word. People sometimes disagreed about what the Bible said, but they did not question its authority or its contribution to higher education. Thus the study of the Bible had a close and fundamental connection to higher education in this age.

Deism

The seventeenth century witnessed sharp disagreements among Christians as to what the Bible taught. Those discouraged by this infighting and encouraged by the advance of human reason began to shift their world view away from Christian theism towards deism. Deism taught that God created the world and then left the stage, allowing the world to hum along on its own apart from any sort of divine intervention or communication. The world was now viewed as a closed system in which natural causes give birth to natural effects, which in turn become the causes of new effects. God is gone. Because no miracles were allowed, the Bible's divine inspiration was gone and its contribution to society was reduced to that of any other book. Into this authority vacuum, people poured their ability to think and reason. If mortals could just use those reasoning skills well enough, they could logically deduce the fundamental truths that make the world work. In sum, what is most reasonable is considered to be universally true.

Rationalism

By the close of the eighteenth century, the reasoning ability of the human mind appeared to be limitless, promising to provide the key to interpreting all dimensions of life and the key to identifying what we should regard as true and cherished. Thus it was a short step from deism, which put God on the sidelines, to rationalism, which denied his existence altogether. This heightened regard for rational thinking gave birth to the period known as the Enlightenment, which further pushed the frontiers of science while elevating reason above all other paths to truth. In many colleges, the Enlightenment pushed God and the Bible to the intellectual margins. Rationalism became the world view of the intellectual community. Its influence was so powerful that any subsequent attempts to refine world view thinking have had to respond to it.

Romanticism

The coldness of rationalism and its failure to address all dimensions of life effectively gave rise to competing world view theories, including romanticism. The romantics argued that the cold mechanics of reason alone were insufficient to define what is true and cherished, and the frigid rhythm of cause and effect eliminated both the value of mortals and their creative processes. Truth seeking needed to take into account evidence from feelings and intuition. Thus the romantic movement argued that beauty and things that create beauty were just as valuable as the objects and ideas deemed rational. It was feeling, not merely thinking, that makes humans appreciate the wonder that fills their world.

Empiricism and Pragmatism

Another competitor to Enlightenment rationalism was empiricism, which found its footing in Great Britain. John Locke argued that truth is more than an intellectual construct; it is the product of experience achieved through careful experimentation and observation. This view is closely linked to American pragmatism as it grew up in the 1870s. Truth was what we could observe to be true through carefully controlled experimentation and the replication of results in such experimentation. Something was regarded as true and cherished if it was observed to work consistently. Combined, the export of empiricism and pragmatism have shaped and supported the scientific method that remains the basis of scientific inquiry to this day.

Existentialism

During the twentieth century, the horror of two world wars led philosophers to question the hope of finding one universal system that could effectively define what is true and cherished. Although the orderly patterns within our world may tempt us to look for one universal way of defining what is true and cherished, existentialism argues that life is much too complex to be explained by any one operating principle. Thus the existential world view divides truth into truth that is objective and subjective. And it further observes that subjective truth is more valuable for society. This kind of truth is not spelled with a capital *T* nor is it best described in the singular. Rather, many "truths" exist that are defined by the experiences of various thinkers. This personally experienced truth is that which best restores a sense of value and dignity to mortals, a dignity that was stripped away by the cold simplicity of rationalism. As we relate our experiences in truth-seeking to one another, we recapture what it means to be alive.

Postmodernism

The current stop on the search for a viable world view has been dubbed postmodernism. Because this approach to truth seeking is still evolving, an enduring definition is premature. But here is a snapshot of how this world view perceives and pursues truth. Postmodernism eclectically draws from a variety of the previous world view approaches. In doing so, it emphasizes the limitations of truth-seeking by highlighting the imperfection of people, methods, and language. Because all forms of inquiry are conducted by people with biases, all results are compromised by those biases. Because every method of inquiry is marked by its own imperfections, the results will always be compromised by the imperfections of the method. And because language is an imperfect tool for communicating discovery, even our attempts to share what those methods reveal are compromised. Thus the search for a grand truth will never be successful. The seeker is merely part of a truth-seeking game that celebrates the quest more than discovery. In the end, postmodernism champions a quest using a variety of approaches and uncritically honors many different conclusions, even those that appear to formally contradict one another.

The Christian World View and Higher Education

What is the Christian thinker to do in this swirling bath of natural philosophy? Christians may choose from two options: separate themselves completely from natural world views, or integrate biblical teaching with natural world views.

Separate

First, Christian thinkers may attempt to separate themselves completely from the influence of natural philosophy. The church father Tertullian seems to propose this idea as early as the third century AD when he considered the role of Greek philosophy in the life of the church. He said, "What is there in common between Athens and Jerusalem? What is there in common between the academy and the church?"[2] Carried to its ultimate conclusion, this would limit Christian schools to the study of the Bible and make them what one secular school president called them: "gated communities" closed to the new ideas and directions revealed by natural thinking. Although the Enlightenment began the process of driving the contribution of the Bible from the halls of higher education, it would be unwise for the Christian university to follow suit and presume that it is a good idea to drive the benefits of natural thinking from its classrooms.

Integrate

By contrast, it is very possible for Christians to integrate natural philosophy and the product of such thinking into their approach to learning. You may find the thought initially disturbing. But we must acknowledge that the Bible simply does not answer every question that we might ask. The biblical poet acknowledges that fear of the Lord is the *beginning* of knowledge (Prov 1:7), but this same author does not argue that it is the sum total of all knowledge. Thus we are left to explore the world using natural philosophy to discover and appreciate the truth that lies hidden within creation itself. The Bible affirms this integration when it tells us that we may even learn things about God by exploring the world around us. "The heavens declare the glory of God; the skies proclaim the work of his hands." (Ps 19:1)

Christian schools then are not "gated communities," but schools whose libraries are filled with the best thinking of the ages. Natural philosophy permeates the hallways and classrooms of the Christian school. The principles of rationalism are employed every time a thesis is demonstrated in a term paper using the flow of cause and effect. Appropriate use of the scientific method will earn an A on lab reports. Romanticism and existentialism operate in the literature class in which students are asked to report on the beauty and personal meaning they find in a Shakespearean sonnet. And postmodernism reminds us to think critically about all our conclusions given the risks of subjective perception, imperfect methodology, and the limitations of language.

But in the same laboratories and classrooms that honor the voice of rationalism and romanticism, the voice of the Bible is also a welcome visitor and its contribution to higher education is honored. Rather than accepting the premise that reason, experimentation, and personal experience are the only pathways leading to truth, the Christian school acknowledges that revelation from God found in the Bible is also Truth (John 17:17; 2 Tim 3:16–17; 2 Peter 1:21). Although Christian colleges and secular colleges ask and seek to answer the same academic questions, the Christian school uses the Bible as a resource in pursuing answers to those questions. This integration is certainly helpful when addressing questions of a more spiritual nature—for example, What will happen to me after I die? But the Bible is also a critical contributor to other conversations about the human experience: What is the origin of life on this earth? How can I feel better about myself? Where can I find the key to life's meaning? Certainly the various natural world views have a contribution to make in answering such questions, but their answers are not always satisfying. The writer of Ecclesiastes purposely eliminated God from the equation in a quest to find meaning in life. The results of that search are captured in this memorable quote: "Everything was meaningless, a chasing after the wind; nothing was gained under the sun." (Eccl 2:11)

By contrast, the pursuit of truth that includes divine revelation is rewarded with insights and comfort that natural philosophy cannot provide. When Peter came to understand the power of Jesus' message, he acknowledged that Jesus is the sole source of information on certain critical topics, exclaiming, "Lord, to whom shall we go? You have the words of eternal life." (John 6:68) Consequently, the Bible becomes a textbook in the Christian college. It is defined as a source of truth, placed next to the other textbooks on the college student's shelf, and regularly consulted to ascertain its contribution to the matter under investigation.

Resolving the Tension

But what is to be done when the truth claim of natural philosophy conflicts with a truth claim made in the Bible? In this regard, not all Christians have taken the same approach. But most evangelical Christians have validated the Bible as the ultimate source of truth. Its message rather than the observations of natural philosophy are given pride of place. This is based not only on a confidence in the accuracy of God's perspective as it is communicated in God's Word, but also on the imperfections associated with the reasoning ability of mortals. Here the Christian acknowledges a problem with mortal perception that goes well beyond the reservations of postmodernism. The Bible teaches that human beings were created to think perfectly with wills and minds created in the image of God (Gen 1:27). But the fall into sin ruined this gift, and immediately the evidence of impoverished thinking became evident. Adam and Eve "hid" from an all-powerful and all-knowing God (Gen 3:10). Their act of poor thinking is only the first of many recorded in the Bible giving evidence that even those who believe in God have lost the ability to think perfectly. That means that every conclusion that is a product of natural philosophy is subject to error. But through the Holy Spirit, Christians are enabled to read the Bible and access the Truth that God alone can deliver because he lies outside the ruined world in which we live. That is why the poet of Proverbs encourages us with these words: "Trust in the LORD with all your heart and lean not on your own understanding." (Prov 3:5)

Planning Your Academic Program

Successful college students not only understand the larger idea of the Christian university, but also know how to efficiently and effectively plan their academic program. If your high school experience has led you to believe that someone else will pick your classes and register you for the next term, you will need to change your perspective. That responsibility belongs to you. A bit later in this chapter, we will talk about the academic advisor assigned to assist you with program planning and registration. This person can be of great help to you. But in the end, you must know your own academic program better than anyone else. Your time and money will be at risk if this planning is done poorly, so make it your business to know the requirements of your program intimately. Toward that end, we will talk about the outline of your academic program and how you can more effectively plan your course of study. We will talk about how to investigate the requirements of your academic program, design a plan for completing your course work, and give you tips on selecting and using your academic advisor.

I Don't Have a Major!

If you have not decided on a major or have great reservations about the major you have selected, all this talk about knowing your academic program and registering for classes may be somewhat upsetting. Perhaps you have even asked whether you should be in college if you do not know what career you want to pursue. We want to assure you that even if you are undecided, college is the right place to be because here you have a better chance of surveying all the potential career paths that lie before you. Furthermore, the career services office on your campus can help you identify the kinds of work you might like to do and specific careers that are associated with your interests. Nearly half of all college students change their major at least once during their time in college. See yourself as one step ahead of them because you are going to do some career exploration before they know they need it. While you are coming to greater clarity, speak to your advisor about a strategy for registering for classes. You still can move forward with your college plans even if you have not declared a major.

The Catalog

The best place to discover the outline of the academic program on your campus is the college catalog that your school publishes every year, in either paper or electronic format. In either case, it is critical for you to acquire a copy of the catalog published the same year you began to attend, because that edition will govern your relationship with the school. Consider this catalog a binding contract between you and your school. In it, the school promises to give you a degree when you have successfully completed the program described in that catalog. From time to time, the requirements of your major may change. In that case, you typically have the right to either upgrade to the new requirements or stay with the plan they had promised you when you matriculated.

Outline of Your Academic Program

In the academic catalog you will find the outline for your academic program. It may consist of four or more parts that define different categories of classes you will need to complete. A typical college program consists of a set of general-education classes (sometimes called the core classes), courses associated with your major, courses associated with your minor, and courses that are free electives.

The general-education core is the part of higher education still rooted in the liberal arts college tradition. It is the part of the educational experience that all graduates from your college will have in common no matter what their major course of study may be. The size and content of the general-education core is set by your school's faculty and generally includes courses in writing, literature, speech, religion, art, music, science, and philosophy.

These courses have two functions. First of all, they are designed to deepen your understanding of topics in which all well-educated people are conversant. Second, they are designed to improve your thinking and communication skills. By practicing and improving those skills in these initial classes, you will be able to perform more effectively in your major and minor course work.

Apart from this general-education core, you will also be taking focused course work in a major. The major is a collection of courses that is designed to give you more specialized and advanced training in one area. Among the college majors offered on your campus you will find programs of study in subjects such as accounting, communication, nursing, and education. Within your college catalog, you will find both a list of majors offered by your school and a list of courses that must be completed in order to graduate with that major. The catalog also contains a brief description of each course offered by the college, including a note about any prerequisite courses you must complete before registering for the course you are considering.

Aside from a major, most college students also complete a minor. Think of the minor as a subspecialty that requires fewer classes than the major. The ideal minor complements the major course of study and enhances it in some way. For example, an interior design major may minor in business because she plans to open her own interior design store. As with the major, the catalog will provide both a list of the minors available on your campus and the course work associated with them.

Your school has established a minimum number of credits that you must earn before graduation. You may acquire all the academic credits you need to graduate by just completing the general-education core, your major, and your minor. But many college students also have room left in their college program for elective courses. Elective courses are just what their name suggests. They are courses that you are free to choose from across the spectrum of courses offered by your school. You may elect to take courses that further support your major, or you may complete several classes in areas not formally associated with your major but of personal interest to you. Here is the place to take the class in cross-country skiing, the course in Near Eastern archaeology, or the course in women's studies that has always intrigued you.

Registering for Your Classes

Once you have the big picture of what your academic program requires, you are ready to think about registering for your classes. In this portion of the chapter, we will present a plan for completing your registration. This plan will be more generic; you will have to modify it to suit your own situation. But we believe that having a plan to follow in registering for classes will help you avoid mistakes that could cost you time and money.

Organization is the key, so make sure that you dedicate a file folder to all items related to your academic program. This folder will contain advanced-placement credits you have earned, an updateable worksheet that indicates what courses you have completed and what courses you still need to complete, grade reports of those completed courses, and any letters of waiver you might receive. Meticulous record keeping not only will keep you better organized but will also provide you with the necessary evidence if one of your accomplishments is disputed at the time of your graduation.

When it is time for you to register for your courses, take that file folder in hand. In particular, you will need to get or make a worksheet that identifies each class or category of classes required by your academic program, a list of courses offered in the next term, and a blank weekly calendar on which you can work out your schedule. Whether you will be registering electronically or by submitting a hard copy of your registration form, be sure that you know what information you will need to avoid unnecessary backtracking.

The first step in the process of registering for next term is to make sure you have updated your academic program worksheet so that you are aware of what required courses you have already completed. Be sure to take into account the course work you are doing in the current semester, plus any transfer or advanced-placement credits you have earned. The next step is to make a list of courses that you could take in the coming term. Be sure to keep in mind special requirements of your major, courses that may require prerequisites, and course rotation (because not every course is offered each term).

Set aside that list of potential courses for a few minutes and put the blank weekly calendar in front of you. On that calendar, block out any times during the week when your weekly schedule will not allow you to be in class. This may include time previously claimed by work, family, an athletic team, or a social organization. After you have completed this step, you are ready to blend the list of courses you need to take, the course schedule for next term, and your weekly schedule to determine what classes to take. Through trial and error you will find the right combination of classes that fits both your schedule and your program needs.

If you become frustrated with the process, do not give up. The sooner you register for your classes the better. As the current term comes to a close, more and more of the seats in any given class will be filled by other students. And typically a limited number of people are permitted to register for a given class. If you get your name in too late, you may be able to put your name on a waiting list, but this is no guarantee that you will find your way to a seat in that room next term. Register early and save yourself the grief of having to weave around closed classes as you prepare your schedule.

Should I Be Working While Going to School?

The answer to that question depends on how much you are planning to work. A college student who is taking fifteen or more credit hours already has a full-time job. If you add the hours you spend in class to the hours set aside for doing homework, you will easily fill a forty-hour week. If you plan to work another full-time job, you are taking on a workload that very few people can carry. It is certainly possible, even desirable, for you to have a part-time job. How much you can work at a part-time job will depend somewhat on your academic ability and your ability to successfully juggle a busy schedule. But if you are going to truly succeed in college and enjoy life as a college student with all the benefits it offers, limit the amount of time you spend in your part-time job to fifteen hours per week.

Academic Policies

The academic catalog of your school will also contain the institution's academic policies. These general policies impact every student on campus, no matter what major he or she may be taking, and include additional graduation requirements (such as community service projects or portfolios), final exam waiver policies, and the minimum grade point average required to be a student in good standing. Although these policies may not directly affect your program planning for any one term, they are important policies that will impact your overall plan. Read them carefully and be certain that you ask about any policy that is not clear to you, because it will be difficult to get an exemption merely based on the fact that you did not know the policy. For example, if you wish to add or drop a class and fail to get your request in within the time set by the catalog, do not expect the school to allow ignorance of a published policy to lead to an exemption from that policy.

Academic Probation and GPA

At most colleges, you will be required to maintain a minimum grade point average (GPA) to continue as a full-time student. Check your college catalog to determine the minimum GPA required to be a student in good standing and the policies that govern students who find themselves on academic probation. Remember that attending college is not a right but a privilege extended to those who can successfully accomplish the work. Be aware of your GPA and have an academic plan that keeps you as a student in good standing.

You can use the following model to calculate your GPA, which is a mathematical average of your course grades. It is easy to compute your current GPA by using the following procedure. For each course, multiply the number of credit hours by the number assigned to that grade you have received (A = 4, B = 3, C = 2, D = 1, and F = 0). For example, if you received an A in a three-credit history course, you would multiply $3 \times 4 = 12$. The number 12 in this case represents the "quality points" you have earned for this class. Do this for each of your classes. Then add up the quality points and divide them by the total number of credit hours you took that semester. This is your GPA.

Course	Grade	Credit Hours	Grade Value	Quality Points
History	B	3	3	9
Chem.	C	4	2	8
English	D	3	1	3
Math	B	3	3	9
Total		13		29

$29 \div 13 = 2.23$ GPA

Emily Smith

Major: History
Hometown: Mustang, Oklahoma
School: Oklahoma Christian University

My advisor is wonderful, and talking to him is easy. I bring my laptop and take notes when we discuss papers. When I go to schedule my classes, I make sure I've looked at the schedule so that I know what classes I will need. I check my own record keeping so that I can keep up with my progress. That makes it easier to know what questions I need to ask him.

Your Academic Advisor

Your school will provide you with a faculty or professional staff member who will function as your personal academic advisor. He or she is your ally in designing and implementing an academic program that will help you accomplish your personal goals within the least amount of time and with the least investment of money. Your advisor is also aware of other support services offered by your school and may be able to assist you with personal challenges you face as well as those directly linked to academics. But as you read earlier, do not assume that your advisor will be willing to do the planning for you or will intuitively know your needs. As the name suggests, an advisor is there to give you advice, not make decisions for you. Know what your professional goals are, know the academic program that will help you achieve those goals, know what you want to do in any given term, and then let your advisor edit and support your plan.

Choosing an Advisor

Your first advisor will typically be assigned to you by the school. If this advisor is a specialist in the area of your academic major, you may remain in that advising relationship for your entire college career. On the other hand, your first advisor may be a general advisor who will help you make the transition into college and then transfer you to someone in the area of your major. Of course, there is always the chance you will change your major. In the latter cases, you may need to interview and pursue a new academic advisor.

If so, realize that no two people look for exactly the same qualities in their advisor, and advisors differ considerably from one another. Some are very friendly and personal, willing to spend a great deal of time with you listening to your concerns and offering you direction and encouragement on both the personal and professional fronts. Other advisors are more conservative in the use of their time and more businesslike. Some advisors are very direct in the advice they give; others take a more hands-off approach. Some advisors are more knowledgeable than others. Some advisors are very interested in helping you make professional contacts that lead to either a job interview or graduate school application; others are less helpful in this area. The point is that advisors come in all shapes and sizes. Be sure that you select an advisor who has the qualities you would like. And if you do not have an advisor with the qualities you like, start the process that will pair you with an advisor more suited to your needs.

Using Your Advisor

In all these cases, you will be more satisfied with your advising relationship if you follow a few simple guidelines in working with your advisor. If you have something to talk about with your advisor that is important to you, make an appointment rather than dropping in unannounced. You are much more likely to get the amount of time you need and the quality of time you require by following that simple rule. When you make an appointment, be sure that you show up and are on time. Advisors are very busy people who are typically glad to meet with you, but have little patience for students who either do not show up for their appointment or come late. Be prepared. If you are coming to talk about registering for classes, be sure that you have done as much planning as you can on your own. Do not expect your advisor to have the time or patience to work through planning steps that you could have accomplished yourself.

In this regard, it is a good idea to come with questions written down that you need answered. This will prevent you from leaving the office only to remember an important question you had failed to ask during the session. It is also wise to write down the answers or advice you receive. With all the things you have going on in any one day, it is easy to forget helpful advice you have received. Taking notes during an advising session not only will aid your memory, it will also demonstrate that you are serious about the appointment. In general, treat your advisor as a professional who is there to help you. Your respect for your advisor will earn his or her respect for you.

The Class Syllabus

In each of your college classes, you will receive a class syllabus. This important document outlines the learning objectives for the class and the various ways your progress will be guided and measured as you work toward completion of those goals. Typically your class syllabus will include your instructor's name and methods for contacting him or her, the class attendance policy, a daily assignment schedule, and a schedule reflecting the dates for papers and exams. Keep the class syllabus in a safe place, and transfer the due dates for all assignments and tests to your weekly and monthly calendar.

Exercises for **Success**

Review Questions

1. Define *world view*. Explain how your school's world view will impact the design of your education.

2. What role does the Bible play in the search for truth within a Christian college?

3. Explain the primary goal of liberal arts courses in contrast to vocational courses.

The History of My School

The history of your college or university has played an important role in shaping the school you are attending today. Make a list of questions you would like answered about your school, such as the following: What year was my college founded? Who were the people that supplied the driving force for bringing the school into being? What is the relationship between my Christian school and the tradition that founded it? What events were most dramatic in shaping the history of my school? After you have created your list of questions, ask a member of the history department what sources would be most efficient in helping you answer those questions. Prepare a two-page summary of what you find.

Our School Seal

The official school seal has something important to say about the unique nature of your institution and presents it in an artistic way. Obtain a copy of the school seal and study it carefully. Look at every detail and determine what message the artist is communicating about your school. Write a one-page paper that describes what the school seal says about the history and purpose of your institution.

World View Summary Report

This chapter offered you a very brief introduction to a variety of world views. Do a more detailed study of one of them: rationalism, romanticism, empiricism, pragmatism, existentialism, or postmodernism. Pursue questions such as the following: What historical circumstances helped give birth to this world view? Who were the key individuals who championed this world view? How does this world view define what is to be true and cherished? How does this world view integrate or conflict with my Christian views? After you have completed your personal study of that world view, interview at least three faculty members at your school to get their impression of the last question. Summarize your findings in a four-page paper.

Ongoing Issues in Higher Education

Your experience in college is taking place in the middle of a continuing debate about how higher education should look and what it should be doing for our culture. The following is a list of topics presently being debated. Investigate the current state of one issue using library and Internet resources, and then present a two-page paper that summarizes the current state of the conversation in America.

Should students in higher education be more deeply immersed in liberal arts courses or in courses that are more narrowly designed for application in a profession?

How does the current relationship between the federal government and higher education, played out in matters such as federal financial aid and the use of universities to do federal research, create a conflict of interest?

Given the expanding base of knowledge available to study, should higher education become more specialized in its course work or focus more on integrating all the knowledge on a topic that is available?

Is there a definite list of "Great Books" that every American college student should read, or should education be more elective, allowing students to pursue areas of study unique to their own interests?

Identifying Key Campus Resources

Every university campus has an array of resources available to support the health and well-being of its student population: health center, counseling center, advising center, financial aid office, and so on. Consult your campus Web page or directory and determine what campus services may be most useful to you. Pick six of those services and complete the following resource outline.

Resource	Contact Person	Phone Number	E-Mail Address	Web Page	Hours	Location

Critical Dates

Your school catalog contains important dates that will affect your semester. Consult your current school catalog for the following dates and make certain that they are recorded in your semester calendar.

First day of class

Last day of class

Last day to add a class

Last day to drop a class

Date of final exam week

Dates of all holidays and breaks

SPIRITUAL REFLECTION JOURNAL

Read Daniel 1 and reflect on the higher-education experience of Daniel and his friends. They were taken away from familiar surroundings and forced to meet a world view that challenged their spiritual beliefs. Where do you see similarities and differences between your experience in higher education and that of Daniel, Hananiah, Mishael, and Azariah (Belteshazzar, Shadrach, Meshach, and Abednego)? What attitudes and behaviors do you see in them that you wish to adopt as you pursue your education?

Time in Prayer

In your personal time in prayer or in connection with others in your class, take time to pray for the following people and needs:

- For those in your class who are uncertain about their career plans

- For all Christian college students facing world view challenges to their faith

- For the church body that supports your Christian school

- For the faculty and administrators who work to define the world view presented by your college

- For your academic advisor

On the Web

The Internet can be a helpful resource as you look for ideas to make yourself a happier and more successful student. Visit the College Success page offered by Thomson Wadsworth for Web links that will help you grow further on this topic. Go to http://www.success.wadsworth.com/ and click on Resource Web Links.

In particular, we recommend the following:

http://www.christianworldview.net/index.html

http://www.christianworldview.com/

http://www.as.ua.edu/ant/Faculty/murphy/436/pomo.htm

http://www.utm.edu/research/iep/

http://careerservices.rutgers.edu/CareerHandouts.html

Endnotes

1. For an accessible and detailed treatment of this topic, see James W. Sire, *The Universe Next Door: A Basic Worldview Catalog*, 4th ed. (Downers Grove, IL: IVP Academic, 2004).

2. Tertullian, *De praescriptione haereticorum,* 7.

Making Time for Everything 3

There is a time for everything, and a season
for every activity under heaven.

Ecclesiastes 3:1

- **How can I use my time more efficiently?**

- **How can I become better organized?**

- **How can I limit distractions?**

- **How can I avoid procrastination?**

Time is a gift from God that can be used either well or poorly. This is illustrated in the story of Mary and Martha (Luke 10:38–42). When Jesus came to visit their home, Mary and Martha used their time in very different ways. Mary sat down and listened to Jesus as he taught, but Martha scurried about investing herself in the household details that would make Jesus' visit comfortable. One could argue that both Mary and Martha were involved in activities that were worthwhile and meaningful. But when Martha expressed dismay that Mary was not helping her, Jesus replied that Mary had made a better choice by using this time to listen to his teaching. Certainly there are times when housework must be done. But because Jesus' time with them would be brief, the household preparations could wait. Mary seized an opportunity she would not always enjoy, so Jesus affirmed her choice over that of Martha.

A Habit That Can Be Changed

So how does your time-use habit look? Are you easily distracted from your work? Do you forget when assignments are due? Do you run out of time when working on a project? Some people mistakenly assume that they were "born" to be poor time managers or that they have less time to use than others. This is not the case. We all have twenty-four hours each day and we all make choices about how we use those twenty-four hours. That is why we are calling your use of time a *habit*, a habit that may be edited and changed if you so desire. This chapter invites you to carefully inspect your time-use habit at several levels to determine where your current habit contributes to your success as a college student and what portions of your habit may need improvement. This means looking at how you organize your time, how you prioritize tasks, how you manage distractions that challenge your use of time, and what you do when confronted by the appeal of procrastination.

Be warned ahead of time. The assessment of your habits may indicate the need to change, and change is hard. But the need to edit your old time-use habits should not come as a surprise. As a new college student, you are in a very different learning environment. You will need to set aside more time for reading. You will have to manage assignments that are more widely spaced and that consume more time. And you will have more free time to manage. Some of your default time management skills will transfer easily to your college environment, while others will need to be changed.

The Gospels report that Jesus took time with his disciples to rest, to celebrate with others at weddings, and to pray quietly by himself. There is a right time for everything. Balance is the key. So rather than seeing time management as your enemy, see it as a friend that will help you find time for all the things you want and need to do.

My Perceptions

We will start with a look at your perception of how you use your time. Estimate the amount of time you spend in a typical week in the following categories and then add up the hours at the end of the chart on the next page. Do not worry about being too specific. Just write down your general impressions of how a typical week looks by using the chart on page 35.

After completing this exercise, you will track your activities during the course of one week and record the actual time spent in these categories. A comparison of perceived versus actual time usage can be an invaluable tool in the effort to change your time-use habit.

My Actual Time Use

Tracking your actual time use will allow you to see how closely your perceptions match your weekly reality. Use the chart on page 36 to record your use of time over one week. Take a few moments every four hours that you are awake

My Perceptions

Time in class	_____ hours
Studying	_____ hours
Work	_____ hours
Commuting	_____ hours
Family time	_____ hours
Volunteer work	_____ hours
Exercise	_____ hours
Athletics	_____ hours
Social time with friends	_____ hours
Sleeping	_____ hours
Eating	_____ hours
Worship services	_____ hours
Prayer and Bible study	_____ hours
Grooming, dressing, cleaning	_____ hours
Fun (TV, music, dating, video games, hobbies, shopping)	_____ hours
Other	_____ hours
Total Hours	_____

(Do not exceed 168 hours!)

and write down what you have been doing during the last four hours. Once the week is complete, add up the amount of time you actually spent in each of the categories and write them on the chart on page 37.

How Is Your Habit?

You should now have a more accurate picture of your time management habits. Reflect on that picture and compare it with your perceived use of time. Where do your perceptions match your reality and where do your perceptions and reality part company? Talk over what you have discovered about your habit with a friend or teacher who successfully manages his or her time. Then write out three positive things about your time management habits and three things most in need of improvement in the chart on page 37.

Calendar for the week of _____

	SUN	MON	TUES	WED	THUR	FRI	SAT
6:00 am							
7:00							
8:00							
9:00							
10:00							
11:00							
12:00 pm							
1:00							
2:00							
3:00							
4:00							
5:00							
6:00							
7:00							
8:00							
9:00							
10:00							
11:00							
12:00 am							
1:00–5:00 am							

Building a Better Time Plan

Now that you have had a chance to reflect on your time use, this is the opportune time to make some changes. As you set about designing an improved time plan, review the goals you established for yourself in Chapter One. Those goals will play an important role in shaping your time-use plan at every level. Just as those goals are unique to you, so the particular way you will design your time plan will be unique to you. But in general, a healthy time plan addresses the way you organize your time at three levels: the semester plan, the weekly plan, and the daily plan. Here we will explore suggestions and ideas that you can use to tune up your time-use habits.

Actual Time Use

Time in class	_____ hours
Studying	_____ hours
Work	_____ hours
Commuting	_____ hours
Family time	_____ hours
Volunteer work	_____ hours
Exercise	_____ hours
Athletics	_____ hours
Social time with friends	_____ hours
Sleeping	_____ hours
Eating	_____ hours
Worship services	_____ hours
Prayer and Bible study	_____ hours
Grooming, dressing, cleaning	_____ hours
Fun (TV, music, dating, video games, hobbies, shopping)	_____ hours
Other	_____ hours
Total Hours	_____

Time Management Habits

LOOKS GOOD:

1.

2.

3.

NEEDS IMPROVEMENT:

1.

2.

3.

The Semester Plan

Not every week of your semester looks the same. One week, you may have a paper due. Another week, you may have two exams. Your best friend is getting married in February. A semester plan will help you keep track of the unique events that occur in any given month of your semester, events that can easily get lost if you focus only on the regular rhythm of your week. A semester plan calls for you to identify and place on a monthly calendar all the birthdays, weddings, athletic events, church meetings, and family gatherings that punctuate your year. Then carefully review all course syllabi for exams, papers, presentations, and the dates on which they will be due. Once you have placed everything on the calendar, you may even color-code them by class or type of activity for easy reference. A typical month might look like this:

February

SUN	MON	TUES	WED	THUR	FRI	SAT
			1 History exam	2	3	4
5	6 Persuasion speech	7	8	9	10 Sociology paper	11
12	13	14 Dad's birthday	15	16	17	18 Winter festival
19	20	21	22 Church meeting	23	24	25 Pat's wedding
26	27 English paper	28				

Now consider what you do to manage these details in your life. If you would like to experiment with building this type of semester plan, obtain a calendar with room to write. Then gather information on your personal activities and meetings, extracurricular commitments such as sport schedules or organizational meetings, and all your class syllabi. Place each of the items you need to remember in their appropriate place on the semester calendar and post that calendar for easy reference. As your semester marches forward and as you have more and more things you need to remember, you will come to value having a calendar like this that relieves you of the need to remember the date of every assignment and every birthday.

The Weekly Plan

The semester plan will help you remember the unique commitments of your month. The weekly plan is designed to help you organize the regular components of your week such as studying, socializing, attending class, or going to a tutoring session. By being more intentional about the time you spend doing these things, you will be more likely to find the balance you are seeking in your weekly schedule.

As you plan your week, study time will be critical. Most college teachers expect you to invest between one and two hours of studying per week for each hour you are in class. You will want to distribute those twenty-five hours of study time throughout the week at times when you will be alert and energized for the task. Not only the time during the week but even the time during the day when you plan to study can be critical. Many students have found that working during daylight hours tends to be more productive than work done at night. But you know better than anyone else when your "prime time" occurs. That is the time during the day or week when you know you are at your best. As you prepare a weekly plan, be sure to exploit that time for studying.

Your happiness and success as a college student will be influenced greatly by the way you balance your time. All work and no play is a recipe for disaster. Plan to set aside regular time in your week for spiritual growth. When will you pray, read your Bible, have quiet time with the Lord, and worship with others? That weekly schedule will also need to be balanced with time for your social life and exercise. When during the week will you plan your aerobic workouts, time with friends, and time alone when you can rest and rekindle your energy?

As you think about your current time-use habits and consider editing what you are doing, do not view a weekly plan as enslaving. Think of it as a guide, not a taskmaster. This is your plan and you will always remain in control of its composition. As you become more sophisticated in your understanding of college life, your weekly plan will go through several drafts. At a minimum, you will want to reevaluate your weekly time plan at midterm and make the changes that seem prudent to you at that time.

If you would like to experiment with a weekly plan, use the grid on page 41 to help you design it. First enter the fixed elements of your week. Put in things such as your class schedule, work schedule, commuting time, and practice time for your athletic team. Then use a pencil (because you may need to erase) to enter the more flexible parts of your day, such as time for studying, worship, recreation, and exercise. It will be insightful to return to the time-tracking exercise you prepared earlier in this chapter as a guide. Do you need to increase the amount of time you are spending in some areas? Do you need to decrease the amount of time you are spending in other areas? Can you work out your schedule so that you are doing two things at once, such as doing laundry and reading your history assignment? But as you design your plan, be aware of one important reality. The first three weeks of the semester will look very different from those that follow. These weeks typically will see few if any papers due or exams to take. So if you are planning based only on your experience in these early days of the school year, be ready to adjust your weekly plan so you can respond to the rhythm of the rest of the semester.

Example of Weekly Plan

	SUN	MON	TUES	WED	THUR	FRI	SAT
6:00 am			Breakfast		Breakfast		Sleep
7:00		Breakfast	Study	Breakfast	Study	Breakfast	↓
8:00	Breakfast	History	↓	History	↓	History	
9:00	Church	Study		Study			Exercise
10:00	Bible study	↓	Speech	↓	Speech		Study
11:00	Laundry						↓
12:00 pm	Lunch	Lunch	Lunch	Lunch	Lunch	Lunch	
1:00	Fun		Study		Study		Lunch
2:00			↓		↓		Family
3:00	↓	Psych.		Psych.		Psych.	
4:00			Exercise		Exercise		
5:00	Dinner	Dinner	Dinner	Dinner	Dinner	Dinner	
6:00	Work		Math	Work		Fun	
7:00		Tutoring			Tutoring		
8:00		Study			Study		
9:00	↓			↓	↓		
10:00		↓		Bible study		↓	
11:00	Prayer	Prayer	Prayer	Prayer	Prayer	Prayer	Prayer
12:00 am	Sleep	Sleep	Sleep	Sleep	Sleep		Sleep
1:00–5:00 am	↓	↓	↓	↓	↓	Sleep	↓

The Daily Plan

Even though you have designed a weekly plan for yourself, there are still portions of any one day that you may use in different ways. The third part of building a better time plan means creating a list of things you could do today and prioritizing that list so that you know which items are more important than others. Some days you may use your designated study time to read an assignment; on other days that time might be used to start a term paper. One week you may spend your exercise time playing intramurals; another week may find you lifting weights with a friend. Clearly you will have various ways

Schedule for the Week of _____

	SUN	MON	TUES	WED	THUR	FRI	SAT
6:00 am							
7:00							
8:00							
9:00							
10:00							
11:00							
12:00 pm							
1:00							
2:00							
3:00							
4:00							
5:00							
6:00							
7:00							
8:00							
9:00							
10:00							
11:00							
12:00 am							
1:00–5:00 am							

of filling in the study time, social time, volunteer time, or fun time blocked out on your weekly calendar. That is where a daily plan can come in handy; not only can it help you organize your day, it can also help you feel progress toward the larger goals to which you have committed yourself that semester.

Of course, not everything on your list will be of the same importance. That is why it is helpful to divide your list into categories of significance. You can prioritize that list by thinking in terms of things that are critical, important, and possible. Give the highest quality time to critical items, filling in with the possible items only when you have extra time. A typical daily plan may look like this:

CRITICAL	IMPORTANT	POSSIBLE
❐ Prepare for history exam	❐ Outline Eng. paper	❐ Movie
❐ Bible study	❐ Birthday gift	❐ Call home
❐ Research on Eng. paper	❐ Laundry	
❐ Exercise		

Today's plan _____   Date _____

CRITICAL	IMPORTANT	POSSIBLE
❐	❐	❐
❐	❐	❐
❐	❐	

Distractions and Procrastination

We need to make one last stop in our review of your time habit, because your careful planning may be undone if you are victimized by either distractions or procrastination. Distractions can come in all shapes and sizes. You may be distracted by your neighbors' music down the hall, by a phone call from a friend, by something that happened at work earlier in the day, or by your own physical exhaustion. You may procrastinate because you feel overwhelmed by the assignment or because you are waiting for just the right moment to start. What can you do to manage your distractions and procrastination?

Distractions

Some of the distractions you face come from the environment in which you are trying to work. One way to minimize those distractions is to have a specific place set aside to study. When you discipline yourself to study in the same location, your body and mind become conditioned to that space and actually move into the study mode more quickly and attentively. That environment should be comfortable, well lighted, and away from sounds, sights, and memories that may distract you.

We also consider multitasking a distraction when it involves doing college homework. The high degree of concentration required for the completion of such homework will preempt your ability to focus on more than one task at one time. If you do attempt to do multiple tasks at once, you are more likely to find yourself not multitasking but sequential-tasking, moving from one point of focus to the next and losing time in the process.

Your friends or family may also distract you from accomplishing your goals with invitations and conversations that invade the time you have set aside to work. You are responsible for controlling the way you use your time. Either you will control your use of time or someone else will. Because you know what is best for you, learn to say "no" when their invitations or conversations prevent you from following your plan.

You may find yourself distracted by your own thoughts. Problems you are trying to manage in life can dominate your thoughts, even when you try to put them out of your mind. Unsettling news can come to us from many places: a relative may be seriously ill, the stress of work may invade our thoughts, or we may have lingering concerns over an argument with a close friend. If you find yourself distracted by a problem, it is unlikely you will be able to concentrate fully on your work. Take a few minutes to pray about the situation. Remember that God has promised to hear and to help. You may also find it helpful to write down the matter that is distracting you. By doing so, you can give yourself permission to set that topic aside for the time being. The written record will remind you to take it up again when the time is right.

Finally, old habits can be a distraction. Maybe you are in the habit of doing most of your studying at night after a full day of work and class. Perhaps you are in the habit of studying with music or in front of the TV. Maybe you find yourself surfing the Internet for fun whenever you are using your computer to write a paper. One way to identify and eliminate these kinds of distractions is by making a "not-to-do" list. Make a list of the habits you wish to avoid and post it in your study environment as a reminder of old habits you are willing to change.

Procrastination

Distractions can prevent us from accomplishing our goals, and so can procrastination. Procrastination is the postponing of tasks that are perceived as unpleasant. Your procrastination may be caused by a number of factors working in isolation or combination with one another. Think about your situation for a moment and put a check next to any of the following items that cause you to procrastinate.

Factors Affecting Procrastination

- I am not confident.
- I am easily frustrated.
- I am not motivated.
- I am bored.
- I have difficulty starting a task.
- I feel overwhelmed by this project.
- I think the task will take less time than it actually does.
- I will avoid the anxiety by resorting to old escape routes.

Samuel Cocar

Major: History
Hometown: Mundelein, Illinois
School: Trinity College

I wrestle bravely with procrastination because, as a sign of respect for my professors, I do not want to turn in shoddy or incomplete work. Furthermore, as a Christian student, I do not want to place myself in a position of ethical or scholarly compromise. This negative reinforcement usually provides the kick start I need to get working. If not, I internally insist that I need *more discipline*. I only need note that Napoleon could concentrate on his students for a solid twenty hours, or that Cyrus the Great memorized the names of his million soldiers, and I immediately regret my idleness.

Lack of confidence and frustration can be both a cause and a symptom of procrastination. One way to rebuild your confidence and defeat your frustration is to begin with a smaller task that you know you will achieve. The success you have with a smaller task will build momentum and help you break the procrastination cycle. And when you overcome the temptation to procrastinate and are successful in completing even a small task, celebrate that fact and reward yourself in a way that is meaningful to you. That will help you associate good time management behaviors with pleasure rather than pain.

Alternatively, you may have difficulty beginning a project because you lack motivation or feel bored with it. If that is the case for you, reread the section on motivation in Chapter One. Identify what creates passion in you and link that passion to whatever project lies before you. That internal motivation will be more powerful than the pressure others place on you. But remember that you can ask a friend, a teacher, or a relative to help hold you accountable for tasks you are committed to completing. Motivation can also be impacted by the way we conceptualize a task. When we use negative language to describe a task, it constructs a task that is harder to engage. But positive language can provide incentive. For example, see the paper you are writing as an "opportunity to improve" your communication skills rather than as a "burden" that prevents you from attending a party.

Sometimes people have difficulty starting a task because they are waiting for just the right moment to begin. In general, that magic moment does not exist and this simply becomes an excuse to delay the project. When you are tempted to delay the start of a project, commit to sitting down for ten minutes of work on the project. After ten minutes, decide whether to continue. More often than not, the momentum you build during the first ten minutes breaks the inertia and moves you forward. As you get started, be aware of escape routes you have used in the past that have contributed to the delay. Do not let the habit of taking a nap, cleaning, or watching TV prevent you from getting started.

Perhaps you find yourself easily overwhelmed by the size and complexity of an assignment. But like the builder of a house, you do not do everything at once. The construction of a home is a very complex project with many dimensions to it. First the builder lays the foundation, and then the frame of the house is erected. Electrical and plumbing components are added before the finishing work is done. When facing a big task, look for ways to break it down into small parts that you can manage and complete. These segments of the larger task can then be composed into a to-do list. That list will help you prioritize the steps you need to take and give you sense of progress as you check off completed segments. Whenever possible, make the first step an easy one that can be accomplished in a short amount of time. This will give you an early sense of success that will foster your motivation for the steps that follow.

On the other hand, you may be prone to underestimate the size and complexity of an assignment. Consequently, you miscalculate the amount of time needed to complete a task and delay starting the work. If you do not catch this miscalculation early, you will be rushed to get it in on time. The result is often work of inferior quality or work that is handed in after the due date. In either case, you will likely receive a lower grade than what you could have earned. One way to address this problem is to set a starting date that is well before the time you believe you need to start the project. Of course, you may complete the assignment before it is due, but there is no penalty for completing a project early.

Time is a great gift from God that may be either used well or poorly. The story of Mary and Martha clearly illustrates that point. We have seen that time use is a habit over which you have great control. This chapter has given you the opportunity to reflect on that habit. Now is the time to experiment with changes in your habit that will improve your chances for success as a college student.

Exercises for **Success**

Review Questions

1. Explain the meaning of the following sentence and what it suggests about your ability to edit your use of time: "Time use is a habit."

2. Compare and contrast the contents of a weekly plan versus a daily plan.

3. How can you design your study environment so that it becomes a place that prevents the distractions which can interrupt your study time?

Create Your Plan

Throughout this chapter you have read suggestions on how you might assess and improve the way you organize your time. Pick one or two of the exercises suggested in the chapter and look for a way to improve your semester planning, your weekly planning, or your daily planning. Again, you must tailor those exercises to make them your own. You may organize your weekly plan using a different scheme, or you may use technology such as an electronic calendar or organizer to create your plan. Failure to plan amounts to planning to fail. This is the time to experiment with something that will improve your time planning.

Assess Your Weekly Plan

Because it is unlikely that you will get your planning absolutely right the first time, it is important for you to assess the outcome of your time management experiment. Assess the effectiveness of your weekly time management plan on or around midsemester. How closely have you been able to adhere to your schedule? Have you allocated enough time for homework? Are there new commitments that need to be integrated into the plan? What adjustments could you make to your schedule? Are you spending enough time during the day on your studies? If necessary, create a new weekly time management plan that meets your needs.

Examine Other Plans

Find three people whom you believe are good time managers. They could be students, faculty, staff members, co-workers, friends, or family members. Interview them about their time management habits. How do they organize their commitments? How do they stay motivated to keep their schedules? What types of tools do they use (day planners, calendars, computer software, etc.)? Ask if you can examine their time management tools. What sorts of techniques and ideas can you incorporate into your time management plan? Write a brief summary report of your findings and incorporate the helpful discoveries into your time management plan.

What Distracts You?

Keep a sheet of paper near you as you study. On the top of the page, write down the date, the time of day, and the location of where you are studying. Every time you find yourself distracted from your work, write the reason. Was it a phone call, a knock on your door, music down the hall, or a family member watching TV? Did you fall asleep? Did your own thoughts distract you from your task? Now, analyze and categorize your list of distractions. Knowing what distracts you is the first step in defeating them. Once you know your distractions, develop a plan to limit them.

SPIRITUAL REFLECTION JOURNAL

The Bible records many of the activities of Jesus. Although most of this record reveals Jesus' teaching and preaching, it also records that Jesus spent his time doing activities that were necessary and healthy for a balanced life. Read the following Bible verses and write down the different types of activities in which Jesus engaged: Matthew 4:23, Matthew 8:23– 24, Mark 6:31–32, Mark 14:32, Luke 5:29, Luke 6:12, John 4:6, and John 11:35. Now make a list of the different activities in life that call for your time. As you think about that list, consider how you have balanced your time. Write about where you have balanced your time well and where you feel a need to make adjustments.

Time in Prayer

In your personal time in prayer or in connection with others in your class, take time to pray for the following people and needs:

- For the ability to balance my time wisely

- For the ability to organize my time in a meaningful way

- For the motivation to stick to my time management plan

- For other students who may be struggling with managing their time effectively

- For change in my procrastination habits

- For a sense of peace when I feel overwhelmed

On the Web

The Internet can be a helpful resource as you look for ideas to make yourself a happier and more successful student. Visit the College Success page offered by Thomson Wadsworth for Web links that will help you grow further on this topic. Go to http://www.success .wadsworth.com/and click on Resource Web Links.

In particular, we recommend the following:

http://www.psychwww.com/mtsite/page5.html

http://www.mdx.ac.uk/www/study/Timetips.htm

http://www.mindtools.com/page5.html

http://studytips.aac.ohiou.edu/?Function=TimeMgt& Type=timeWasters

http://www.dartmouth.edu/~acskills/success/time .html

Defining My Style of Learning 4

I praise you because I am fearfully and wonderfully made.

Psalm 139:14

• **Why does my friend have an easier time learning in lecture classes than I do?**

• **What is my preferred style of learning?**

• **How can I use my dominant learning style to become more successful?**

The desire to explore our world and to understand its complexity comes as standard equipment in every human being. We may not be curious about exactly the same things, but we all have a curiosity about our world, a curiosity that fuels our desire to learn. Why is the sky blue? How were the pyramids built? Why did my friend act the way she did? What happens to people when they die? Ever since their creation, humans have pursued questions like these because they have an innate desire to learn.

God created us not only with this desire to learn but also with preferences for the way we learn. These are often called *learning styles*. The term may be new to you, but the reality that lies behind it is not. Some of your classmates would rather read to find the answers to their questions, while others would prefer to learn by listening. One of your friends may be able to look at a graph and instantly interpret its value, while another may puzzle over the same graph for hours before obtaining the same insight. You may prefer to learn by quietly thinking over the question yourself, while another person would prefer to talk about it in a small group. The God who created humans with a questioning mind created those same people with preferred ways of finding answers to their questions.

Initial Impressions of My Learning Style

Imagine that you have just purchased a vacuum cleaner. You bring it home and need to assemble the vacuum cleaner before it can be used. You open the box and remove the contents. What would be your next move? Check the box that describes your most likely course of action.

❑ I would read and follow the written instructions.
❑ I would study the diagrams and look at the picture on the box.
❑ I would pick up each of the pieces and assemble them by trial and error.

Although you may use each of these techniques at some point in the assembly process, chances are you have a certain preference for the way you would complete this task. There is no right way or wrong way to assemble the vacuum, but there is your preferred way.

In a small way, this exercise illustrates the unique way that God has fashioned you and how you prefer to learn. The role of this chapter is to deepen that insight so that you may learn more about your learning preferences and how you may use that knowledge to improve the quality of your work. It is certainly possible to learn and grow as a college student without a formal awareness of your learning style. But successful students typically know something about their learning style and how to use it to their advantage both inside and outside the classroom.

Just as we are different from one another on the outside, so also are we different on the inside. And just as there is no "right" way to look on the outside, there is no "right" way to learn. Consequently, this chapter is not about checking the correctness of your learning style but about exploring the way you learn more naturally. The learning style we are going to investigate is your preferred way of studying the world and of sharing what you have learned with others.

Verbal, Visual, and Kinesthetic Modes of Learning

There are many ways to assess your learning preferences, but one way is to consider which mode of learning is more natural for you: verbal, visual, or kinesthetic. In the exercise with the vacuum cleaner, you may have noticed that we offered options that appealed to each of these modes of learning. The typical student employs all three modes of learning during any one month of school but feels more natural using one or two of them.

The following exercise will help you discover more about the modality of learning you prefer. Place a check next to the statements that best describe you:

Verbal

❑ I usually remember what I read or write down.
❑ I like to listen to my instructors talk.

❏ I would rather call someone on the phone than write a letter.

❏ I like talking about interesting topics.

❏ I would rather have directions written in sentences ("Make a left on Spring St.") instead of drawn on a map.

❏ I would read the directions when assembling a vacuum cleaner.

Visual

❏ I usually learn more from diagrams, maps, charts, and pictures.

❏ I would rather have a map than written directions.

❏ I usually remember what my instructor projects on the screen during class.

❏ I like textbooks with lots of colors and pictures.

❏ I like to put jigsaw puzzles together.

❏ I like to figure out mazes.

❏ I would rely on the diagrams to assemble a vacuum cleaner.

Kinesthetic

❏ I like working with my hands.

❏ I enjoy classes that have a lab.

❏ I like to move around when I study.

❏ I like teachers who have us move about the room instead of sitting or standing in one place.

❏ I learn more by doing than by listening.

❏ I would assemble the vacuum cleaner by trial and error—putting the pieces together that seem to fit.

Where did you place your checks? Your approach to learning may be more balanced or may suggest a strong preference for one learning mode. In either case, check out the following descriptions of each learning mode and read the accompanying suggestions to see how to exploit your preferred learning mode(s).

Verbal Learners

Verbal learners usually learn better with written or spoken language. They enjoy discussions and prefer verbal explanations and directions. Students who are strong in verbal learning also tend to take in more information by reading. Many college classes favor verbal learners because many teachers rely on lecturing, class discussions, and reading assignments. If you believe you are stronger in the verbal area, here are some things you can do to help you study.

• Rewrite your notes so they are clearer.

• Create outlines for reading material.

• Recite your notes out loud.

• Discuss the class material with a peer or in a study group.

• Teach the material to another person.

• Ask someone to quiz you from your notes, study guides, or textbook questions.

- Rewrite your class notes while adding notes from the textbooks.
- When learning mathematical or scientific formulas, write out or talk through the steps in order ("First, do the necessary computations within the parentheses").

Visual Learners

Visual learners usually learn better with information presented visually, as in pictures or images. Students stronger in visual learning are drawn to videos, films, maps, charts, diagrams, tables, and other types of visual presentation. If you believe you are stronger in the visual area, here are some things you can do to help you study.

- Examine the diagrams and charts in your textbooks, add additional information to them, or redraw them in your notes.
- Think about how you can translate verbal information into visual pictures. For example, rewrite conceptual information using mind maps (see the chapter on taking notes) and historical information with timelines. If you have a list of statistical information such as percentages, draw a pie chart.
- Highlight your notes and textbooks with different colors that are coded for specific information (for example, yellow for important facts or concepts, green for new vocabulary words, blue for definitions).
- Lay out your notes on your desk or post them on a wall to study them. Visualize the location of information on your desktop or wall when taking an exam.
- If you are trying to learn a sequence of steps or process, draw boxes around each concept and connect each step with an arrow. Visualize the boxes in your mind as you study and take a test.
- Create multicolored flash cards and use symbols and pictures on the cards.

Kinesthetic Learners

Kinesthetic learners usually learn better when they are physically moving about or actively doing as they learn. Students who favor kinesthetic learning are drawn to laboratory work, fieldwork, demonstrations, and other types of "hands-on" activities. If you believe you are stronger in the kinesthetic area, here are some things you can do to help you study.

- Recite your notes out loud while moving about your room.
- Create flash cards and study them while pacing. Be sure to recite the information out loud.
- Teach the material you are studying to another person. Use a chalkboard, whiteboard, or large sheet of paper to write or draw some of the information for your "student."
- Draw mind maps or pictures to accompany your notes.
- Learn critical information by creating outlines, mind maps, or pictures on a chalkboard, whiteboard, or large sheets of paper.

For the sake of simplicity, we have discussed these modes of learning as if they exist in isolation from one another. In reality, though you may favor one style, you can learn by experiencing life in all three modes. Try the preceding suggestions that fit your learning style preferences. If you are a visual learner,

STUDENT VOICE

Hilary Hurst

Major: Undeclared
Hometown: San Jose, California
School: Brigham Young University

I am a very introspective, independent person, so I learn best when I do most of the learning on my own. I also am a very hands-on person. When it comes to learning something, I like to physically do something with it. For example, I like to take notes and then reread them, explaining how ev-erything fits together. I also like to make flash cards. After I have a good grasp on the subject, I like to talk it out with someone. I like to go back and forth, asking questions and explaining in detail the different aspects of whatever subject we are learning.

use visual techniques to study. But remember that this is only a preference. Do not hesitate to experiment by tapping into various modes of learning. Try using some verbal and kinesthetic learning techniques to supplement your dominant preference. We believe that you will find that learning information with a variety of techniques will create a more interesting learning experience and help you strengthen your retention.

Take the VARK!

If you would like to investigate your preferred learning modalities further, we suggest you take the VARK Inventory online. VARK also uses visual and kinesthetic categories, but it separates the verbal category into "aural learn-ers" (people who like to receive information that is spoken or can be heard) and "read/write learners" (people who like to receive information that is written in words). This inventory is another helpful tool for exploring your learning pref-erences. Once you have taken the inventory, spend some time on the Web site reading about the study strategies associated with each type of learning mode. You can find this inventory at http://www.vark-learn.com/english/index.asp.

Learning Styles and Personality Type

Another way to investigate our preferences for learning is to examine the unique personality that God has given each of us. In this portion of the chap-ter, you will be able to explore your learning style by studying the personality types described in the work of Isabel Briggs Myers and Katharine Briggs.[1] They

"Professor Smith is driving me crazy . . ."

Do you find yourself frustrated in a class and do not know why? Maybe your instructor's teaching style is at odds with your learning style. Instructors tend to teach the way they learn. If you are a visual learner in a class with an instructor who only lectures, you probably feel a bit frustrated. It is critical at times like these to design personal study time that translates the material into a learning mode that is more amenable to your style of learning. Find a student in the class who is having similar difficulties. Together, you may be able help each other "translate" all the verbal information into a visual format that is easier for you to grasp. In this case, you might also consider asking the verbal learners in the room to help you identify the key concepts that you may not identify as quickly.

developed a personality inventory based on Carl Jung's theory of psychological types. This inventory explores four aspects of personality preferences that combine to form sixteen distinct personality types. The following exercise is based on these personality preferences as they are related to learning styles. You will discover things such as whether you prefer to work in groups or individually, whether you like to make decisions based on fact or feelings, or whether you prefer to plan or be spontaneous.

In the extended exercise that follows, you will be introduced to four scales with opposite personality poles. For each scale, you will be asked to identify which of the opposite poles more accurately describes your current personality. Please do not feel that one side of the scale is more appropriate than the other. Your success as a college student is not based on which side of the scale you find yourself. The "right answer" is the one that best describes you.

Extravert/Introvert Scale

The first scale reveals where people like to focus their energy and attention. Some prefer the inner world of thoughts and ideas, while others prefer the outer world of people and action. Of course, we all function in both worlds, but we tend to prefer one or the other.

Extraverted people like to focus their energy on the outer world of people and activities. Are you outgoing and talkative? Do you like working with people? Do you feel energized at a party? Do you like to relax by talking with a group of friends? If you have a problem, are you most likely to "talk it out" with a trusted friend? Then you are probably an extravert. Extraverts focus on the world around them and enjoy interacting with the people in that world. Extraverts also draw on that energy from the outer world in order to "recharge" themselves. For example, extraverts often seek out a group of friends or make some phone calls when they need a study break.

Introverted people like to focus their energy on the inner world of thoughts and ideas. They are refreshed by time spent alone in quiet places. Do you enjoy quiet times and relaxing by yourself? Would you be more likely to ponder and think through a problem than discuss it with others? Would you prefer to work alone rather than in a group? Are you bothered by interruptions? You may be an introvert. Although introverts like people, they prefer to work or study quietly by themselves. Introverts are not shy, as some may mistakenly believe. They "recharge" by spending time alone or engaging in mental activities rather than social interaction.

As stated previously, you are likely to be a blend of both introversion and extraversion, but one of these preferences will be stronger than the other. Estimate what percentage of your personality is more extraverted and what percentage is more introverted. Combined, they should total 100 percent.

EXTRAVERTED (E) ____%

INTROVERTED (I) ____%

In the upper left half of the following circle, place either an E (extraverted) or an I (introverted) to reflect the higher percentage from the preceding scale. Place that percentage value in the lower right half of the circle.

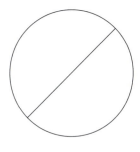

Sensing/Intuitive Scale

The next scale expresses your preference for acquiring information. We all gather information that helps us understand our world and manage our lives within it. But we have different preferences for the way we gather information and the value we place on the information-gathering process.

Sensing people like to work with the facts that they have obtained from their five senses. Do you prefer to deal with present and concrete information such as facts and figures? Do you see yourself as being practical? Are you good with details? Do people describe you as realistic? You are probably a sensing individual. Sensing people can engage in theoretical discussion, but they prefer the world of facts. They tend to place more importance on the information they gain from their experiences in the sensory world, value common sense, and have realistic expectations. Sensors trust information that is based on concrete data drawn on what they can hear, see, feel, or touch.

Intuitive people prefer to deal in the world of ideas. Do you enjoy a discussion about an abstract, philosophical concept or theory? Do you move quickly from the bare facts to their relationship to one another? Do you tend to look for the "big picture" and spend less time on the details? Do you tend to think ahead to future possibilities and pursue nontraditional rather than traditional solutions to problems? You may be an intuitive person. Intuitive types understand details and facts, but prefer to find the relationships and meaning beyond the facts. They may gather information via their senses, but they tend to trust their intuition and try to find the meaning beyond the data.

Again, you are likely to see a bit of both the sensing and intuitive personality in yourself, but one of these preferences will be stronger than the other. Estimate what percentage of your personality is more sensing and what percentage is more intuitive. Combined, they should total 100 percent.

SENSING (S) _____%

INTUITIVE (N) _____%

In the upper left half of the following circle, place either an S (sensing) or an N (intuitive) to reflect the higher percentage from the preceding scale. Place that percentage value in the lower right half of the circle.

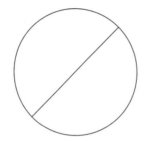

Thinking/Feeling Scale

The third dimension reveals your preference for making decisions. As with the differences in gathering information, we differ on how we use that information to make a decision. The thinking/feeling scale shows the way we prefer to make decisions.

Thinkers prefer to make decisions based on logical analysis. Do you make decisions after carefully collecting and weighing all the facts? Do you pride yourself on remaining objective when making a decision? You are probably a thinker. Thinkers obviously have emotions and feelings like everyone else; they just give feelings a diminished role and prefer to base their decisions on facts and evidence. Thinkers place a high value on fairness and logic. They try to be objective and carefully analyze all the aspects of situation before making a decision that passes the test of being both logical and fair.

Feelers prefer to make decisions by considering values and emotions. Do you usually make decisions based on how you feel or how others may be impacted by your decision? Do you try to maintain harmony with those around you? You are probably a feeling type. Feelers take into account the logic and facts of a decision. However, the facts are a secondary consideration behind their own emotional cues. This does not mean that feelers are overly emotional or irrational. But they place a premium on the personal consequences of a decision.

We all blend both the thinking and the feeling qualities as we make decisions, but one of these preferences will be stronger than the other. Estimate what percentage of your personality is more the thinker and what percentage is more the feeler. Combined, they should total 100 percent.

THINKING (T) _____%

FEELING (F) _____%

In the upper left half of the following circle, place either a T (thinking) or an F (feeling) to reflect the higher percentage from the preceding scale. Place that percentage value in the lower right half of the circle.

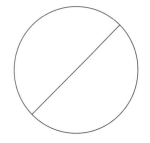

Judging/Perceiving Scale

The last scale reveals your preference for designing your daily activities. Again, we are likely to be a blend of the following types. As you read the following, think about how you prefer to plan your life as a college student.

Judgers prefer to plan and approach life in a very organized way. Do you prefer structure to your day and week? Do you like organizing information and making concrete plans? Do you set goals and stick to them? Do you make lists of things to do? Do you have a carefully organized work space and closet? Do you have a calendar that keeps track of your assignments? Do you complete tasks you begin? Judgers like to live in an orderly world. They make plans and stick to them. When judgers have to make a decision, they are happy when the decision is made and follow through with a plan to implement the decision. They often feel a strong sense of satisfaction at the completion of a project they have planned.

Perceivers like flexibility and spontaneity. Do you like to experience life without feeling the need to plan your day? Do you like to "go with the flow"? Do you put off decisions while you continue to gather information? Do you struggle with procrastination? Do you see yourself as flexible and spontaneous? Do you resist organizing your work space or closet? Do you find it easy to leave tasks uncompleted? Perceivers often feel unduly constrained when asked to live by a daily or weekly plan. They like the spontaneity of life and can handle changes or unusual circumstances without much problem. Perceivers like to gather a lot of information before making a decision and may feel tension if forced to make a decision before they feel ready. They often feel satisfaction when starting new projects, but because of their reluctance to create a schedule and their propensity to procrastinate, projects may be rushed, late, or forgotten completely.

Think about this dimension as it relates to your life. Again, you are likely to demonstrate a blend of both judging and perceiving traits, but one of these preferences will be stronger than the other. Estimate what percentage of your personality is more judging and what percentage is more perceiving. Combined, they should total 100 percent.

JUDGING (J) _____%

PERCEIVING (P) _____%

In the upper left half of the following circle, place either a J (judging) or a P (perceiving) to reflect the higher percentage from the preceding scale. Place that percentage value in the lower right half of the circle.

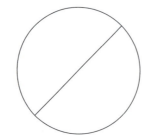

Now it is time to bring this information together. In each circle you have placed a letter that represents your preference in each of the four scales. Collect the letters from the four circles and enter each letter on the following lines.

_____	_____	_____	_____
E-I	*S-N*	*T-F*	*J-P*

This is how you see yourself at the moment. No personality is without strengths and weaknesses, so we can explore how your preferences impact the success of your learning. Examine the following box for possible strengths and weaknesses of your personality type.

Strengths and Weaknesses of the Types

	Possible Strengths	**Possible Weaknesses**
Introvert	is independent works alone reflects works with ideas avoids generalizations is careful before acting	avoids others is secretive loses opportunities to act is misunderstood by others dislikes being interrupted
Extravert	interacts with others is open acts, does is well understood	needs people to work needs change and variety is impulsive is impatient with routine

Strengths and Weaknesses of the Types (continued)

	Possible Strengths	Possible Weaknesses
Intuitor	sees possibilities works out new ideas works with the complicated solves novel problems	is inattentive to detail is inattentive to practical matters is impatient with the tedious loses sight of here and now jumps to conclusions
Sensor	attends to detail is practical has memory for details/facts is patient is systematic	does not see possibilities loses the overall picture in details mistrusts intuition is frustrated with complexities prefers not to imagine future
Feeler	considers others' feelings understands needs, values is interested in conciliation demonstrates feelings persuades, arouses	is not guided by logic is not objective is less organized is overly accepting
Thinker	is logical and analytical is objective is organized has critical ability is just stands firm	may not notice others' feelings misunderstands others' values is uninterested in conciliation does not show feelings shows less compassion
Perceiver	compromises sees all sides of issues is flexible decides based only on data is not judgmental	is indecisive does not plan does not control circumstances is easily distracted from tasks does not finish projects
Judger	decides plans orders makes quick decisions remains with a task	is stubborn is inflexible decides with insufficient data is controlled by task or plans wishes not to interrupt work

Source: From Your College Experience: Strategies for Success *4th Edition by Gardner/Jewler, 2001.*
Reprinted with permission of Wadsworth, a division of Thomson Learning.

You and Your Instructors

Now that you are more aware of your own personality profile, see if you can guess the personality style of your instructors. They may have taken a similar personality inventory and can tell you what their own results were. But it is more likely that you will have to investigate their personality based on the evidence they have given you. Check out the syllabus and the classroom presentations of your teachers. Is this instructor more introverted or extraverted, sensing or intuitive, feeling or thinking, judging or perceiving? If your roommate says that she absolutely loved the professor that you find nearly intolerable, it may be because the personality style of your roommate and that instructor match more closely than your own. And that leads to some interesting facts about college students and those who teach them.

Research from the Center for Applications of Psychological Type[2] (CAPT) indicates that first-year college students tend to be about evenly mixed between extraverts and introverts, but that college faculty are more likely to be introverts. In the general U.S. population, CAPT research indicates that sensing types make up about 65–70 percent of the population. This statistic seems to be fairly representative of most first-year college classes as well. Curiously, CAPT reports that most college faculty are intuitive types. What is more, college faculty are also more likely to be judgers rather than perceivers.

Do not despair if you are feeling at odds with your instructors. First, note that the Myers-Briggs personality preferences focus on only four aspects of our personalities. Human nature is much more complex than those four dimensions can reveal. What is more, having differing preferences on this measurement does not mean you cannot learn from that instructor. Also be aware that the personality preferences on these four scales are not cut into stone. We all change and grow. Having a professor with a more extraverted personality teaching you as an introverted personality may cause you to explore new ways of interacting and make you a stronger person in the process. In the same way, if you are a strong sensor, a highly intuitive instructor can provide you with opportunities to hone your conceptual and creative-thinking skills. Let yourself be challenged by these instructors and be ready to grow as a learner.

Multiple Intelligences

Up to this point our discussion of learning styles may seem to have focused mainly on cognitive processes. Traditional education in the United States has equated intelligence with the traditional standards of "reading, writing, and arithmetic." When students perform well in these subjects, they are considered "intelligent." Sadly, when students struggle in one or more of the traditional areas, they are sometimes considered less intelligent by the old standards.

Dr. Howard Gardner, an education professor at Harvard University, argues that humans have many forms of intelligence, not just the traditional math and verbal forms. Have you ever met a person who claims she is not "book smart" but can easily play several musical instruments? Dr. Gardner would say she has *musical intelligence*. Let's look at the different types of multiple intelligences so you can start to think about your own strengths.

- *Verbal/linguistic intelligence* focuses on spoken and written language. People strong in this intelligence like to read and write, play word games, and tell stories. Lawyers, speechwriters, and journalists are often strong in verbal/linguistic intelligence.

- *Logical/mathematical intelligence* emphasizes logical problem-solving and mathematical ability. People strong in this intelligence favor deductive reasoning and scientific thinking and often are accountants, mathematicians, detectives, and computer programmers.

- *Visual/spatial intelligence* involves the ability to visualize and manipulate mental images. Students high in this intelligence are often drawn to images such as maps, charts, diagrams, and pictures in their textbooks. Their notes are often filled with doodles, as they like to draw images and pictures. Cartoonists and graphic designers are often high in visual/spatial intelligence.

- *Bodily/kinesthetic intelligence* links bodily movement with mental learning. People strong in this intelligence are often physically coordinated and enjoy activities in which they are physically doing something. Athletes, dancers, artists, surgeons, and carpenters usually rate highly in bodily/kinesthetic intelligence.

- *Musical/rhythmic intelligence* involves a keen sensitivity to sound and rhythmic patterns. People who favor this intelligence are good at remembering melodies and sounds, can pick up different tunes and harmonies, and may play musical instruments. Of course, people such as musicians and conductors are high in musical/rhythmic intelligence.

- *Interpersonal intelligence* focuses on the ability to relate well to other people. Effective communication and the ability to mediate conflicts are often traits of someone strong in this intelligence. Counselors, religious leaders, and social workers usually have strong interpersonal intelligence.

- *Intrapersonal intelligence* involves understanding one's own self, understanding one's emotions and motivations, and being able to use that knowledge to pursue a goal. Intrapersonal learners may prefer working alone and like their contribution to reflect their originality. Philosophers, poets, and artists are often strong in intrapersonal intelligence.

- *Naturalist intelligence* emphasizes an understanding of the environment, the natural world in which we live. People high in naturalist intelligence are good at observing, identifying, and classifying plants and animals in nature, but they also enjoy exploring the natural surroundings. Biologists, forest rangers, and zoologists are usually high in naturalist intelligence.

Are you interested in exploring your own multiple intelligences? We encourage you to explore Dr. Gardner's theory of multiple intelligences further by taking the full inventory for yourself. The link to that inventory is available for you among the exercises that follow.

The same God who created people with a desire to learn blessed them with preferences for the way in which they learn. This chapter has helped you learn more about the options. Although there is no one correct way to study or to learn, there is *your* way. And the more you know about your own learning style preferences, the greater success you will come to know as a college student.

Exercises for **Success**

Review Questions

1. How do the preferences of a verbal learner and a kinesthetic learner differ from one another?

2. Compare and contrast the strengths that a perceiver and a judger would bring to their college week.

3. How might the learning style preferences of a faculty member impact your success in their classroom?

Applying What I Know about My Learning Style

Throughout this chapter, you have been gathering information about your learning style. It is now time to put that information to work. Using the material from the chapter, describe what you have learned about your learning style. Which learning modes did you favor? What did the four Myers-Briggs scales teach you about your learning personality? How does your learning personality favor your success as a college student, and how do those habits threaten your success? Complete each of the following sentences to gain a clearer understanding of what you have learned.

My personality preferences and learning type is. . . .

When it comes to learning, I believe my greatest strengths are. . . .

When it comes to learning, I believe my greatest weaknesses are. . . .

Fitting My Style to My Classes

It is vital that you think critically about how your learning style will function in each of your classes. Ask yourself questions such as the following: How has the instructor designed the class? Does the instructor's presentation favor a visual, verbal, or kinesthetic mode of learning? Does the class favor an extraverted learner or an introverted learner? Does the class require that I deal more with ideas or concrete facts? How does my preference for making decisions and organizing my life impact my ability to be successful in this class? Once you have answered these questions, write out three specific techniques that you can use when studying for that class. Keep in mind both your learning style and the nature of the class.

Class:

The class presentation favors. . . .

The exams in this class favor. . . .

Because of the nature of this class, I plan to use the following techniques:

1.

2.

3.

My Multiple Intelligences, Your Multiple Intelligences

Take the multiple intelligences inventory at http://www.ldrc.ca/projects/miinventory/mitest.html. In each category, put a check next to each statement that applies to you. When you are finished, add the number of checks in each section:

_____ Verbal/Linguistic   _____ Musical/Rhythmic

_____ Logical/Mathematical   _____ Visual/Spatial

_____ Interpersonal   _____ Intrapersonal

_____ Bodily/Kinesthetic   _____ Naturalist

You should have a number between 0 and 10 for each section. Any sections with a high number (7 or higher) indicates you may be stronger in that type of intelligence.

Discuss Your Intellectual Strengths

Find a classmate who shares one of your intelligences. Discuss how both of you can use your strength to be successful in school. If necessary, explore some of the Web sites that follow for more information on your multiple intelligences.

SPIRITUAL REFLECTION JOURNAL

As God designed the very unique person that you are, he did not do so serendipitously but very purposefully. He designed you to fit in the world in a way that no one else could. One of the goals of that unique design is to forward the message and cause of the church. Read 1 Corinthians 12. What unique gifts do you have that will advance the church of Christ?

Time in Prayer

In your personal time in prayer or in connection with others in your class, take time to pray for the following people and needs:

- For an understanding of your learning style

- To praise God for the unique person he has made you

- For the ability to successfully apply your learning style in your classes

- For a love for learning

- For wisdom

- For insights on the gifts you have for advancing the church

- For your instructors who can help guide your learning

On the Web

The Internet can be a helpful resource as you look for ideas to make yourself a happier and more successful student. Visit the College Success page offered by Thomson Wadsworth for Web links that will help you grow further on this topic. Go to http://www.success.wadsworth.com/ and click on Resource Web Links.

If you would like to investigate more how personality inventories can help you, visit the following Web sites.

http://www.metamath.com/lsweb/dvclearn.htm

http://www.keirsey.com/

http://www.capt.org/

http://www.infed.org/thinkers/gardner.htm

http://www.newhorizons.org/strategies/mi/dickinson_mi.html

http://www.learning-styles-online.com/inventory/

http://www.edwebproject.org/edref.mi.th.html

Endnotes

1. Isabel Briggs Myers, *Gifts Differing: Understanding Personality Type* (Palo Alto, CA: Davies-Black, 1980).

2. *Estimated Frequencies of the Types in the United States Population* (Gainesville, FL: Center for Applications of Psychological Type, 1996).

Pursuing Careful Thought 5

A simple man believes anything, but a prudent man gives careful thought to his steps.

Proverbs 14:15

- **What does it mean to think well?**

- **How can I use my college experience to improve my thinking?**

- **What is critical thinking and how can I develop it?**

There is a time for faith that is sure of what is hoped for and confident about what is not seen (Heb 11:1). God calls us to use such faith when he tells us that he is both three and one at the same time. This math stands outside the bounds of every human experience and defies all attempts at logical explanation. Yet in faith, we take God at his word. However, this call to faith is not a call to be gullible. God does not expect us to believe everything we are told. If the high school student delivering pizza to your residence hall room asserts that he is really the owner of the entire food chain, you would do well to be skeptical of the claim. The call of the Christian is not a call to stop thinking, nor is it a call to abandon the quest for better thinking. In this chapter, we will see that the Bible contains not only examples of effective thinking but also a challenge to think carefully. "A simple man believes anything, but a prudent man gives careful thought to his steps." (Prov 14:15)

Effective Thinking

The reason that certain careers are open only to college graduates and the reason that college graduates receive a higher wage for those kinds of careers is intimately linked to the fact that college, by design, produces better thinkers. Although much of your formal learning to this point has entailed memorizing "facts" and returning them to your teacher for a reward, your college education will consist of much more than that; what is regarded as a "fact" in one generation of learners can quickly become a falsehood for the generations that follow. For example, students like you were once taught that human flight was impossible, that women were not capable of voting, that Native Americans needed to be civilized, and that computers would never replace the typewriter. In a world where the "facts" are edited so frequently, well-educated people will pursue thinking skills well beyond rote memorization so that they can be effective in the boardroom, in the city council chambers, and in parent-teacher meetings.

Who Is the Smartest?

If being smart is more than just the ability to memorize facts, then what is it? Who is the smartest one in the classroom? A young teacher came to realize that this weighty question was already being discussed among the members of her first-grade class. The students all claimed to know who the smartest student was in the room. Can you guess to whom they quickly pointed? These first graders claimed that the smartest person in the room was the girl who always handed in her quiz first! Assuming that you believe there is more to it than that, how would you complete the following sentence?

The smartest person in the room is the one who:
- A. answers the question correctly.
- B. asks the best questions.
- C. thinks beyond the boundaries of the question.
- D. questions all of the answers.

If you are feeling frustrated by the question, you are already thinking well—because the right answer to the question is not A, B, C, or D, but "all of the above." The most effective thinkers are those who know how to frame a question, how to pursue the answer to the question they raise, how to think beyond the boundaries of questions others have asked, and how to carefully evaluate traditional answers for potential problems and weaknesses.

Your college education seeks to improve your thinking in each of those arenas: content knowledge of the facts, logical organization of the facts, creative thinking that goes beyond the facts, and critical thinking that examines the credibility of the facts. In this chapter, we invite you to do some careful thinking about thinking by exploring each of the four components of effective thinking. The more you know about what effective thinking is, the better you will understand the goal of your college education and the individual assignments that are designed to improve the quality of your thinking.

Know the Facts

Effective thinking starts with knowing the facts as they are currently conceived. This process of learning the basics began long before you attended your first formal class in grade school. As you explored your world, you learned the relationship between pain and a hot stove as well as the social appropriateness of sharing your toys with others. Once you began your formal education, you began to meet more facts—long lists of "who," "what," "when," "where," and "why" facts in subjects such as math and English. These basic facts enable you to function in life: balancing your checkbook, balancing your meals, and even reading the words on this page.

Being a college student does not mean that you will be free from increasing your knowledge of facts. It is assumed that well-educated people have a grasp of even more "who," "what," "when," "where," and "why" facts than the average person who did not graduate from college. Of course, what facts should be taught to all college graduates is an ongoing debate in itself. But be confident that your college education will require you to know basic facts.

Facts for College Freshmen

The physics behind the operation of a lever

The grammatical components required in a well-formed English sentence

The rules that govern the balance of power between the legislative, judicial, and presidential offices of our government

The name of the waterway that links the Great Lakes with the world

The English meaning of words in your French class vocabulary list

The location of the Sistine Chapel and the artist who painted its ceiling

The dates of the Civil War

The difference in musical value between a half note and a quarter note

The difference between modern and postmodern models of truth

Your school is full of specialists in areas such as theology, art, politics, biology, physics, and literature. As you meet them in your general-education classes and eventually in your major courses, they will expect you to learn the basic jargon used in their discipline and the truths currently held in their respective areas. As you are tested and evaluated, you will be asked to demonstrate an advanced knowledge of "who," "what," "when," "where," and "why."

This dimension of thinking that challenges you to remember certain important facts is reflected in a variety of Bible stories, but one stands out in particular. When God was ready to bring the Children of Israel out of captivity in Egypt, he established an annual festival, Passover, which was associated with this event. This festival required the worshipers to reenact a portion of the deliverance known as the Exodus from Egypt. Read Exodus 12 and you will see that the meal they ate, the way they ate the meal, and how they dressed during the meal were all choreographed to review the "facts" of the Exodus. God expected the younger children who participated in this ceremony to ask questions about this unique family behavior. The answer to their questions would bring the details of the Exodus to life in a new generation (Exod 12:26). Facts remain important. Good thinkers—*careful* thinkers—are those who know those important facts.

Logically Organize the Facts

The second component of effective thinking is the logical thinking that organizes facts in a meaningful way. That organization may take the form of placing items in chronological order or of placing items together that have a similar theme or quality. It may mean determining the relative importance of facts or their degree of intensity, allowing them to be placed into a hierarchy. It may mean organizing an experiment into certain steps that must follow in order. Or it may mean deciding how best to design the structure of an oral presentation so that the audience may more easily grasp it.

Your college education will give you plenty of practice in improving your logical-thinking skills. For example, learning a second language is one way for you to improve your ability to think logically. As you study the way another culture carefully structures its communication, you will develop a fresh appreciation of the unique way in which thoughts are structured and communicated in your first language. In a Bible history class, you may be asked to learn the chronological relationship of various Bible stories. Did the story of Noah come before or after the story of Abraham? In a political science class, you may participate in a formal debate that calls for the use of logic in defending your views on campaign finance reform against those who hold a contrary view. In a lab session, you may be asked to observe the reaction of various metals as an electric current is applied to them and then draw logical conclusions from your observation. And each time you are asked to write a research paper, you will practice the art of carefully organizing that presentation so that it pleases the reader with a logical and coherent flow. In these ways, college classes and assignments will give you many opportunities to improve your logical-thinking skills.

When reading your Bible, you will see many examples of people demonstrating logical-thinking skills. Consider the apostle Paul. During one of his missionary trips, Paul found himself in Athens as he shared the Gospel with its residents (Acts 17:16–34). When Paul delivered his message in that city, he began a conversation with a group of Epicurean and Stoic philosophers. Their interest in his teachings led to an invitation; Paul was to speak publicly at a meeting of the Areopagus, where the latest ideas were publicly discussed and debated. Paul logically deduced that these individuals had not had previous contact with the Old Testament, so his traditional teaching approach used in the Jewish synagogue was not going to work in this context. In fact, he knew that if he claimed to bring them a message from God that was completely disassociated from their culture, they would quickly close their ears. Consequently, Paul began his address by observing that the citizens of Athens must be very religious people, given all the idols that lined their streets. "As I walked around and observed your objects of worship, I even found an altar with this inscription: TO AN UNKNOWN GOD. Now what you worship as something unknown I am going to proclaim to you." (Acts 17:23) He preached the same message of forgiveness of sins, but logically framed it in a way that was more winsome for this new audience.

Creatively Think beyond the Facts

Effective thinkers know the facts and can logically organize those facts in a meaningful way. But effective thinkers can also creatively think beyond the facts, seeing and exploring possibilities and connections that others have failed to see. To achieve this level of creative thinking, we must defeat the inertia placed in our path by the demands of conformity and the demands of time. Creative thinkers look at the question before them and then look through the question and beyond the boundaries of the question itself. Creative thinkers release themselves from the bondage of searching for only one "right answer" and even from the bondage of needing a question before they begin to search. What is more, creative thinking requires time that is not easily given by a culture that is in a hurry for quick and simple answers. During this extended time, creative thinkers practice strategic daydreaming that unlocks their mind's eye, allowing it to wander and rove to new and unique places. The creative thinker is the artist who takes a formless lump of clay and turns it into a sculpture that once existed only in his or her mind. Creative thinkers are inventors who play with problems and think where others have not thought before, giving us products such as self-sticking notes and microwave ovens. Creative thinkers are problem solvers who think outside the logical box to see solutions in places others do not.

Mature Thinkers . . .

Know the facts
Logically organize those facts
Creatively think beyond those facts
Critically question the value and validity of those facts

This creative thinking is evident in inventors such as Orville and Wilbur Wright, who took time to lie on the beach and watch seagulls in flight. In doing so, they conceived of an airfoil design that would allow them to become the first humans to enjoy mechanically powered flight. This creative thinking is alive in the fingers of Maya Angelou as she reflects on life and turns those reflections into poetic verse. This creative thinking was alive in the mind of George Frideric Handel, who meditated on the Word of God and then brought it to life in the music of *Messiah*.

You too can further develop this creative thinking ability by carefully living your daily life. Remember that creative thinking requires time. Walk a bit more slowly as you go about your daily routines. Observe things and relationships that might have gone unnoticed before. Try to see and think about things in ways you have not before. And remember that conformity can be the enemy of creative thinking. If your classmates are all doing their class presentation in the same way, make a point of communicating what you have to share in a different way. Learn to play the guitar or another musical instrument and spend quiet time playing combinations of notes that no one before you has played. Set aside time for strategic daydreaming when you are writing a paper. Think about how you might approach the topic differently. What have others missed that you may see during your reflective time? And take classes that formally develop the creative dimension of your personality. An art class, an acting class, a music class, or a creative-writing class can give you the opportunity to develop your creative side.

Perhaps the most striking example of creative thinking in the Bible is Solomon's judicial ruling, offered when two women came to him with an infant boy. Each woman asserted that the child was her own son (1 Kings 3:16–28). Solomon knew that one of the women was lying, but he had to discover a way to reveal the real mother of the child. After careful reflection, he gave his judgment, causing all those who heard it to gasp. "Cut the child in half and give each woman one half of the child." His creative thinking on this topic led to this unorthodox verdict, assuming that the compassion of the true mother for the child would reveal itself in the face of such an unthinkable verdict. He was right. Immediately after hearing this verdict, the real mother of the child was overcome with compassion and immediately withdrew her claim to the child. Once the true mother revealed herself in this way, Solomon then returned this child to his rightful home. This remarkable demonstration of creative thinking caused all Israel to stand in awe of Solomon.

Critically Question the Facts

The fourth dimension of effective thinking involves what we narrowly define as critical thinking. Critical thinking is thinking that questions the answers. It does not see the first answer to a question as a stopping place but as a temporary resting place. It is skeptical thinking that asks the even harder questions: Is the answer true? Does it make sense? Are there other alternatives that have not been considered? Does it work in application? Critical thinking probes the presumed answer with these kinds of questions to test its value and validity.

As a student, you will have increasing amounts of practice with critical thinking in your advanced course work. But even in your first semester, you may be asked to refine this dimension of effective thinking. For example, your professor may assign you a critical-response paper in which you are to react to an assigned reading or to the views of a speaker. Be careful that you do not fall into the trap of writing a summary paper rather than a critical-response paper. Such a paper will, of course, require you to briefly summarize the main points of the reading or speech, but your professor is asking you to do much more than that. He or she is asking you to critically evaluate what you have read or heard.

Critical Thinking

1. Identify the thesis.
2. Identify the evidence used to support the thesis.
3. Evaluate the truthfulness, validity, and value of the evidence.

Consider using the following model as an outline for completing this kind of assignment. First, identify the thesis statement within the reading or speech. This is more than a topic. It is the "point of view" or the perspective that the writer or speaker is taking on that topic. For example, you may be asked to listen to a speaker who is addressing the president's foreign policy in the Middle East. That is the topic of the speech. But you will need to isolate the thesis of the speech, the point of view on that topic. "The president's current plan for peace in the Middle East is flawed." That is a thesis statement.

The second step in the process is to identify the evidence summoned to support the thesis statement. That evidence often reveals itself if you turn the thesis statement into a "why" question: "Why is the president's current plan for peace in the Middle East flawed?" The speaker may argue that the president's plan is flawed because it is based on a misunderstanding of Middle Eastern culture. Or she may argue that the plan is flawed because it is not as aggressive as it needs to be. This sort of evidence provided in support of the thesis statement needs to be identified.

Once those arguments have been identified, the third step in the process is to evaluate the quality of the evidence being used to support the thesis statement. This is where the hard questions need to be asked. Is the evidence true? If it is true, does it really support of the thesis? Are there other explanations that the speaker has not taken into account? Does the entire argument make sense when it is assembled as a whole? Any evidence of logical fallacies will undermine the argument and should be noted in your response paper. Your paper will need to honor the fact that most thesis statements are supported by a collection of arguments that vary in quality. Acknowledge those with merit and critique those that fail.

This kind of critical thinking is also encouraged and illustrated in the Bible. The Apostle Paul traveled extensively, sharing the message of God with people throughout Asia and Europe. But of all the places that he stopped, he was particularly happy with the reaction of those in the Greek city of Berea. These members of the Jewish synagogue listened carefully to Paul's ideas, but then thought critically about them. "Now the Bereans were of more noble character than the Thessalonians, for they received the message with great eagerness and examined the Scriptures every day to see if what Paul said was true." (Acts 17:11)

Logical Fallacies

Logicians have identified and labeled a number of arguments that are inherently weak. Hence they are called logical fallacies. Several logical fallacies are given here, along with the Latin names that are often used as shorthand for them.

FALSE CAUSE-EFFECT (*Post Hoc Ergo Propter Hoc*)

This fallacious argument assumes a direct causal relationship between two events that occurred at approximately the same time. For example, you may assert that your stomach cramps are being caused by food poisoning because the food you ate at the local restaurant did not taste like it usually does. You have taken two events that are correlated in time and assumed that they were causally related. But in the absence of other evidence, your stomach cramps may be caused by a case of the flu rather than food poisoning. Correlation does not always equal causation.

APPEAL TO AUTHORITY (*Argumentum ad Verecundiam*)

This fallacy is in play when the authority being used to support a thesis has questionable credentials as an expert on the thesis in question. For example, the plea from a nationally known athlete to use a certain type of sports shoe in an advertisement may be a legitimate use of that person's expertise. But why should I take that athlete's advice on the type of automobile to buy from the local car dealer?

APPEAL TO PITY (*Argumentum ad Misericordiam*)

The appeal to pity seeks to divert attention away from the evidence and instead asks the evaluator of the thesis to respond with mercy toward the presenter of the thesis for mercy's sake. The college student who cannot afford to fail his or her first-semester history class may seek to divert the professor's attention away from the evidence found in failed quizzes and exams and instead ask that he or she not be failed because it would affect the student's financial aid package for the next semester.

APPEAL TO FORCE (*Argumentum ad Baculum*)

The appeal to force, like the appeal to pity, seeks to divert the evaluator's attention away from the evidence. But in this case, the evaluator is threatened with the consequences of not agreeing with the thesis. Unfortunately, the Christian church used such an appeal to force when dealing with Galileo in the seventeenth century. Using his telescope, Galileo was finding growing support for the theory of Copernicus that identified the sun, rather than the earth, as the center of the solar system. Feeling threatened by this evidence, the church condemned Galileo as a heretic and threatened to burn him at the stake if he did not retract his thesis.

ARGUMENT AGAINST THE PERSON (*Argumentum ad Hominem*)

This fallacious attack on a thesis is not an attack on its ideas but on the person who is presenting them. It assumes that if you can discredit the messenger, you will then have discredited the mes-

Logical Fallacies (continued)

sage. This popular fallacy often takes the form of giving someone a label designed to discredit them. For example, if a Democratic candidate for governor comes up with a sound idea for dealing with unemployment, she may be attacked as being a "bleeding-heart liberal," a label that is designed to turn people against her argument without engaging the argument itself.

ARGUMENT FROM IGNORANCE (*Argumentum ad Ignorantiam*)

The argument from ignorance presumes that a thesis is valid as long as it has not been proved wrong. Even if there is no evidence to support the thesis, it claims to be correct in the absence of any evidence that defeats it. If this form of argumentation is allowed, then I may assert that the oddly shaped cloud in the sky is actually a UFO. I may not have any evidence to support my thesis, but I can claim it true so long as there is no evidence to deny it.

HASTY GENERALIZATION (*Dicto Simpliciter*)

This fallacy occurs when one draws a general conclusion from too few cases or exceptional cases. For example, it has been argued that college athletes should be paid because they make money for the university. This argument fails because although some universities make money from their athletics programs, most do not. The argument fails because it is an inappropriate generalization.

Effective Thinking Is a Symphony

For the sake of this presentation, we have broken effective thinking into four parts: knowledge of facts, logical organization of facts, creatively thinking beyond the facts, and critically questioning the truthfulness of the facts. In reality, we do not think in these little compartments. Our thinking is a symphony in which the sound of individual instruments is not noticed in the grand synthesis of the music produced by the orchestra. Such thinking allows us to look at a declared fact in a number of different ways.

For example, let's take the case of the Italian navigator Christopher Columbus. You may have been taught that he discovered America in 1492. Consider how this "fact" might be addressed by the careful thinker. It can be examined logically to determine whether such a journey would have been possible given the technology of the fifteenth century. Did the construction of ships in this period permit such a journey? Would there have been room for sufficient supplies to make this kind of journey? What methods were available to navigate effectively on such a trip? In the end, the logical thinker could come to a conclusion on whether such a trip and such a discovery seemed plausible.

The declared fact could also be explored creatively by thinking beyond the mere details of the trip to explore the character of a person like Columbus. What kind of personality did it take for a man to captain a ship on such a voyage? How did this man manage a crew and keep them motivated for such an uncertain voyage? The creative thinker thinks beyond the details of the thesis to explore regions of the topic that had not been explored by previous inquiry.

Finally, the same fact can be explored critically by questioning the truthfulness of the statement. Although for many decades the activity of Columbus was called a "discovery," the appropriateness of that description itself can be called into question. Did Columbus discover America, did he happen upon it by chance, or did he invade America to the harm of those already living there?

STUDENT VOICE

Anne Rasschaert

Major: French/International Business
Hometown: Brussels, Belgium
School: Bethel College

After a year of college, many different things make you a more effective thinker. I truly believe that the *whole* college experience—living on your own, attending classes, meeting new people—makes you a much more effective thinker. College is very different from high school basically because you really feel as if you are on your own for the first time. You have a lot more responsibilities that fall on you that really challenge you to think well.

Grow as an Effective Thinker

The acceptance letter from your school is evidence that you are off to a good start as an effective thinker. But what is good can become even better through repeated practice. Let me give you an analogy to consider. As a college student, I enjoyed playing tennis in the summer with a close friend. Tim was an excellent tennis player who went on to play tennis professionally for a time. On all the afternoons we played together, I never won a match. From time to time, I would win a game and once or twice I won a set. But I never beat him in a tennis match. Still I kept playing because I noticed something about my tennis game. As I played against a partner who was better than I, the quality of my play improved.

There is an analogy between the author's experience with Tim and your experience in college. Your school has hired people to teach your classes who are expert thinkers. As you listen to their lectures, as you take their tests, as they grade your papers, you will improve your thinking week by week. Just as playing tennis with someone who is better than you can improve your tennis game, so thinking with people who think well will improve the effectiveness of your own thinking. That is the positive way of viewing research papers, critical-response papers, lab assignments, and essay exams. They are all chances to improve your thinking.

"A simple man believes anything, but a prudent man gives careful thought to his steps." (Prov 14:15) The same God who created us with the ability to think has also challenged us to think more effectively as we take our steps in this life. In a world where so much changes, you as the future leaders in your professional fields, as the future leaders of your country and communities, and as the future leaders of God's church would do well to become as effective in your thinking as you can.

Exercises for **Success**

Review Questions

1. Explain the difference between creative thinking and critical thinking.

2. Give an example of a logical fallacy. Define it and illustrate it.

3. Identify assignments and classroom experiences you are enjoying right now that are improving your logical-thinking skills.

Analogies

One way to see and practice your thinking skills is to practice word puzzles called analogies. The following four examples are from the guidebook for the Miller's Analogies Test. To answer them all correctly you will need to know certain facts and think logically, creatively, and critically. Look for a relationship between the first two terms and then seek to replicate that relationship on the second side of the double colon by choosing one of the words in parentheses.

Light : Dark :: Pleasure : (Party, Sunlight, Pain, Eyesight)

Centrifuge : Mixture :: Prism : (Water, Spectrum, Light, Sound)

Green : Blue :: Red : (Orange, Yellow, Brown, Pink)

Swan : Butterfly :: Dive : (Fly, Sink, Stroke, Smell)

Answers:

Light : Dark :: Pleasure : Pain
Light is the opposite of dark; pain is the opposite of pleasure.

Centrifuge : Mixture :: Prism : Light
A centrifuge divides a mixture; a prism divides light.

Green : Blue :: Red : Orange
Green is the product of adding the color yellow to blue; orange is the product of adding yellow to red.

Swan : Butterfly :: Dive : Stroke
The swan is a type of dive; the butterfly is a type of swimming stroke.

In order to get each of the analogies right, you had to practice the four forms of thinking described in this chapter. Go back and determine which forms of thinking were necessary to answer each analogy correctly and where weaker thinking blocked your progress in solving these word problems.

Box Challenge
Using only four straight lines and without lifting your pencil from the page, connect all of the following dots.

.   .   .

.   .   .

.   .   .

Creative Circle Sculpture
To work the creative side of the thinking process, make a copy of the following circle on a piece of cardstock. Cut out along the lines and color the shapes different colors. Place the shapes before you and manipulate them again and again to form figures that your mind has not yet seen.

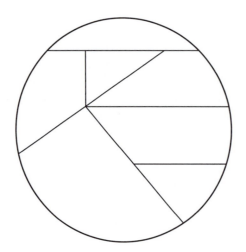

What Can You Do with That?
Another way to practice creative thinking is to think of uses for a common device that have not occurred to others. Take an everyday object such as a paper clip in your hand. In three minutes, write down as many different uses for the paper clip as you can imagine. Of course, the obvious use is for holding papers together. But what about using a paper clip as a screwdriver, as a twist tie, or as a hanger for Christmas ornaments? Have fun!

Critical Reaction to a Television Commercial

Television commercials are enacted thesis statements that seek to persuade you to purchase a product or service. Record several television commercials and practice your critical-thinking approach on them. Commercials in support of political candidates are particularly good. Identify the thesis of the commercial. Look for evidence presented that supports the thesis statement and then put that evidence to the test. Where does the logic fail in the evidence? Where do you see examples of logical fallacies at work?

Answer to Box Challenge:

Did you assume you needed to stay within the borders defined by the "box" of dots?

SPIRITUAL REFLECTION JOURNAL

We have seen that effective thinking consists of knowing certain facts and thinking logically, creatively, and critically. When the Apostle Paul was called before the Sanhedrin with his teachings on trial, we see him thinking in all four categories of effective thinking presented in this chapter. Read Acts 23:1–11 and point to places in this story where you see each of those four components of effective thinking at work. Now think about your own life as a Christian thinker. Which dimensions of effective thinking have you practiced the most? Which dimension of thinking do you enjoy the most? Where can you improve your thinking, and how will you do it? How do you see improved thinking in your life strengthening your church?

Time in Prayer

In your personal time in prayer or in connection with others in your class, take time to pray for the following people and needs:

- For your professors, that they might carefully design classes and assignments that will improve your thinking

- For God's blessing on your growth as an effective thinker

- For God's direction in using your thinking as a tool that will glorify him and advance the Gospel message

On the Web

The Internet can be a helpful resource as you look for ideas to make yourself a happier and more successful student. Visit the College Success page offered by Thomson Wadsworth for Web links that will help you grow further on this topic. Go to http://www.success.wadsworth.com/ and click on Resource Web Links.

In particular, we recommend the following:

http://www.criticalthinking.org/index.cfm

http://www.sjsu.edu/depts/itl/

http://www.nizkor.org/features/fallacies/

http://www.fallacyfiles.org/

http://www.virtualsalt.com/crebook1.htm

http://www.jpb.com/creative/creative.php

Engaging in the Classroom: Listening and Taking Notes

So Jeremiah called Baruch son of Neriah, and while Jeremiah dictated all the words the LORD had spoken to him, Baruch wrote them on the scroll.

Jeremiah 36:4

- **Why should I take notes in class?**

- **How can I improve the quality of my listening?**

- **What system of note taking will work best for me?**

- **When and how should I review my notes?**

It is too hard to remember everything that is important. That is why we take the time to write down the things that are most important to us. We write down the time and location of our intramural basketball game. We write down the date of the midterm exam in history class. And we write down the phone number of that special person whom we intend to ask out on a date.

God also had things written down that were important to him. Rather than just count on the memory of eyewitnesses and the reliability of oral communication, God inspired writers to record events, laws, speeches, and poetry meant for our comfort and growth. "While Jeremiah dictated all the words the LORD had spoken to him, Baruch wrote them on the scroll." (Jer 36:4) Baruch was one of the men whom the Lord selected to record the Word of God for us.

Like Baruch, you too will take notes on the important things that you see and hear in your college classes. Of course, the notes you take during your classes will not have the powerful impact of the Bible. But they will impact your personal success during college, because they will help you organize and recall critical details from your classes. In this chapter we will discuss how you can become more active as you engage with the lectures, discussions, and demonstrations that fill your week in college. This discussion will include an overview of strategies that will help you improve your attentiveness during class, the quality of the notes you take, and the effectiveness of the review process. Because you have been taking notes in class for years, you may assume that you will have nothing to learn from this chapter. You are likely to be affirmed in many of the things you are already doing. But because college classes and college exams are different from the ones you have experienced before, this is a good time to experiment with new approaches and practices. So make it your goal to find something new in this chapter that will advance your habits in a meaningful way.

Why Take Notes?

Taking notes during a class is a distraction. Clearly, it would be better if we could just listen to and discuss the topic without the burden of also keeping a written record of key points. The problem with that is our inability to recall the key elements of a class session even one day after we have experienced it.

One solution would be to audio-record the entire class so that you could just listen during the session and take notes from the recording later. This particular approach may work well in the occasional class that is more challenging for you. But this strategy is usually far from desirable. The audio-recording and listening process doubles the amount of time you must spend "attending" any one class session. Consequently, it is much more desirable to gather the key components of a class session the first time you experience it rather than create the time management nightmare of "attending" the class session twice.

So is taking notes really that important? Yes; until someone discovers a better solution, the traditional practice of taking notes is still the most effective way to defeat the inevitable forgetting that occurs after a class session. Consider the following statistics: Most people quickly forget half of what they hear, even if they pay close attention to the speaker. After two days they can recall only half of what they originally remembered. That means that after

Recording a Class Session

If you audio-record a class session, ask the instructor's permission to do so. Because the class presentation contains the instructor's intellectual property, he or she may have a policy that forbids or limits such recording.

only two days, most people recall only one-fourth of the original presentation.[1] Although it would be convenient to just listen and discuss the material during your classes, notes and note taking are a reality for every college student.

Be Attentive

Because note taking is an inevitable part of the college student's life, we will now explore what kind of notes and note taking will best meet your needs. This begins with evaluating the level of attentiveness you bring to the note-taking process. We will see that your attention is connected to your attendance, your pre-class preparation, and your ability to stay focused during the class session.

Attendance

Be there and be on time. Your commitment to be in class and to be on time sends an important signal to the instructor about your level of commitment, a commitment that will not go unnoticed during the grading process. What is more, on-time attendance is also critical to your firsthand knowledge of what was said and done in that room. You may already know students who skip class and then rely on the someone else's notes or the lecture notes on the instructor's Web site. By doing this, they have missed out on a key step in the learning process. First, there is no guarantee that the notes they borrow truly capture the essence of the session they have skipped. But even if they do, their experience with the class session will lack the animation and emphasis of the real thing. Using someone else's notes may be helpful to you when you have to miss a class. But those notes are a weak second to being there. If you want to have the best notes possible, be there and be on time.

Preparation

The second key to attentiveness is pre-class preparation. Your instructors will typically assign reading and exercises that set the context for that day's class. Complete all reading assignments and exercises before coming to class. This preparation will provide important landmarks you may expect to meet on the way, which will translate into better notes because it will improve your attentiveness and allow you to listen with greater understanding. Your preparation will also identify difficult concepts or ideas for which you can seek clarification during the class session. Remember that this opportunity extends right up to the moment the class begins; you can use those pre-class minutes spent waiting at your desk to review the key points and questions from the assigned reading.

Staying Connected

Then there is the matter of staying connected during class and avoiding "thought vacations" that take you off topic. Staying connected begins with acknowledging the difference between listening and hearing. You can hear sounds such as a clock ticking, cars rushing past an open window, or someone shouting your name across a crowded room. But listening is more than hearing

Would You Like a Partner?

Consider asking another student in class to be your note-taking partner. This is not a tag-team event in which you trade dates going to class, but an opportunity for two people who were in the same class session to grow from each other's experience. Here is how it may help you.

- A note-taking partner provides a safety net to ensure that you do not miss important information from the session.

- It may motivate you to take more complete notes, because you know that you will be comparing notes with your partner.

- It will provide an alternative for learning the class content if you must miss class because of illness or a family emergency.

- It may lead to a weekly review session with your partner.

- It may lead to phone or e-mail conversations about a class session that sharpen your understanding.

sounds move through the air; it is about actively attending and engaging with the words that are spoken and the demonstrations that are given.

Complete honesty demands that we admit this can be a problem. Even when we are in class, have prepared for the session, and have committed ourselves to paying close attention, we can find our focus drifting away. One reason for this is that our brains can process much more information than can be delivered in oral speech. The brain processes 400–800 words per minute, but most people speak at a rate of 120–150 words per minute.[2] The difference between the brain's processing time and the average speaking rate can work to your advantage because it means you will physically be able to keep up with your instructors. But it also presents a problem. Because your brain can process information so quickly, the comparatively slow speaking rate gives your brain "lag time" in which to wander. And with some speakers and some classes, all we need is a brief lag in attention to send us off on an extended thought vacation.

So what can you do in light of that reality? First, acknowledge that staying connected in class is a habit. And if you tend to be less attentive during class, you are empowered to change this habit. Attending class is not like watching television. It requires action, expectation, and participation. If you're looking to improve, here are suggestions to improve your attentiveness.

- Say to yourself "I am going to actively listen now" when the instructor starts. This calls your attention to focus and prevents you from getting started on the wrong foot.
- Create several questions from the reading assignment. If you keep a list of questions on your desktop, your presence in class can become an active quest for the answers. If the lecture is leaving the topic without addressing your question, raise your hand and ask the question out loud.

Maher Saab

Major: Political Science
Hometown: Abilene, Texas
School: Abilene Christian University

Each student has a distinct way that helps him or her focus. Some chew gum, others fiddle with their pens or doodle, and still others make a point of maintaining eye contact with the professor for the entire class. For me, I work to intentionally pay attention to my point of focus.

- As you think about the subject matter being discussed, try to anticipate the next points. What line of logic is the presentation following?
- If you disagree with something that is being said, make a quick note of it so that you can think about it later, rather than allowing it to consume your attention space during the lecture. Be sure to listen to the entire message before you respond.
- If the subject matter is difficult or you feel your attention starting to slip, remind yourself that this class is important to your success. Briefly recall the goals you set for this class and push yourself to listen.
- Watch for changes in the instructor's enthusiasm, intensity, and use of visual aids. These clues will direct you to lecture content that is particularly important to your instructor.

Proceed with a System

Apart from paying attention, effective note taking in college classes also means proceeding with a system for taking those notes. By now you have discovered that each class in your schedule is unique. Not only are college classes different from high school classes, one college class differs from the next. If you are going to take notes in classes that differ so widely from one another, it makes sense to have more than one note-taking system. Compare it to the toolbox you have in your car or at home. This box is filled with different types of tools because it will be used to address different kinds of repair. One repair may require a screwdriver; another may require a hammer. You would not think of trying to make one tool do every repair, so it is a stretch to assume that one form of note taking will work in every class. Here we will consider the options you have and how they may apply to different classes. As you evaluate an individual class's subject matter and the instructor's teaching style, and as you consider the various note-taking systems that you can modify to suit your needs, you will find just the right tool for the job.

Outlines

Outlines work well with instructors whose lectures are clearly organized into major and minor ideas that flow in an orderly way. If your instructor offers a main idea, then expands on the idea with more detailed minor points, try taking notes using an outline format as illustrated here. The advantage of taking notes in this way is that you can rely on the structure of the outline to recall the key points and their relationships. This will diminish the amount of writing you need to do and present a visually appealing structure that can help you recall the lecture.

Example of an Outline

Topic: Narrative Criticism
Date: September 21, 2007

I. What Is Narrative Criticism?
    Narrative criticism is the careful analysis of the author's artful selection of content and form when telling a story.

II. What Components of a Story Need to Be Analyzed?
    A. The Plot
       The plot is the organizing principle of the story.
       It has a beginning, middle, and end.
    B. The Characterization
       Authors invite us to meet characters in a variety of ways.
       1. The character speaks.
       2. The character is spoken about.
       3. The character acts.
       4. The character's appearance is described.
       5. The character is named.
    C. The Shaping of Time
       1. Duration
       2. Sequence

Paragraphs

Not all lectures can be easily recorded using an outline. What is more, some people find the outline a less helpful review tool. When your instructor likes to present a main theme and then discuss examples and ideas that relate to the theme, a paragraph format may work well for you. This method of note taking groups thoughts under broader headings. The notes under those headings do not have to be grammatically complete sentences. However, they should cap-

Should I Use a Laptop?

Your laptop computer will be portable enough to take to class, but may not be the best way for you to take notes. The only way you will know for sure is to conduct an experiment. Take notes in the more traditional way by writing them out. Then transfer those notes to a computer file via your laptop after the class session. You are likely to find that pen-and-paper notes have some advantages you may wish to retain.

ture the main elements of the idea being presented. Leave lots of space within your notes if you choose this style. Later when you review your notes, you can add extra information or rewrite sections to make your notes clearer.

Example of Paragraph Notes

Topic: Narrative Criticism
Date: September 21, 2007

What Is Narrative Criticism?
Narr. criticism = careful analysis of the author's artful selection of content and form when
           telling story

What Components of a Story Need to Be Analyzed?

Plot is organizing principle of story . . . a beginning, middle, + end.
    Ex: David and Goliath—tension of Philistine invasion moves to victory of Israelite army.

Characterization
    How? Watch for the character speaking, spoken about, acting, appearance, and naming.
        Ex: Goliath—writer of 1 Sam 17 gives description of Goliath and directly quotes Goliath as
          he speaks to David

Shaping of Time
    How? Duration and sequence of time.
        Ex: time slows to emphasize the speech and character of David

Cornell Recall Columns

This system is based on the Cornell format developed by Walter Pauk.[3] For each page of your notes, draw a vertical line the length of the page three inches from the left edge of the paper. This will create two columns, one wider and one narrower. During class, take notes only on the wider, right side of the page. This is called the record column. After class when you are reviewing your notes, reduce the notes from the right side of the page to single words, phrases, or questions. Place them in the smaller column on the left side of the page. The item in this recall column may become the memory hook that serves as a path to the fuller discussion. After studying the record column of your notes, cover the record column and use the recall column to quiz yourself on the main points. Can you recite the information that is covered?

Example of a Cornell Recall Column

Topic: Narrative Criticism
Date: September 21, 2007

Definition	Narrative criticism is the careful analysis of the author's artful selection of content and form when telling a story.
Components: Plot	The components of a story that need to be analyzed: The plot is the organizing principle of the story. It has a beginning, middle, and end.
Characterization	Characterization is achieved when . . . 1. The character speaks. 2. The character is spoken about. 3. The character acts. 4. The character's appearance is described. 5. The character is named.
Time	Time is shaped by duration and sequence of events.

Visual Maps

A fourth format for taking notes can be used on its own or in conjunction with any of the methods previously described. Sometimes the information presented in class may be easier to remember if you turn the data into something with more visual appeal. One way to do so is to create a visual map (also known as a concept map). If the instructor leaps from one point to another and then backtracks to what was said earlier, it can be difficult to take notes using an outline or paragraph format. So instead try recording the information using a visual map. When creating a visual map, you will place the theme or topic in the very middle of the page. Draw a circle or square around it using a heavy line or bold color. Whenever a new point is introduced you can add that point to the picture and connect it with a line to the main point or one of the other subpoints you have already put in place. In the end, your notes will look like a large spider web with strands that connect various data to one another.

If you favor a visual or kinesthetic learning mode, you may find this a helpful way of turning a more verbal lecture into a picture. This is particularly true if you experiment with various shapes and colors to differentiate between types of information or between information of various levels of importance. Some students may hesitate to use this as their primary technique because it is so different from what they have done before. If that is the case for you, try converting some of your notes into a visual map as part of the review process.

Example of a Visual Map

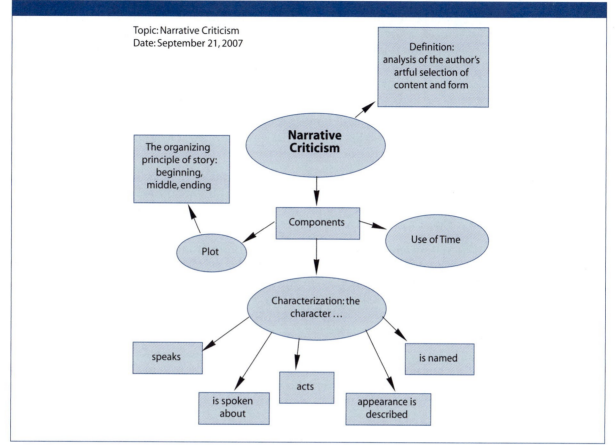

Topic: Narrative Criticism
Date: September 21, 2007

Definition: analysis of the author's artful selection of content and form

Narrative Criticism

The organizing principle of story: beginning, middle, ending

Components

Plot

Use of Time

Characterization: the character …

speaks

is spoken about

acts

appearance is described

is named

Nothing will be lost in the experiment and you may discover another tool that will function well for you in certain class settings. Remembering has much to do with seeing relationships, and visual maps easily illustrate relationships between concepts. Thus you may find yourself recalling information more easily when using a visual map rather than an outline or paragraph form.

General Tips for Any Note-Taking System

As you consider the various systems you can modify to meet the needs of your current classes, here are general tips that are helpful and applicable to any method.

Always date your notes. Dating your notes leaves no doubt regarding the chronology of the information presented in class. This is particularly helpful if the pages of your notes get mixed up or if you miss a day of class. In the latter case, you will be able to easily identify which day is missing so that you can fill in the gap with a classmate's notes.

Write on one side of the paper. Writing on both sides of a piece of paper means that you must consult both sides of the paper when reviewing your notes. The greatest advantage to writing on just one side of the paper will come during the review process. If you write your notes just on one side of the page, you will be able to lay your notes out in front of you on a large surface and be able to see everything at once. This can be of great help when you are attempting to define a chronology or logical flow that would be interrupted by flipping the page. At times, you may even remember an item from your notes by its position on the tabletop.

Leave blank space. Always be generous with the blank space you leave in your notes. This will prevent them from feeling crowded, even when you add additional insights you gain from a review session or when you compare your notes with those of a classmate.

Record information from boards, overheads, or computer-generated images. Because creating visual aids takes time and energy, your instructor will typically create them only for important information. Make sure you take note of them.

Ask if you do not understand something. Your education is important, and you deserve to understand all that you can. If the class session heads in a direction that is not clear to you, ask for help either during class or after class. You can even use e-mail. As long as you do not fault the instructor for your failure to understand, you are likely to find the classroom leader ready to help you in any way possible.

Use a "lost" signal. If you get lost in class and cannot complete a section of your notes, mark your notes so that you know where they are going to be incomplete. The "lost" signal will remind you to recover what you missed, from either the instructor or a classmate. Failure to mark such a location is a recipe for review frustration.

Develop your own shorthand. Many words or concepts will repeat when you take notes in a class. Save yourself space and writing time by developing shorthand symbols for commonly used words and concepts.

Record main ideas, not each word. Class lectures are typically structured to have several major points with supporting evidence and examples. Your goal in note taking should not be a word-for-word transcription of the lecture. Instead, your goal is to record the main points of the class and any evidence or examples that help you understand those main points. If you are having trouble figuring out what to write, listen for important themes. At some point in your college experience, you are likely to meet an instructor whom you have difficulty decoding. This is when an informal study group, Supplemental Instruction group, or note-taking companion can be helpful.

Taking Notes during Science and Math Classes

Taking notes in a math or science class is different from taking notes in a history or theology class. Math and science courses communicate more information through formulas, equations, graphs, charts, and pictures. Merely recording the formula, equation, or picture may not be enough to give you the

Should I Take Notes Now? Yes!

Learning experiences come in many shapes and forms. Just because today's class is not a traditional lecture hour does not mean that it is a good idea to leave your notebook in your backpack. Clearly, it is better to have notes that you may not need rather than realizing you need notes you do not have. The following are examples of learning experiences that your instructor may offer in connection with a college class. Do not be fooled into thinking this is "time off" when you can let your guard down.

- Guest speakers: People who are invited into a classroom generally bring some expertise, knowledge, or unique experiences to share. Note new concepts they bring to class and note how their perspective relates to what you have read and heard from your instructor.

- Videos or other electronic media: The information presented through videos could be brand-new information or examples that reinforce class readings and lectures. In either case, create a written record of those things that are important to you.

- Class discussions: Because college is about developing your communication skills as well as your listening skills, expect to be involved in group discussions. It may be more difficult to take notes and participate, but it is worth the effort. Pay particular attention when the instructor enters the conversation and expresses a criticism, compliment, or different point of view. Furthermore, if your instructor makes statements such as "That is an excellent example of . . ." or "That is the key to . . . ," be sure to note them. These are verbal cues that your instructor finds those comments important.

- Lab experiments or demonstrations: Lab experiments and demonstrations provide hands-on experience for students. Keep your notebook within arm's reach to record any important information that can supplement your lecture notes.

- Student presentations: Some instructors involve students in the learning experience by assigning individual or group presentations. Take notes during these presentations just as you would if your instructor lectures.

- Field trips: Bring along some type of notebook that is easy to carry as you engage in out-of-classroom experiences. You never know when something memorable will be said on a field trip.

understanding you seek. If you have math and science classes, we suggest the following.

- Be prepared: Complete all reading assignments before each class. Familiarize yourself with new vocabulary and new math or scientific symbols. Study examples of equations and formulas. This will give you a head start when they are used during class.

- Get a three-ring notebook: It is especially important that all your course materials stay organized. We suggest that you use a three-ring notebook for math and science courses. This way, you will be able to keep handouts, your own class notes, and homework problems in one place and grouped by topic.

- Think big, write large: A page that is densely filled with marks is less inviting to review. Give your eyes a break by writing larger and by leaving white space on the page. This is particularly useful when recording diagrams, formulas, or pictures.
- Review previous material: Higher-level math and science concepts usually build on basic information. If the foundation starts to erode over time, you will find it very hard to understand the advanced concepts. Refresh your memory by routinely reviewing the basics.

End with Review

Class is over and you have a set of notes in hand, but the most important part of the learning process still lies ahead: the review. It is vital to review your notes because this is where you will do most of the encoding that will secure the information in your long-term memory.

When?

Because you will forget much of the lecture within a day or two, plan to do the first review of your notes within twenty-four hours of taking them. Designate review sessions in your time management plan if you have not done so already. Do not recoil too quickly from the idea, because we are not talking about a significant block of time. Ten minutes per class session, set aside the same day the class has met, should do it. Even a student with a busy schedule can manage this brief review time to revisit the key points of the class. In addition to those brief sessions, we recommend a longer period of time each week during which you review and assimilate the data from that week's class. We will have more to say on that topic when talking about exam preparation. But an early review coupled with regular review will beat cramming every time.

How?

You have produced a valuable study tool. But the real value of that tool will not be realized unless you design creative ways to revisit the material during your review time. If you have been in the habit of just rereading your notes, we understand why the idea of reviewing your notes might seem a burden. Because you are in charge of how you use this time, make it as active, interesting, and diverse a time as you can. Here are a few suggestions that you can creatively combine and modify to meet your needs:

- Enter key words in the recall column of your notes and give yourself a quiz.
- Create a visual map to supplement the notes you took in class.
- Combine insights you obtained from the readings with your class notes.

- Recite your notes out loud.
- Try teaching what you have learned.
- After reciting the concepts, try to describe them in your own words without looking at your notes.
- Review foundation material for math and science courses.

Whatever you choose to do, make your review time an active learning time. And if you get bored with your routine, change it. You have the power to design this time in a variety of ways.

Baruch had an important job to do as he recorded the words of Jeremiah. Because his note taking was under the inspiration of the Holy Spirit, his notes could not be improved! That is not true of us. Because you will be taking notes every semester that you are in college, this is a great time to experiment with ways to improve the quality of your work. Try new techniques for improving your attentiveness in class. Experiment with different systems of taking notes to find one that fits the style and content of each class. Then design a review plan that is both timely and interesting. Old habits are hard to change. But changing old note-taking habits can be very worthwhile because it can improve your education across many classes.

Exercises for **Success**

Review Questions

1. In what ways can pre-class preparation contribute to better listening during class?

2. Compare and contrast the strengths and weaknesses of at least three note-taking systems presented in this chapter.

3. Identify three ways to use your review time to improve what you remember from your notes.

Stare and Compare

Pick a class that requires a lot of note taking. Ask three of your classmates for photocopies of their notes from one of the class sessions. Look at the product they have produced. Did they record the same content that you did? Compare their note-taking system to your own. How is it similar? How is it different? In which ways are their note-taking systems weaker or stronger than your own?

Defeating My Distractions

Not paying attention during class is a habit. You can blame the instructor, the class subject, or the person across the aisle, but your level of attention is also a habit. If you are in the habit of becoming inattentive during class, try the following exercise. Put a blank sheet of paper next to your notes on the desk. Put a check on the page every time you catch your mind wandering from the lecture. At first you may have a lot of marks on the page because you do not realize how often you give in to distracting thoughts, but the number of marks will decrease over time. By thinking more actively about where your attention lies during class, you will begin the process of defeating distractions.

Fit the System to Your Class

College classes differ from one another in terms of content, presentation technique, and testing. In this exercise, we challenge you to find a system of note taking and review that fits the uniqueness of each of your classes. Use the following chart to identify each class you are taking. Then give careful thought to the method of note taking and review that will allow you the best opportunity for success.

Class:

The best system for taking notes in this class would be:

The best time to review my notes for this class is:

I will review my notes using these methods:

Class:

The best system for taking notes in this class would be:

The best time to review my notes for this class is:

I will review my notes using these methods:

Class:

The best system for taking notes in this class would be:

The best time to review my notes for this class is:

I will review my notes using these methods:

Class:

The best system for taking notes in this class would be:

The best time to review my notes for this class is:

I will review my notes using these methods:

Note-Taking Experiment

Nothing ventured results in nothing gained. Now is the time to experiment with some dimension of your note-taking habits. After completing the previous exercise, pick one class and try the new approach you have described. Spend two weeks using the new techniques for note taking and reviewing. Then evaluate how successful your approach is and make adjustments as needed. Write a two-page paper that summarizes both your experiment and its outcome.

Time in Prayer

In your personal time in prayer or in connection with others in your class, take time to pray for the following people and needs:

- For the ability to focus and listen during classes

- For the diligence to study your notes on a daily basis

- For the ability to keep personal problems from distracting you during class

- For students who are feeling homesick and overwhelmed with work

On the Web

The Internet can be a helpful resource as you look for ideas to make yourself a happier and more successful student. Visit the College Success page offered by Thomson Wadsworth for Web links that will help you grow further on this topic. Go to http://www.success.wadsworth.com/ and click on Resource Web Links.

In particular, we recommend the following:

http://www.dartmouth.edu/~acskills/success/notes.html

http://www.d.umn.edu/kmc/student/loon/acad/strat/ss_notetaking.html

http://www.ucc.vt.edu/stdysk/notetake.html

http://www1.chapman.edu/arc/goodnotes.html

http://www.sas.calpoly.edu/asc/ssl/notetaking.systems.html

http://www.canisius.edu/jff/notetaking.asp

Endnotes

1. Michael P. Nichols, *The Lost Art of Listening* (New York: Guilford, 1995).

2. Florence I. Wolff and Nadine C. Marsnik, *Perceptive Listening,* 2nd ed. (Fort Worth, TX: Harcourt Brace Jovanovich, 1992).

3. Walter Pauk, *How to Study in College,* 6th ed. (New York: Houghton Mifflin, 1997).

Reading to Remember 7

Then Philip ran up to the chariot and heard the man reading Isaiah the Prophet. "Do you understand what you are reading?" Philip asked.

Acts 8:30

- **What types of reading occupy the time of a college student?**

- **How can I read so that I do not become tired and distracted?**

- **Where and when is it best for me to do my reading?**

- **How can more intentional reading improve the quality of my reading time?**

- **How can I recycle my reading in ways that improve what I remember?**

"Do you understand what you are reading?" The high-ranking Ethiopian official from Acts 8 was a very frustrated reader. This well-educated man was attempting to read the Book of Isaiah and find significance in the passage. He knew the meaning of all the individual words in the text, and he was correctly decoding each of the grammatical structures. But he still had difficulty comprehending the passage until Philip stepped up to his chariot and helped him understand what he was reading.

Many first-year college students have a similar experience. College textbooks are very different from the textbooks used in high school and from popular publications such as newspapers and magazines. They are written at a higher reading level, with more complex sentence structure and less familiar vocabulary. Like the royal official from Ethiopia, college students can turn every page in the chapter and read every word but still be frustrated in their bid to comprehend and remember what they have read.

Did You Say 150 Pages a Week?!

Do you understand what you are reading? If you find yourself answering this question with "no" on a regular basis, that can spell trouble for you as a college student because so much of college homework involves reading textbooks. Think about your assignments for any one week and you will likely find that textbook reading accounts for more than half of the homework you have been assigned. Those numbers can really add up. A typical undergraduate student can expect to read 2,500 pages or more every semester—more than 150 pages of reading every week! Consequently, anything you can do to improve your textbook reading will have a significant impact on your success.

Of course, as with all changes you make in old habits, changing your reading habit will take time and effort. You may feel frustrated during the process and want to quit, but we encourage you to stick with it. Commit yourself right now to improving your reading habit. Sample the ideas from this chapter, experiment with a new approach for several weeks, and then evaluate it. There is no magic bullet. Not everything you read in this chapter will work for you. But as you consider where and when you read, as you experiment with a new system for reading that is more intentional, and as you explore a method for recycling your reading, you will find something new that will help you read those 150 pages a week more effectively. That prize alone is worth reading this chapter and experimenting with methods for reading your college assignments. Take heart, because effective readers are made, not born.

Not Every Kind of Reading Is the Same

The first step toward improvement is to realize that a one-size-fits-all method for reading does not do justice to the wide variety of reading you do. Different types of reading invite different methods of reading. Consider the different approaches you may take when doing devotional reading, recreational reading, and analytical reading. The Lord invites us to hear his voice in our daily lives through the reading of his Word. In your quiet time, you may read and then meditate on the meaning of what you have read in God's Word. In contrast to this style of devotional reading, you will employ a different reading style in your recreational reading: when you sit down to read a popular magazine on a Saturday afternoon, when you read the daily newspaper at the breakfast table, when you pick up an adventure novel, or when you surf the Internet for a good deal on a used pair of in-line skates. This form of recreational reading is faster and lighter than analytical reading. Analytical reading is very careful and slow reading whose goal is to get every last detail just right. If you are attempting to troubleshoot a problem with your computer using the help menu, or if you are reading the contract you will sign for a student loan, or if you are reading a recipe for making a new dinner, you will employ this slow and careful form of analytical reading.

Textbook reading is different from devotional reading, recreational reading, or analytical reading in that it combines a higher level of concentration, a greater amount of time, and a greater need to retain what has been read. Textbooks are written using language that is more difficult than the language in a newspaper. The readings are longer than most magazine articles, and yet textbooks must be read more quickly than we would read a contract. Once you see that college textbook reading is different from other types of reading, you will see that it is important to have a distinct method and style that will help you read those textbooks for the valuable information they contain without committing more time than necessary to the task.

Primary and Secondary Sources

Your college reading assignments will take place in both primary and secondary sources. Primary sources are the original documents that record the prominent thinking of a notable individual or group from the past or present. The Bible, the U.S. Constitution, the letters written by Dr. Martin Luther King, and the audiotapes of President Richard Nixon are all examples of primary sources. When you read a primary source, your goal is to learn as much as you can about the views and perspective of the author or speaker. Sometimes it is helpful to read such documents out loud, changing your volume and tone to replicate the voice of the author to get a feel for the flow of language being used.

By contrast, secondary sources comment on and critique primary sources. They reflect the opinion and views of a subsequent reviewer who analyzes and interprets the material from the primary source. A commentary on the Book of Romans, an essay that discusses the application of the First Amendment to Internet pornography, or a book on the Watergate scandal are examples of secondary sources that use and seek to interpret primary resources. When reading secondary literature, your goal is to understand the perspective being argued in the secondary literature and to evaluate the evidence that the author is using to support his or her view of the primary source.

Nyanna Potter

Major: Public Relations/Advertising
Hometown: Denver, Colorado
School: Oklahoma Christian University

My frustration levels were high when I picked up my ultrathick textbooks from the bookstore and realized that I needed to read several hundred pages. There was so much reading to do and I instantly felt pressure in my chest. I was downright scared. I needed a plan like this. When looking ahead on my syllabus at a lengthy reading assignment, I normally take an hour, sit down, and read away. If I am crunched for time, I take a book with me as I run errands or go to meetings. That way I could whip out that book and get my assignment done on the fly!

Picking the Right Time and Place to Read

As you create a plan for reading your textbooks more effectively, you need to pick the right place and time to do that kind of reading. Remember that going to college is a full-time job, and reading is your primary responsibility in completing that job. That makes picking the right place and time for doing this work critical. Some types of reading can be done in almost any place and at almost any time. You can surf the Internet in a noisy café, or you can read a romance novel in a crowded bus that keeps stopping and starting. But neither place would be conducive to reading a textbook assignment that requires a higher amount of focus and concentration.

Distraction

Read your textbook in the wrong place or at the wrong time and you open the door for distractions to ruin your reading session. Think about your own habits for a moment. When you take a thought vacation from your textbook reading, what usually causes that distraction? The following is a list of items that could be the culprit. Circle each item that has been a problem for you and list any others we may have missed.

Television
Children
Music
Video games
Temperature
Lighting
Eye fatigue
General noise
Uncomfortable seating
Worry
Headache
Checking and rechecking the length of the assignment
Feeling drowsy

Right Time

One way to address these distractions is to be particular about when you plan to do your textbook reading. Reading at different times during the day will result in varying levels of success for the time you invest. Given the importance of reading your textbook effectively, you must pick times for your textbook reading when you are well-rested and most alert.

That prime time of the day will not be the same for everyone. Some have more energy and focus in the morning; others are more alert and focused at night. By setting aside the hours during the day when you are at your peak and reserving them for reading, you accomplish two things. First, that scheduled time keeps you from rushing through a reading assignment because you did not get around to reading it until just before it was due. Second, you can read at the times of the day that give you the best results in the least amount of time, lowering your level of frustration with the task.

Competing Noise

Selecting the time you read will give you some control over the level of competing noise you experience when reading. Some students require absolute quiet when they read. Others find that absolute quiet itself can distract them from their reading. Background noise is not necessarily harmful to your reading so long as the background noise does not change in volume or intensity. For that reason, it may be helpful to listen to very quiet background music while you read. But the noise associated with television, radio, and video gaming will be harmful to the reading process.

Length of Time

It is to your advantage to increase your reading time between breaks as much as you can, because each break you take introduces some inefficiency into the reading process. You may already have noticed that when you begin reading an assignment, you are reading with less focus and connection than after you have been reading for several minutes. The first five minutes is a time of light concentration during which you are easily distracted. Only after ten minutes of reading do you find yourself at a place of deep concentration. Thus the more often you take a break, the more often you go through the cycle that begins with minutes of less focused and less effective reading. If you reduce the number of breaks you take during any hour of reading, you will be reading more efficiently.

Of course, there is a limit to how long you can read in one sitting before you need to stand up and take a break. Consider forty-five minutes a realistic mark after which fatigue can diminish reading effectiveness. If your current habit allows you to read for only ten minutes without taking a break, do not be discouraged. You can lengthen the reading time you invest before taking a break by increasing the time slowly. Start with ten minutes, if that is your habit, and then increase it to twelve, fifteen, twenty, and so on until you are able to sit and read for thirty-five minutes or more without a break.

Studying with Sound

If you have been in the habit of studying with the television or radio playing in the background, you may be studying less effectively than you could be. Most students report that they can study better with some background noise than with absolute quiet. But studying with the television or radio on in the background can impede your focus and concentration. Programs on television and the radio are sponsored by people who want you to listen to their advertising. Thus they design the advertisements to recapture the lagging attention of the listening and viewing audience by changing the volume and intensity of the sound of their commercials. You can grow accustomed to having a television or radio playing in the background, but you will not be able to avoid the distraction that such advertising causes.

Once you have read for forty-five minutes, it is wise to take a ten-minute break that rejuvenates you mentally and physically. Just be cautious about how you use that break time. If you engage in an attractive alternative to reading such as watching TV or playing a game on your computer, that brief break could turn into an unintended hourlong distraction. Get up and stretch, walk around, get some fresh air, and you will be ready to engage your reading again. If you take a longer break or will not resume your reading until the next day, make a quick note to yourself about what you have been reading and what you expect to encounter next in the reading assignment. This diminishes the warm-up time and allows you to get back into the more effective reading zone more quickly.

Right Place

Selecting an appropriate place for reading can be as important as selecting the right time to read. Defining one location where you plan to do all your textbook reading enables you to control environmental factors that will help you read more efficiently. At a minimum, the place you select for reading should have comfortable seating, adequate lighting, and a temperature that is just right for you. Do not assume that just because your residence hall has a desk and chair that it will be the best spot for you to read. Be strategic and intentional about the choice of location. It could be the patio, the kitchen table, or a desk in the library.

By selecting a spot designated exclusively for studying, you will be able to control the noise and other distractions that prevent you from reading most effectively. Furthermore, when you study in the same place time after time, you move into a more effective study and reading mode more quickly because you have unconsciously associated that location with studying. For this reason, it

Rereading Is a Habit

Many students become frustrated when reading a textbook because they end up having to read a page more than once. If you are reading very difficult or technical language, rereading can be helpful. But if rereading is your regular habit, here are some things you can try. If you have eliminated all the other distractions in your reading area that could impede your focus, then it is time to address your habit of rereading a page of your textbook. You may have gotten into the habit of lowering your attentiveness the first time you read a page because you know that you always go back and read the page again. Here is one way of breaking that habit. The next time you read a page, place a piece of paper on the page and slide it over the sentences that you have completed reading. As you move your eyes from the top to the bottom of the page you will be covering up sentences that you have already read. You may need to employ this technique for a while before you notice that your habit is changing. But by using this method you are continually reminding yourself to pay attention to what you are reading the first time.

is unwise to read in bed or to nap in your reading spot, because it can cause role confusion. If you are accustomed to socializing while sitting at your desk, try reading in a different location. As you rethink the method you will use in reading your textbooks, give careful thought to the time and place you choose to read. You will be more efficient in your reading if you follow a routine and study in the same place and at the same time every week. Let that spot be one that is environmentally comfortable, has the tools you need at arm's reach, and is free from as many distractions as possible.

Reading with Intention

Once you have determined the best place and time to do your reading, it is time to check the method. Just as there is more than one kind of reading material, there is more than one method that can be used when reading. The variety of reading methods may be compared to the various ways in which people shop.

Different Ways to Shop

At times, you may travel to a store to do some recreational shopping. When you do recreational shopping, you are not really shopping because you need something from the store; you are there for the fun of it and would be content to leave the store without making a purchase. Consequently your feet wander through the aisles and your eyes wander haphazardly from one shelf to another. By contrast, another time you may be shopping for a special gift for someone. You may not know exactly what you want to buy, but your feet travel more intently past the lawn mowers and refrigerators, and on to the jewelry department. As your eyes light on an item, you pick it up and turn it over in your hands. You may set it down and walk away only to return later to reflect and mull over its merits as a gift for this special occasion. This thoughtful, reflective shopping not only looks different from recreational shopping, it also looks very different from the intentional shopping you may do in the grocery store. As an intentional shopper, you are not interested in browsing or mulling; you are interested in efficiency. You have made a list of things you need and your feet travel in a very direct line between the front door of the store, the shelves on which the items lie, and the checkout line. You waste no time as you get what is on the list and nothing else.

Different Ways to Read

Of course, there is nothing right or wrong about each of these shopping methods. They are simply different approaches that you would use on different types of shopping trips. Just as you use a different method for different types of shopping, you need to use different methods of reading for the different types of reading you do. The recreational shopping method is similar in style to the method you might use when doing your recreational reading. When you read the Sunday morning paper, your eyes glide haphazardly from one place to the next, looking at this or that article or advertisement between sips of coffee with no concern for time or efficiency. By contrast, the thoughtful shopping for a gift is comparable to the devotional reading we do in God's Word. We may read a passage of Scripture because it promises to offer us a word of direction or encouragement that we can immediately apply to our day. We read the passage thoughtfully, pausing to reflect and meditate on it. Finally, there is the intentional shopping that is done with a list. This form of shopping is most analogous to the style of reading we may best employ when reading a textbook chapter. If we read the textbook assignment with a list of questions to pursue, we convert our reading from an aimless journey into a focused quest for information. We believe that this kind of intentional reading will save you time as well as the frustration of reaching the bottom of the page completely unaware of what you have just read. This more intentional form of reading can be done in more than one way. But here we offer a process of reading that has three steps: preview, question, and pursue.

Reading with Intention!

1. Preview
2. Question
3. Pursue

Preview the Reading

In the first step of this process, we encourage you to spend at least five minutes previewing the reading assignment. This time helps you warm up your mind and clarify the context of all that you read. Before you engage in any form of serious physical activity, you should warm up your body. The drills you do before your athletic team practices or the stretching you do before running prepares the muscles in your body so that they are switched on and ready to go when you push them more aggressively. The same is true of your brain. Just a bit of warming up helps you think more effectively and efficiently when you get aggressive in your reading.

In addition, this preview provides a context for the steps that follow. Consider the following short story.

> *A man left home, ran for a while, and then turned left. After a brief pause he started running again, and again he turned left. He continued running and turned left just before meeting a masked man. Nevertheless, he arrived back home safely.*

If you are unclear about the meaning of this story, it is not because you do not understand the vocabulary and the grammar, but because you do not understand the context of this communication. Now reread the story but do so in the context of watching a baseball game. Suddenly the message being communicated is clear. Someone has just scored a run! Context is critical to reading a textbook chapter, and a preview of the reading can get you that context.

During this five-minute preview, turn the pages of the chapter quickly and look for clues about its contents and organization. Read the chapter title and the subheadings within the chapter. Look at the pictures, charts, or illustrations. Read the introductory and concluding paragraph of the chapter. In these five minutes of preview reading, you will not get everything you need but you will have a clearer idea of what the author is talking about in the chapter and how the ideas are organized. Remember, context is critical to your understanding of every sentence and paragraph in that assignment. If you fail to grasp the context before you read it, you are requiring your mind to do two things at once—figure out the context and figure out how what you are reading applies to that context. This requires you to read more slowly, to back up, and to reread portions of the assignment that were less clear. The first step in reading your college textbook with greater intention is to conduct a preview reading of it. This step alone can increase your retention by 20 percent.

Question the Reading

Once you are warmed up and have set the context with a preview, now it is time to question the reading by developing a list of things you want to learn from the reading assignment. That list will take the form of questions. Look again at the chapter heading, the subheadings within the chapter, the introduction and conclusion, the words and phrases that are in italics or bold. You can then turn these smaller segments of information related to the overall theme of the chapter into questions that the chapter promises to answer.

For example, suppose you are studying the chapter in your Old Testament history book that discusses the Book of Leviticus. As you preview the chapter, you notice a subheading titled "Sacrifices and Offerings." During this step of the reading process, you can turn that subheading into two questions related to the larger context of the chapter topic: What sacrifices does God request of his people in Leviticus? What offerings does God request from his people in Leviticus? A further subheading in this section is titled "The Significance of Blood." This also can become a question: What is the significance of blood in the Levitical worship rites? Perhaps the author of this chapter has also put some important terminology in italics, phrases such as *whole burnt offering* and *peace offering*. These words can also become questions: What is a whole burnt offering? What is a peace offering? When you finish this step of the reading process, you have identified the most important topics the chapter discusses and have turned them into questions.

Watch Your Speed!

The typical college student has an average reading speed of about 240 words per minute. If you are attempting to do all of your textbook reading at the same speed, whether it is faster or slower than that, you are making a strategic error. The most effective college readers change the pace of their reading according to the type of assignment they are reading. For example, preview reading and reading of literature assignments may be done at a faster-than-average pace. By contrast, more technical reading for a science or math assignment may demand a slower pace and strategic rereading of certain paragraphs. Successful college students watch their reading speed and vary the speed with which they read from one assignment to the next.

Pursue the Answers

The preview and question phases of this method are followed by pursuit. With the questions in hand, it is now time to read the chapter. That does not mean that you will read every single word in the chapter. That is no longer your goal. Now you are pursuing the answers to your questions, reading only the portions of the chapter that are necessary to complete that task. Consequently your reading has become more intentional, directed, and focused. And each time your pursuit is successful, you will feel the reward.

Your search for the answers also becomes more efficient if you read with an awareness of how the author organizes most textbook paragraphs. Typically a textbook paragraph has a topic sentence that introduces the topic or thesis the paragraph will address. The topic sentence is followed by sentences that either illustrate or support the statement. You can use that organization to determine whether the paragraph contains information that is important to your quest. Remember that the goal is not to read every paragraph, but to read only those that answer the questions you have raised.

One word of caution is in order here. As you begin to use this approach to reading your textbook, you may fall into the unhealthy habit of stopping too soon and too often. Remember that context is important, so read an entire section of the chapter before you pause to write down the answer to one of your questions; otherwise you may miss the larger picture the author is attempting to convey. This can result in the frustration of landing on either wrong or incomplete answers to your questions. Be sure that you read an entire section and then articulate the answer to the question that section promises to offer.

Recycle Your Reading

If you read with intention in the way we just described, you will get more out of the textbook than you would otherwise. But the information you encounter in that reading and the answers to the questions you have raised will not stick with you unless you also recycle that reading. This method of review requires that you record the questions and answers just discussed and then actively review that material by using a recycling plan.

Design a Reading Record

The first step is to design a *reading record* of your questions and answers. This reading record can be generated in any number of ways.

Textbook Marking For example, you may write the questions you want to answer in the margin of the textbook. As you read through a section and discover the answers to your questions, mark the textbook to call attention to those answers. Alternatively you may use a highlighter to highlight the answers to the questions in different colors in order to discriminate between major and minor points. Another way to mark the answers to your questions is to create a shorthand method of notation. Answers to your questions could be double underlined. Critical points could be marked with a "!" and matters that you want to clarify later could be marked with a "?."

This system has its advantages and disadvantages. It permits you to write the questions and mark the answers right in the book. This saves time rewriting the answers. But on the other hand, there is a distinct advantage to putting the author's ideas in your own words, as is required in the other recording systems noted shortly. When you mark the textbook with a highlighter, you risk marking too much of the text. A textbook page that is colored completely in yellow is of very little value to you! So if you elect to highlight the answers to your questions, be sure to read the entire section of the chapter before you mark. And then mark only the items that are critical to you in answering your questions.

Example of Textbook Marking

Psychoanalytic Psychology

what is the unconscious?

As mainstream psychology grew more scientific, an Austrian physician named Sigmund Freud was developing his own theories. Freud believed that mental life is like an iceberg: Only a small part is exposed to view. He called the area of the mind that lies outside personal awareness the **unconscious.** According to Freud, our behavior is deeply influenced by unconscious thoughts, impulses, and desires—especially those concerning sex and aggression. Freud's ideas opened new horizons in art, literature, and history, as well as psychology (Westen, 1998). Freud theorized that many unconscious thoughts are threatening, which causes them to be **repressed** (actively held out of awareness). But sometimes, Freud said, hidden thoughts and wishes are revealed by dreams, emotions, or slips of the tongue. ("Freudian slips" are often humorous, as when a student who is tardy for class says, "I'm sorry I couldn't get here any later.") Freud believed that all thoughts, emotions, and actions are determined. In other words, if we probe deeply enough, we will find the causes of everything we think, feel, or do. Freud was also among the first to appreciate that early childhood experiences affect adult personality ("The child is father to the man"). Most of all, perhaps, Freud is known for creating psychoanalysis, a method of psychotherapy that explores unconscious conflicts and emotional problems.

what is unique about Freud's psychoanalytic psychology?

Source: From Introduction to Psychology: Gateways to Mind and Behavior *9th Edition by Coon, 2001. Reprinted with permission of Wadsworth, a division of Thomson Learning.*

Note Cards or Self-Sticking Notes   A second way to record the questions and answers is to use note cards or self-sticking notes. As you question the reading, write your questions on one side of the card or sticky note. When you begin to read for the answers, you can write them on the back side of the card or sticky note.

This system has several advantages. First, it gives you the opportunity to write the answer to each question in your own words. This is much more valuable than simply rereading the answer or copying the exact words of the author onto your card. Second, it allows you to manipulate the information on the desk or wall in front of you. You can create separate piles for separate topics in the chapter. You can stick the answers on the wall and create patterns of association that may help you recall the answers to the questions. You can quiz yourself by asking the question and then flipping the card or note to see the answer. But most of all, it allows you to put the textbook aside when you are done reading and focus instead on the parts of the reading that are of the greatest value to you, the ones that you yourself have written on the cards.

What does the Book of Leviticus mean
when it talks about holiness?

(front)

Something that is holy is "set apart" from things that are
common or ordinary in order to be of service to the Lord.

Example: furniture and utensils used in the Tabernacle.

(back)

Reading Notes A third way to design a record of your reading is to use regular note paper. Take a sheet of paper and draw a vertical line three inches from the left margin, leaving a smaller column on the left side of your page and a larger column on the right side of your page. As you question the text, write your questions on the left side of that page; when you hunt for the answers and find them, place the answers to the right of the line you have drawn in the larger column.

Like the card or note system, this has the advantage of allowing you to put the answers to the questions in your own words. It also allows you to put the textbook aside when you are done reading and focus on the work you have written. And it allows you to quiz yourself by covering the right side of the page and asking yourself the questions in the left column. The one disadvantage to this approach is that it prevents you from mixing up the questions when you quiz yourself or maneuvering the questions around on your desktop. But if you find that you study from a page of notes better than from smaller cards, this system may be more effective for you.

What was the role of the person who wanted to make a sacrifice?	1. Present the animal for sacrifice. 2. Place a hand on the animal's head to personally identify with the animal. 3. Take the animal's life.

Design a Recycling Plan

If you have read your textbook using the plan just described, you now have a record of your reading that is ready for recycling. The plan you develop for recycling your reading will require you to spend additional time with the information and concepts you have already met. As you plan your review time, be aware that it is most advantageous for you to review what you have written shortly after you complete your reading, and regularly in brief sessions after that. Multiple review sessions over a longer period of time are worth much more to you than one long review session right before an exam. We recommend that once you have finished writing and answering your questions, you should review for at least half the time you spent in the reading process. For example, if your preview, questioning, pursuing, and recording took forty minutes, it would be wise to dedicate another twenty minutes that same day to recycling your questions and answers.

Be careful how you plan to use that time, because a poorly designed recycling plan will cause you to lose interest and focus. Create as much variety in this time as you can, while giving special time to techniques that work best for you. For example, during this recycling time, you can quiz yourself by using the questions you raised. You can rearrange the questions in different ways on your desktop or wall. You can recite the information out loud. You can work with a partner to develop a game in which you challenge each other to answer the questions from the reading. You can reformat the answers by making a visual map or a timeline. The point is that there are many ways to review what you have gained from the reading. Do not let your recycling time fall flat because of a lack of creativity in its design.

Do you understand what you are reading? A considerable part of your homework time will be claimed by textbook reading. If you are having trouble understanding or remembering what you have read, consider adjusting your reading habits. Realize that different types of reading require different approaches. Select a time and location for your textbook reading that minimizes distractions and optimizes your chances for successful reading. Check your reading method for the level of intentionality that it requires. Establish the context of your reading with a preview of the chapter before you establish the questions that will turn your textbook reading into a pursuit for answers. Then design a recycling program for your reading that allows brief but frequent contact with your reading record. A system like this will go a long way toward building better understanding of what you read as well as help you remember what you need to know.

Exercises for **Success**

Review Questions

1. Describe the location that will give you the best chance to read your textbook without becoming distracted.

2. Explain what is meant by "intentional reading."

3. In what ways can you most effectively recycle your reading?

Design Your Own Textbook Reading System

Within this chapter you have read about a system that you can use when reading a college textbook assignment. Because one size never fits all, use the system described in this book as a starting point and design your own reading system. Be sure to provide as many details about that system as you can. How much time will you spend prereading the text? How will you record the questions and answers you discover in that reading? On what schedule and in what ways will you recycle the reading assignment?

Now pick one of the classes in which you regularly have a reading assignment. For the next two weeks, experiment with the reading system you have just designed.

Following your two-week experiment, write a two-page report for your instructor that describes both your experimental reading system and the results of your two-week experiment in using it.

Develop Your Vocabulary by Building a Word Wall

As a college student, you will encounter new vocabulary every week. Many of those new words will first come to you in the reading assignments you complete. Your professors will expect you to become familiar with these new words used in their area of specialty and to use them in papers you write for their classes. You can be certain that you will meet them again in the exams just ahead. One way that you can build your vocabulary is to make part of the wall in your study room a "word wall." Each time you encounter a word you do not know and want to remember, write it on a sticky note. Put the word on one side and its meaning on the other. Post those notes on the wall and look at them from time to time. As you review them and meet them again in future reading and class discussion, you will add to your vocabulary base. You can even turn this into a game with your roommates. Select five words and quiz each other on their meaning. Loser cleans the room!

SPIRITUAL REFLECTION JOURNAL

God has chosen to communicate with us using the written word. When we read that Word, we are being carried forward in faith to an extraordinary eternity with him. As the Apostle John has said, "These are written so that you may believe that Jesus is the Christ, the Son of God, and that by believing you may have life in his name." (John 20:31) Consequently we hear of people from Moses to Paul who are either reading God's Word or challenging others to do so (Exod 24:7, Neh 8:1–8, Luke 4:13–21, Col 4:16, 1 Tim 4:13, and Rev 1:3). Read those passages and then consider the time you spend reading God's Word. Write about your Bible-reading habits and how you want to improve them.

Time in Prayer

In your personal time in prayer or in connection with others in your class, take time to pray for the following people and needs:

- For the courage to speak with the faculty members in whose classes I am having trouble

- That I, like Philip, may be ready to help someone read God's Word more effectively

- That I may improve on my own Bible-reading habits

- That I may define a method through which I might read my textbooks more effectively

- For my seminar instructor and the well-being of his or her family

On the Web

The Internet can be a helpful resource as you look for ideas to make yourself a happier and more successful student. Visit the College Success page offered by Thomson Wadsworth for Web links that will help you grow further on this topic. Go to http://www.success.wadsworth.com/and click on Resource Web Links.

In particular, we recommend the following:

http://www.dartmouth.edu/~acskills/success/reading.html

http://www.ucc.vt.edu/lynch/TextbookReading.htm

http://www.mtsu.edu/~studskl/Txtbook.html

http://www.coh.arizona.edu/English/Inst/engl108s1/project/reading_college.html

http://www.lemoyne.edu/academic_advisement/academic_support_center/texttip.htm

Scoring on Your Exams 8

> *When the queen of Sheba heard of Solomon's fame, she came to Jerusalem to test him with hard questions.*
>
> 2 Chronicles 9:1

- **How can I design an effective preparation plan?**
- **What can I do during the exam to improve my grade?**
- **How can I control the anxiety that washes over me before and during an exam?**
- **What can I do when I am tempted to cheat on an exam?**

Tests have been around since the beginning of time. After God created Adam and Eve, he invited them to eat from the plants in the Garden of Eden but instructed them not to eat from the tree of knowledge of good and evil. Satan measured their confidence in God's directive by asking them this test question: "Did God really say, 'You must not eat from any tree in the garden'?" (Gen 3:1) After Joseph was sold as a slave by his older brothers, he had every reason to wonder if they would also do harm to his younger brother, Benjamin. So he tested his older brothers to see if they would abandon Benjamin when he came into harm's way (Gen 44). And when the queen of Sheba heard about the incredible wisdom that God had given to King Solomon, she came to test him with hard questions (2 Chr 9:1).

Your life has also been filled with tests. From the time you were in grade school, the week was punctuated by tests and quizzes measuring everything from your ability to spell *luxury* to your skill at summarizing the achievements of Eli Whitney. Those early tests, like your college exams, are designed to give you and your instructor feedback on your progress. But college exams look and feel very different from the previous exams you have taken. In college you are tested less often, so each exam covers significantly more material and has a greater voice in

111

determining your course grade. What is more, your answers are evaluated against much higher standards. For that reason, it is important to rethink and to edit both the way in which you prepare for your college exams and the strategies you use in taking them.

This chapter will give you the opportunity to do just that. When reading this chapter, you may find a number of techniques celebrated and encouraged that you already use as you prepare for and take exams. On the other hand, you may encounter ideas that you have not tried but that are worth exploring. For some, anxiety associated with exams can interfere with the demonstration of their knowledge and skills on the tests. So here you will also read about the anxiety that attends college exams and how you might best manage the stress that you encounter. Finally, each exam you take in college is also an opportunity to demonstrate your integrity. So we will discuss cheating on exams and how to manage the temptations to cheat that will most certainly come your way. In the end, we believe that by checking and editing your approach to college exams, you will receive even better grades on them.

Design an Exam Preparation Plan

At the moment, you have an exam preparation habit whether you formally call it that or not. Portions of that habit may date back to the very first exams you took in grade school. But if you try to prepare for a college exam in the same way that you prepared for a grade school exam, you will not meet with the success you desire. In this portion of the chapter, we offer an exam preparation plan that you can edit to suit your needs. It has several steps: define the scope of the exam, determine the type of exam, establish a preparation schedule, employ effective review techniques, and improve your memorization skills.

Define the Scope of the Exam

Your college instructor determines what knowledge or skills are evaluated on an exam, but students have a right to know on what topics they will be tested. A good place to begin defining the scope of any college exam is the class syllabus. Reread the goals of the course to remind yourself of the outcomes the instructor seeks. Then check the course schedule to determine the chronological organization of the course and where this exam lies. Listen carefully to the description that the instructor gives during class to define the scope of the exam and write it down. Because your instructor wants you to prepare effectively for the exam, he or she may even invite you to ask any questions you have about the exam. Get all the information that you can. Will the exam be based on the assigned reading, the lectures, the discussion, the handouts, the guest speakers? Will the exam be cumulative, testing you on all your learning experiences to date, or limited to the last unit? Defining the scope of the exam is the first step in the preparation process.

Determine the Type of Exam

Exams differ from one another not only in their scope but also in their format. Because you will prepare differently for an essay exam than for a true/false exam, it is critical to determine the type of exam that lies ahead. As a college student you will see exams in many different formats:

True/false	Brief essay	Open book
Multiple-choice	Extended essay	Test bank
Matching	Take-home	

If the exam is going to have more than one type of question, attempt to find out how many points of the exam will be associated with each type of question. Your teacher may or may not be comfortable disclosing this kind of information. But there certainly is no harm in asking and learning all you can about the way your teacher is going to design this evaluation tool. Toward that end, make sure that you attend the last class before the exam. College instructors often spend at least part of that time reviewing for the exam and often give further clues about the exam's content and format. You do not want to miss that!

Establish a Preparation Schedule

As soon as you know the date or approximate date of the exam, it is time to establish a preparation schedule. That schedule of activities may not kick into gear the first day of class, but the first day of class is the time to identify the dates for the exams and establish the schedule that will guide your preparation.

The All-Nighter

Some college students employ a test preparation technique they call the "all-nighter." The night before an exam they literally stay up all night and use the time when they would normally be sleeping to prepare for the exam. This technique is destined for trouble at more than one level. First, this technique assumes that study time is of the same quality no matter when during the day it is invested. But a study session after 2:00 am, when you have already experienced a full day of work and play, will not be high-quality study time. You may be going through all the motions of exam preparation, but studying with a tired mind will not produce strong results. Second, because learning continues during sleep as our brain consolidates and further deepens our recollection of information acquired just before going to sleep, you rob yourself of a critical part of the learning process. And finally, if you stay up all night you will be both mentally and physically exhausted at just the time when you need to be most refreshed. The all-nighter may sound appealing, but it promises only to disappoint those who rely on it.

This approach contrasts with the more serendipitous approach of studying for an exam when there is nothing better to do or leaving all the preparation until the night before the exam.

Just a Little at a Time There is a limit on how much information we can acquire and master in any given amount of time. Furthermore, there is a limit to how long we can maintain the high level of concentration needed for test preparation. So it makes the most sense to design a preparation schedule that extends back several days before the exam to allow you to process and digest the information you need more slowly. We do the same thing physiologically. We need a certain number of nutrients in any given week to remain healthy and to function normally. But rather than attempt to eat and drink everything that we need for one week in one day, we eat and drink smaller portions over several days. This is analogous to what we are suggesting you do as you prepare for an exam. Reintroduce yourself to the information over an extended period of time. This gives you the opportunity to reflect on that information, organize it, consolidate it, and so master it in preparation for the exam.

The Week and Day before the Exam One week before the day of the exam is the latest that a daily review of the material should begin. Depending on the exam's difficulty, set aside one to two hours of time each day for the first six days. Put this time into your weekly schedule and defend it against all intruders. You may spend a bit more time than that the day before the exam, but do not wear yourself out mentally or emotionally on that day. It is wise to keep the day before the exam as typical as possible, putting your final review as close to bedtime as possible. Even when we are sleeping, our mind continues to process and work with the information most recently added. Because of that, you will wake up better prepared than when you went to sleep!

The last day before the exam is also a day to be careful with your sleep and diet patterns. If you have been preparing for the exam over the previous week, you do not need to stay up later than usual the night before the exam and you will benefit from being physically rested when you take the test. What is more, be careful about your food and liquid intake. Eat fruits, vegetables, and foods

Cramming

If you are cramming for a college exam, you are working at a disadvantage. Because we can assimilate only so much information in a given amount of time, this technique always prevents students from achieving true mastery of the material. The only time we recommend this technique is in an emergency when some preparation is better than no preparation at all. If you are forced to cram for an exam, be aware that you must dramatically limit the scope of what you can effectively learn. Focus your time and energy on the big points and on the topics where you feel most vulnerable. And be ready to accept a lower grade for your efforts, because cramming costs you learning.

that are high in complex carbohydrates. These foods help you achieve a more balanced physical and mental state and avoid the peaks and valleys that can occur after using stimulants or foods with an abundance of simple sugars.

Employ Effective Review Techniques

If you are not in the habit of setting aside an hour or more a day to prepare for a coming exam, you may find it difficult to experiment with this approach unless you are aware of the various review techniques you may employ during that time. Hours and hours of just rereading your notes is a recipe for boredom that will not give you the results you are seeking. The goal is to manipulate the material you wish to review through a series of encounters. Early in the exam preparation week, we recommend that you begin a process of reducing, reorganizing, and reformatting your notes. Not every experience you have with a given class is valuable to you on the coming exam. Thus you must reduce the large amount of information that you have read, listened to, written, and discussed into a smaller quantity of information for review. Once you have reduced the data, it is time to reorganize and reformat it. You may use summary sheets, flash cards, or visual maps. By reexperiencing that meaningful core of information and manipulating it in this way, you will be on your way to remembering it.

Once you have reduced, reorganized, and reformatted your educational experience in this class, it is time to create repeated encounters with it. Vocal rehearsal (recitation of that information) deepens both your recollection and your understanding of it. Use flash cards and test yourself out loud. Get together with others in the class who are as serious as you are about success and teach the material to one another out loud, or go for a private walk during which you talk out your review.

Apart from reciting the information out loud, written practice further deepens your total preparation. If the exam requires you to use mathematical formulas, practice using those formulas. If the coming exam includes essay questions, practice writing essays you make up or try answering the questions raised at the end of the textbook chapter. The week before you take an exam can be filled with meaningful practice if you employ review and recitation exercises like these that keep you interested and animated throughout the process.

Improve Your Memorization Skills

Although effective thinking is more than just the ability to recall data, the ability to recall data is a critical part of effective thinking. Consequently, most college exams require you to hold and maintain a significant amount of information in your memory. Anything you can do to improve the memorization process will help you prepare for your college exams.

Short-Term and Long-Term Memory First, realize that God has created us with more than one kind of memory. Psychologists speak about short-term memory and long-term memory. Short-term memory is very helpful in the short run. It allows us to recall five to nine items for thirty seconds or so. This form of memory is wonderful for recalling our meal selection at a restaurant after closing the menu but is inadequate for remembering all the vocabulary needed to translate a paragraph of French literature. We need long-term memory for the latter task. Such long-term memory consists of encoding information, storing it in a meaningful way, and then retrieving it when we need it. If you have taken your French vocabulary through this cycle, it will be there when you need to translate.

Principles to Consider Several principles associated with placing items in long-term memory are helpful to know if your goal is to improve your memorization skills. First, it is easier to memorize something we understand than something we do not understand. For example, college students have a much easier time recalling the words to a German song they are memorizing if they can translate it than if they are just memorizing a series of unfamiliar sounds. In addition, the laws of *primacy* and *recency* confirm that we are more likely to recall things early in a learning experience and late in a learning experience than items in the middle of a learning experience. If your goal is to place something in long-term memory, a simple mathematical calculation shows that multiple review sessions spaced over time are better than one long session, because there will be more cycles with first and last items in them. Those multiple review sessions also give you the opportunity for repetitive practice. And such repetition also speeds the process of memorization. In this regard, many educators suggest that key concepts should be overlearned. *Overlearning* occurs when material is reviewed past the point of mastery by 50 percent. For example, if it takes you thirty minutes to master your German vocabulary list, study that vocabulary for an additional fifteen minutes to get to the point of overlearning.

Memory is also enhanced by adding multiple senses into the learning process. Students in a German class learn more quickly that the word *Tür* means "door" if they tape the word *Tür* to their residence hall room door and say it out loud each time they touch the door. Finally, we are more likely to recall things that are organized for us. A random series of names or dates is much harder to remember than a carefully organized list. If the items do not organize easily on their own, try using mnemonic devices to aid your recall of random lists.

Success on exam day is closely associated with the type of plan you use to prepare for that day. Check the design of your plan. Do you define the scope of the exam? Do you learn all you can about the type of questions you will meet during the exam? Do you establish a preparation schedule that allows you to reduce, organize, consolidate, and review the data? Do you employ review techniques that are both effective and keep your interest? And are you honoring the principles of memorization that will help you recall the data?

Design an Exam-Taking Strategy

Planning for a successful test session does not end when you arrive in class the day of the exam. You can also do some key things during the exam to improve your grade. This portion of the chapter will talk about effective ways to use the first five minutes of your time, strategies for writing different types of exams (e.g., true/false, essay, take-home), and how to manage the anxiety that attends an exam session.

Memory Aids

Poems, acronyms, and phrases can help you recall concepts or lists of facts that are hard to remember. When you needed to figure out how many days there are in the month of April, you may have relied on the poem "Thirty days hath September, April, June, and November; all the rest have thirty-one. . . ." Here is a poem to help you recall the resignation of President Nixon in 1974: "In 1974 Richard Nixon found the door." Or when spelling the word *deceive*, you may have repeated the rhyme "*i* before *e* except after *c*."

Phrases can also help recall details that are hard to remember. For example, the phrase "*Every Good Boy Does Fine*" can be used to recall the musical notes represented on the lines of the treble clef.

An acronym is also helpful when you need to recall a list of things. *AROW* helps pilots remember which documents they need to have in their airplane to fly it legally. *AROW* stands for *a*irworthiness certificate, *r*egistration, *o*perating limitations, and *w*eight and balance information. If you have to recall the names of the Great Lakes, try using the acronym *HOMES*, which stands for *H*uron, *O*ntario, *M*ichigan, *E*rie, and *S*uperior.

It takes a bit of work and creativity to form these memory aids. But that time and effort can pay big benefits if they help you recall details that easily escape into thin air.

The First Five Minutes

On the day of the exam, arrive early and take a few minutes to get comfortable in your seat. Make sure that you have all the tools you will use during the exam, such as a calculator, exam review sheet, and extra pen or pencil. You may also consider bringing a snack to eat, particularly during a long exam period. We are not suggesting you attempt to eat an entire meal, but a quick snack or beverage during the exam can reanimate your focus and energy level. Before you receive the exam, take time to pray that the Lord will help you think clearly during the exam, limit your anxiety, and write at the very highest level that you can.

Once the exam reaches your hands, listen carefully to any oral instructions and guidance that is given. If you direct all your attention immediately to one of the questions, you may miss valuable help being offered by your teacher. After the instructor is done speaking, take several minutes to survey the entire exam and read the directions for each section. You may find that you have options that are different from those you had expected. For example, you may be asked to answer two of the three essay questions offered. Or you may find that in the true/false section, you are to correct answers that you mark false.

This is also the time to determine how much time to spend on each segment of the exam. This decision takes into account both the point value associated with each segment of the exam and a reasonable estimate of how long you need to compose your answers for each section. Consider writing down specific times in the margin of the exam to indicate when you intend to start and finish each section. For example, you may plan to do the multiple-choice questions from 8:35 to 8:45 and focus on the essay questions from 8:45 to 9:15. Of course, having a watch or clock in plain view will help you track your progress. As you plan your time, allow yourself time to return to any questions that gave you difficulty and to do a final check on all the answers. This strategic use of the first five minutes of the exam delays the time between receiving the exam and writing your first answers, but it improves the quality of the time you spend writing down answers and leaves you feeling much more in control of the effort.

Writing the First Answers With that plan in hand, it is time to answer the first question. In almost all cases, there is no rule that says you must begin by answering the first question on the very first page. During your survey of the exam, you may have identified a section of the exam about which you are very confident. This is the place to start, whether it is on the first page of the exam or the last. Completing that portion of the exam will give you a positive start, making you feel more confident about yourself as you move into the portions of the exam that challenge you even more.

As you move through the rest of the exam, expect to encounter questions that are more difficult for you. When you come to a more difficult question, decide whether it is best to wrestle with it now or leave it for later. Many students find that if they mark such a question and leave it for later, another portion of the exam gives them an insight that helps them answer the question they have set aside. This is particularly true of essay questions. When you first encounter an essay question that will be more challenging for you, write down as much as you know at the moment and then move through the rest of the exam. Clues quietly given in the rest of the test may help you further develop the answer to that troubling essay question.

Strategies for Different Formats

The goal of all tests is to measure your progress toward an educational goal. But educational goals differ from one another and so you will meet tests that differ in format from one another. Tests such as true/false, multiple-choice, and matching are primarily designed to measure your knowledge of the facts. Essay tests and take-home tests are designed to measure both your knowledge of the facts and your ability to use higher forms of thinking as you compose your answer.

True/False Exams When you are asked to mark a series of statements as either true or false, consider the following. It is difficult to write a persuasive false statement, so expect that more of the statements in a true/false test will be true. As you approach one of the statements, assume that it is true and stay with that point of view unless you can find something wrong with it. As you do so, watch out for little words that can turn a true statement into one that is false, such as *always*, *never*, and *only*. And keep a sharp eye out for words such as *not* and *except* that completely reverse the meaning of the sentence. For example, the following statement is true: "Jesus healed the sick on the Sabbath." But it becomes false when the word *only* is added: "Jesus healed the sick only on the Sabbath." It also becomes false when the word *except* is added: "Jesus healed the sick except on the Sabbath." Do not become consumed with attempts to find patterns or sequences of true or false statements in the test. Focus on each statement one at a time. Assume that it is true unless you can find something false with it. And if you are absolutely uncertain about an answer, guess that it is true. Remember there are usually more true statements on an exam than false statements.

Multiple-Choice Tests Multiple-choice questions typically consist of a stem (an incomplete sentence) and several answers that would finish that incomplete sentence. Among the possible answers are one or more correct answers that would build a true statement when linked to the stem. Usually there are also one or more distracters, answers that when linked to the stem create a sentence that has the appearance of correctness but creates a false or incomplete statement. Multiple-choice tests can be written in one of two ways. Either you are asked to find just one correct answer, or you are asked to mark all answers that are correct. Be sure to read the directions carefully to determine which of the two is required.

The best approach to answering multiple-choice questions begins with reading the stem and proposing an answer before you look at the choices. Then, rather than searching for the right or most complete answer(s), identify and cross out the answers that are wrong or incomplete. This process of elimination will leave you with the best answer(s) while lowering your risk of being taken in by an appealing answer that is either wrong or incomplete. Consider the following multiple-choice question.

Abraham's son, Isaac, had two sons. Their names were

A. Jacob and Esau.

B. Isaac and Ishmael.

C. Jacob and Joseph.

Be sure to read the stem carefully so that you can imagine the right answer before looking at the options. What were the names of Isaac's two sons? Once you have visualized the answer, try to discredit each of the options. Option A sounds correct. Option B is attractive because Isaac and Ishmael were brothers. But these were the sons of Abraham, not the sons of Isaac. The third option sounds attractive because Jacob was one of the sons of Isaac. But Joseph was the son of Jacob, not the son of Isaac. Thus you can return to option A because it is most correct and complete.

As with the true/false portion of the exam, do not waste time looking for patterns in the answers. Rather, look for words such as *always* or *never* that can turn a good answer into a bad answer by implying a level of consistency that rarely exists in this world. Again, be alert for the introduction of a negative such as *not* into the stem, which completely reverses the direction of the question. If you are uncertain about an answer, attempt to identify at least one of the three options as incorrect to improve your odds in making an educated guess.

Matching Exams College instructors sometimes use a matching exam to check your understanding of factual information or your knowledge of technical vocabulary. The first step in completing a matching exam is to determine whether the answers in the answer column may be used more than once. If not, then match all the items that you know for sure, crossing out the items in the answer column when they have been used. Once you have narrowed the options in this way, you can return to the items you are less sure about with a narrowed field of possible answers. Here is an example of a matching quiz that might be given in your Bible history class to assess your knowledge of the families in Genesis.

_____	1. wife of Abraham	A. Joseph
_____	2. brother of Esau	B. Leah
_____	3. son of Jacob	C. Tamar
_____	4. wife of Jacob	D. Sarah
_____	5. daughter-in-law of Judah	E. Jacob

Essay Questions Essay questions may require either a brief or long answer. In either case, they are designed to measure not only your knowledge of the information but also your ability to think logically, creatively, and critically. The first step in answering an essay question is to make sure that you are answering the question that is being asked. College professors often report reading wonderful essays that had little or nothing to do with the essay question they had asked in the exam!

In order to answer the question effectively, you need to identify and mark three components of the question: the key word, the limiting word, and the topic. The *topic* of the sentence is the part of the learning experience that your instructor wants to evaluate. The *key word* or words ask you to do something specific with that topic—for example, analyze, describe, compare, or contrast. The *limiting word* or phrase reduces the topic to a more manageable size. Consider the following essay question:

> *Identify and describe the geographical features of ancient Israel that led the Lord to select this land as the Promised Land.*

In this essay question, the topic you are to discuss is the geography of ancient Israel. The key words are *identify and describe*. The limiting phrase reduces the discussion to the geographical features of ancient Israel that made it particularly attractive for selection as the Promised Land.

Once you have identified the precise question you are to answer, outline your response before you write. This helps you organize your thinking, avoid rambling, and balance the contents of your answer so that you give fair treatment to each component. In connection with the preceding essay question, you might have two parts to your answer:

I. Location
II. Absence of natural resources

Once you have identified those two features as the major points of your answer, you would then outline the subpoints under each. That outline might look like this:

I. Location
    A. Key international crossroads
    B. News spread effectively via the merchants and travelers
    C. So the Land of Israel facilitated the spread of the Gospel

Key Words and Essay Questions

Here are the key words that instructors may use to ask you to perform a task in an essay question:

Analyze   To break the topic or problem into its parts in order to understand it. Discuss and examine each part and show how the parts work together within the larger framework of the topic.

Compare   To examine the characteristics or qualities of several topics and identify their similarities and differences.

Contrast   To examine differences between topics.

Critique   To evaluate the quality of a statement or an idea. A criticism acknowledges positive and negative qualities. You may need to supplement your opinions with support from recognized experts.

Define   To give the accurate and concise meaning of a word or phrase. Providing an example may help clarify a definition, but an example is not itself a definition.

Describe   To give a verbal account of something. This can be in a narrative or other form of description that lists characteristics or qualities.

Discuss   To examine important characteristics of a topic or issue. Discussion often includes identifying the main points and the important questions within the topic.

Evaluate   To weigh the strengths, weakness, merits, worth, or truthfulness of a topic or argument.

Explain   To make a concept or topic understandable. Explanations often treat how and why things develop.

Illustrate   To give concrete examples of something. This may be either in written form or in a diagram or picture.

Interpret   To explain the meaning or significance of something.

Justify   To argue in support of a position by giving evidence or reason in its favor. Provide logical reasoning and concrete examples to support your argument.

Narrate   To tell a story or describe a series of events in chronological order.

Outline   To give the main points of a topic in appropriate order, focusing on broader concepts.

Prove   To demonstrate the truth of a statement by providing facts or logical arguments.

Relate   To identify the connections or relationships between topics or events.

Review   To summarize the main parts of a topic. Evaluation may also be included.

Summarize   To briefly cover the main points of a topic, omitting details. A summary covers all of the most important points, yet remains a condensed account of the topic.

Trace   To describe the order of events or the development of an idea.

    II.   Absence of natural resources
        A.   Illustrate that Israel is a land with limited natural resources
        B.   The absence of natural resources increases dependence on God
        C.   Thus the Land of Israel nurtures faith in God's care

At times, an essay question may require you to introduce your own opinion into the answer, but generally in an undergraduate class your instructor is asking you to represent the scholarly view of others. If a scholarly consensus was presented on the topic, be careful not to wander far from that in your answer unless you are absolutely convinced you can make an impressive and convincing case. Your instructor will expect you to use the jargon of his or her discipline in the answer, so be sure that you know the language and use it correctly.

Remember that the answer you give will be evaluated on the basis of its accuracy, clarity, and logic. Your instructor will further be impressed by an answer that is succinct, legible, and free from grammatical and spelling errors. An answer to an essay question that makes the corrector work too hard will receive a lower grade. Thus, unnecessarily long answers or answers that are difficult to read will receive a lower grade even if they are generally correct in their direction.

Take-Home Exams Certain essay tests are completed not in class but rather outside class. These take-home exams can be addressed in the same way as the essay exam just described, but also have some unique expectations associated with them. An instructor who assigns a take-home essay exam will expect an answer that is higher in quality than one you would write in class. Carefully follow the instructions you are given, for the take-home exam may require you to use resources other than your textbook and notes. You may be required to cite your sources as you would in a research paper. And you most assuredly will be evaluated against higher standards for the completeness, accuracy, and organization of your answer. Be careful about how you plan your time for writing a take-home exam. Typically such an exam requires you to spend more time writing than you would if you were completing the exam during the class hour.

Open-Book and Open-Note Exams At other times, you will take exams in college that permit you to use written resources during the class hour when you take the exam. Some college students are lulled into a false sense of security when they hear that they will be able to use their textbook and notes during the exam. Consequently, they are disappointed because they spend too much time researching answers and run out of time for writing effective answers to the questions. Look at it in this way: the class hour for an open-book test is not the time to learn the material, but rather to demonstrate your knowledge of that material.

Like the take-home exam, this type of exam will likely contain more difficult questions that carry higher expectations from the instructor. So it is critical that you prepare for such an exam by memorizing and familiarizing yourself with key information just as you would for a closed-book test. Think of the book and notes you bring to class as tools with which to supplement your answer rather than as tools for creating your answer from scratch. In this regard, prepare those tools carefully. Use self-sticking notes and color coding to mark

Hot Topics Card

As you prepare for an exam, you will always find some piece of information or idea elusive and more difficult to understand. Consider carrying around a "hot topics" card. On this small card write down the formula, the vocabulary item, or term you are having difficulty recalling. During the slow moments of your day, waiting for a bus or waiting in line for lunch, do a quick review of the hot topics on your card.

portions of the textbook you are most likely to use, and organize your written notes in a similar way so that you can use these auxiliary tools efficiently and effectively.

Math and Science Exams College exams in math and science courses also have some unique expectations. You must be competent in using scientific terminology and able to perform accurate mathematical calculations. When taking a science exam, be well acquainted with the terminology that your instructor and textbook have used. Your ability to answer the questions begins with your ability to understand the scientific terminology that is used to frame the questions. When science and math exams require mathematical computations, practice the computation process and formulas many times before you demonstrate them on the exam. Be sure to check whether you must memorize formulas or may bring them along on a note card. And allow yourself time to check each of your answers carefully. Does your answer make sense? Have you applied the correct formula? Have you completed each step of the formula in the correct order? Have you made any basic mathematical errors?

STUDENT VOICE

Kevin Sheridan

Major: Sports Management
Hometown: Grafton, Wisconsin
School: Cardinal Stritch University

There is a lot of anxiety when it comes to taking exams, especially at a university. After more than a semester in college, I really believe the best way that I deal with my anxiety is to study extremely hard for these exams. The anxiety never goes away completely, but being prepared helps me feel less stress.

Manage Your Anxiety

Exams and anxiety go hand in hand for most people. All of us would like to do well when we are evaluated, and that creates a level of anxiety that is natural and expected. The symptoms of stress vary from one person to the next but may include the following: butterflies in the stomach, difficulty sleeping, irritability, nausea, loss of appetite, diarrhea, and headaches. If these symptoms become so acute that they interfere with your ability to live a normal life, or if they significantly impact your ability to demonstrate your capabilities on an exam, you should seek the direction and support of a professional counselor. The following suggestions for managing anxiety are not meant to replace such professional assistance, but they may help you manage milder forms of exam anxiety.

The place to begin managing anxiety is with the one who has created us and who has promised to hear and answer our prayers. Read and take to heart this promise from 1 Peter 5:7: "Cast all your anxiety on him because he cares for you." We can experience nothing that exceeds God's power. And in love, he has promised to use that power to bring us peace in the midst of our worry.

A second way to address the anxiety you feel in connection with an exam is to prepare effectively. We tend to worry about things we do not know about or are ill-prepared to meet. The early pages of this chapter speak about a method of exam preparation that empowers you with knowledge and a preparation plan. Following such a plan is another step in limiting the worry you may feel about a coming exam. Remember that information and preparation translate into empowerment.

Third, be careful not to give an exam more power than it is due. Exams are meant to measure a very limited amount of who you are as a person. They have no power to define your value or worth as an individual. They have no ability to absolutely predict your future success. And their outcome can be compromised by your physical and emotional state on the day you take the exam. Let the exam be a tool that measures your growth and provides feedback on how to improve, but do not let exams define you as a person. You are much bigger and more wonderful than the grade on an exam may suggest.

This is particularly important to keep in mind when you encounter a question in the exam that has caught you by surprise. Go into every exam assuming that at least one question will give you trouble. Do not let one or two questions derail your confidence and precipitate negative self-talk. It is entirely possible to pass most exams with a good grade even if you cannot answer one of the questions.

Finally, realize that you have power over your anxiety. On the day of the exam, arrive in class early. Sit in the seat and focus on the task ahead. Use the stress reduction techniques discussed further in Chapter Twelve. Visualize your success and then get to it.

Keeping It Honest

Each time you take an exam, you have a chance to give evidence of your integrity by managing the temptation to cheat. Such cheating can take any number of forms. Some students are intentionally absent on exam day, feigning illness so that they can obtain information on the exam from others who have taken it. Other students smuggle illegitimate information into the room and keep it hidden from the instructor's eyes. Still others devise systems to exchange answers during the exam, even using electronic communication in the process.

Students who resort to this dishonest behavior do so for a variety of reasons. They may have managed their time poorly or dealt with a very difficult personal situation that prevented them from preparing for the exam. They may be angry at the instructor and wish to do well in his or her class despite the perceived unfairness they have experienced from the teacher. Or they may place so much emphasis on their grade that they are willing to sacrifice their integrity by cheating to obtain a higher grade.

To be caught cheating on an exam carries significant consequences. Typically college faculty are empowered to handle the cheating student in a variety of ways. Such a student may be given a failing mark on the exam or for the entire course. In certain cases, cheaters are expelled from the school. Such official consequences, along with the humiliation of failing this character test, are a burden to carry. Cheaters who are caught are clearly harmed, but so are cheaters who are not caught. Those who misrepresent themselves on an exam have lowered the value of their education. They have received a grade that has no connection with their knowledge or skill. What is more, those who cheat on exams rightly feel the guilt of sin and the personal humiliation of claiming to be someone they are not.

Keeping it honest on all your exams will not be easy, but it will be possible because of the promises that God has extended to you. Assume that you will be tempted to cheat on an exam at some point during your college years. Preempt that temptation of Satan by writing out Hebrews 4:15–16 and placing it in your study area. In this verse, the inspired author reminds us that Jesus has been there: "For we do not have a high priest who is unable to sympathize with our weaknesses, but we have one who has been tempted in every way, just as we are—yet was without sin. Let us then approach the throne of grace with confidence, so that we may receive mercy and find grace to help us in our time of need." (Heb 4:15–16) When Jesus was beginning his earthly ministry, he too was tempted to take shortcuts that were only paths to failure (Matt 4). He knows what you are feeling when tempted to cheat and has promised you the power to remain honest and true. If you are tempted to cheat, pray for his help, seek the support of a Christian friend, and even be ready to take a lower grade on the exam rather than misrepresent yourself. If your life has been complicated by personal tragedy, speak to your instructor about delaying the demonstration of your ability. And if you fall victim to this sin, confess it and find peace in the forgiveness of Jesus (1 John 1:9–10).

Test preparation is not new to you. You have been doing it for years. But as you consider your habits related to taking college exams, look for ways to strengthen yourself as a student. How can you improve the process you use to prepare for an exam? How can you strategically use the time during the exam to produce the best results? What can you do to lower your level of anxiety? What are you doing to prepare for the day when you are tempted to cheat on an exam?

Exercises for **Success**

Review Questions

1. Explain the value and the harm associated with cramming for an exam by staying up all night to study.

2. List and define three learning principles that improve the way you memorize.

3. Summarize the key ways in which you can manage your exam anxiety.

Find Your Challenges

Most students find one type of exam more challenging than another. Review the last four or five exams that you have taken and determine on what kind of questions you are losing the most points. Then do some further investigation on that type of exam question that gives you difficulty. Look for new preparation or test-taking strategies associated with that type of question that will produce more positive results for you.

Type of Question	Test #1	Test #2	Test #3	Test #4	Test #5
Multiple-Choice					
True/False					
Matching					
Essay					
Other					

Build an Exam Plan

The ideas offered in this chapter need to be edited and made your own. Pick an exam that is coming up in the next month and draft a preparation plan. Experiment by starting your preparation earlier or using different review and recitation techniques. After the exam, you will have a better sense of what worked or did not work for you.

Exam Plan

Course:

Date of Exam:

Scope of Exam:

Type of Exam:

Study Schedule:

Day	Time	Content	Review and Recitation Technique
Day 7			
Day 6			
Day 5			
Day 4			
Day 3			
Day 2			
Day Before			

Dissecting an Essay Question

The following are two essay questions related to the contents of this chapter. Identify and mark the key word(s), limiting word/phrase, and topic. Then write an outline that would be the framework on which you would build your response.

Compare and contrast the techniques that may be used to answer an essay question versus a multiple-choice question on a college exam.

Explain why a college student needs to be proactive to avoid cheating on exams, and relate what steps you plan to take to avoid that temptation.

Interview a Successful Upper-Class Friend

Many of the best suggestions on how to succeed on tests given by a particular professor may be obtained by asking an upper-class student who has successfully completed the class you are taking. Pick two of your classes and identify competent students who have already completed those courses with high grades. Interview them and find out what techniques they used both in and out of class to do well on those exams.

The Price of Dishonesty

Investigate the student conduct code on your campus under the topic of cheating on a college exam. Write a brief summary of what you find. How is cheating defined in the conduct code? What penalties are assessed against those who are caught? What can you do if you are charged with cheating when you are in fact innocent?

SPIRITUAL REFLECTION JOURNAL

Because you will face the temptation to cheat on a college exam, now is the time to arm yourself with prayer and the Word of God to combat it. Read Genesis 22 and Matthew 4.

Describe the ways in which Abraham and Jesus met their spiritual tests. What do you learn from their experience that you can apply to your life?

Time in Prayer

In your personal time in prayer or in connection with others in your class, take time to pray for the following people and needs:

- That God may motivate you to improve your exam preparation habits

- That those who are thinking about cheating on their next exam may be able to resist that temptation

- That you may find effective ways to keep anxiety from interfering with your ability to succeed on your college exams

- That God may bless the person in your class who is struggling in a relationship

---

On the Web

The Internet can be a helpful resource as you look for ideas to make yourself a happier and more successful student. Visit the College Success page offered by Thomson Wadsworth for Web links that will help you grow further on this topic. Go to http://www.success.wadsworth.com/ and click on Resource Web Links.

In particular, we recommend the following:

http://www.psychwww.com/mtsite/memory.html

http://www.dartmouth.edu/~acskills/success/study.html

http://www.csbsju.edu/academicadvising/help/testskil.htm

http://www.ucc.vt.edu/lynch/SevenStrategies.htm

http://www.ucc.vt.edu/lynch/ImprovConcentration.htm

http://www.mtsu.edu/~studskl/teststrat.html

Saying It Just Right: Writing and Speaking Successfully 9

A word aptly spoken is like apples of gold in settings of silver.

Proverbs 25:11

- **What can I do to improve my writing?**
- **How can I become a better public speaker?**
- **What research tools can help me write and speak more effectively?**

In Genesis 1, we read that God "spoke" and the world came to be. On a much smaller scale, we too have the ability to *create* using language. Through our use of language, we can shape the knowledge, perspectives, and attitudes of those touched by our words. This effective use of language is celebrated in the Bible. The poet in Proverbs writes, "A word aptly spoken is like apples of gold in settings of silver." (Prov 25:11) Your future employer will also celebrate your ability to communicate effectively. According to the National Association of Colleges and Employers, communication skills consistently rank at the top of the list used to evaluate prospective employees. That makes effective writing and speaking a priority for you.

But the mere ability to write and speak does not necessarily entail the ability to communicate effectively. These are skills that can be developed. Consequently, you can expect to have a lot of practice refining those skills as a college student; the mark of a well-educated person is not only the ability to think well but also the ability to communicate that good thinking effectively in both written and oral form. You will likely have classes during your first year of college wholly dedicated to writing and public speaking. This chapter is designed not to be a substitute for them, but rather as a tool to support your basic development. Here we will discuss strategies for improving your writing and public speaking skills and tips for doing basic college research.

Improve Your Writing Skills

College trains you to be a better thinker, and writing has been a traditional player in accomplishing that goal. There may be no better way for you to see and evaluate the quality of your thinking than through the medium of writing. Putting your thoughts on paper will show both strengths and weaknesses in your thinking that had otherwise gone unnoticed. You will see clarity or lack of clarity in your word choices. You will see the logical flow of your thinking or a tangled web of disconnected factoids. You will see a thesis that is persuasive or a presentation that is wholly unconvincing. Because good writers are made and not born, we can discuss practices that will help you become a better college writer. This begins with understanding the assignment, but quickly moves to the topics of creating a writing schedule, getting ready to write, writing the first draft, and revising the first draft.

Understanding the Assignment

The first step in the writing process is to understand the assignment. This may surprise you if you have never thought about the variety of writing assignments you may encounter. Understanding the assignment means more than knowing the mechanics, such as the number of assigned pages or that the paper must be typewritten. It is about the very nature of the project itself. As you consult the syllabus, written guide, or instructor, you need to determine the precise nature of the writing assignment so you do not waste time on an assignment that was never assigned in the first place. Here are some common assignments an undergraduate may meet.

Position Paper Sometimes called an essay, the position paper requires you to discuss your views on a certain topic. For example, your political science teacher may ask you to write an essay about your position on a recent election issue.

Critical Reaction Paper After discussing a topic in class, reading an article, or visiting a Web site, your instructor may ask you to write a reaction paper, which typically requires you to briefly summarize and then evaluate what you have heard or read. Following the summary, write about where you agreed and disagreed with the presentation, and explain why. Study the evidence. Does it clearly support the conclusions? You may have several reactions to the topic, so organize your reactions clearly in the paper.

Case Study Perhaps your instructor wants you to conduct an in-depth review of a person or an event—a case study. Although the parameters of this type of paper vary, provide ample details and anecdotes.

Research Paper This is the most time-consuming writing project you will do as a college student, because it requires you to develop a thesis statement and conduct a significant amount of research. You need to gather information and organize it into a well-crafted presentation. Because of the complexity of this project and the amount of time it consumes, the research paper usually counts more heavily toward your final course grade. An early start on this type of paper is essential.

Creating a Writing Schedule

It is important to create a schedule for each paper, particularly longer research paper assignments in which you have many tasks to perform. This means breaking up the project into smaller steps and assigning your own "due dates" for each step in the writing process.

Schedule for a Research Paper

September 25:	Pick a topic and confirm it with the instructor.
October 15:	Complete initial research on the topic.
October 20:	Create thesis statement and working outline.
October 27:	Complete additional research.
November 10:	Complete first draft.
November 15:	Revise first draft.
November 22:	Go to the writing center for feedback on paper.
November 30:	Complete final draft.
December 3:	Paper due in class.
December 4:	Reward myself with dinner and a movie.

Even if the assignment does not entail extensive research, you can still set due dates for steps in the project that must be accomplished, including a working outline, first draft, and revisions.

Getting Ready to Write

Long before you write the first draft of your paper, you have a variety of tasks to complete, including selecting the topic, completing the initial research on the topic, forming a thesis, and designing a working outline. Each of these prewriting steps has an impact on both your motivation for the project and its final quality.

Skimming for a Topic Sometimes your instructor assigns a specific topic for your paper; at other times you may select your own topic. This freedom can present a problem for some students. Because a paper may go in many different directions, the choices can be overwhelming. If you are subject to procrastination, this may be the only excuse you will need to delay the start of the project. There is no right way to search for a topic. But consider the following approach if you are stuck. Go to the library and start skimming newspapers, magazines, indexes, or journals associated with the larger theme of the project.

As you skim these sources, notice when you stop skimming and start reading an article with interest. Keep a list of the topics that you read. After an hour of skimming, look at your list of topics and identify a potential focus for your project.

Brainstorming   After you have chosen your topic, spend some time thinking about it. What do you already know about the topic? More important, how can the topic itself be investigated? Ask the pertinent who, what, when, where, and why questions as you brainstorm and begin to write down the various facets of the topic you discover in the process. Do not worry about spelling, grammar, and punctuation. Just keep your fingers moving! Set a timer and free-write for ten minutes. Through this process you not only gain a sense of context for the topic but also begin narrowing the topic to a manageable size and zeroing in on the facet of the topic that you find most interesting.

Let us say that you want to do a paper on the death penalty. That is an enormous topic. Brainstorm by yourself or with a friend. *Who* is affected by the death penalty? *What* forms of execution are used? *When* was the death penalty last used in this state? *Where* do the executions take place? *Why* do some states have the death penalty while others do not? Write the topic in the center of a piece of paper and explore all the dimensions and issues related to the death penalty. Your notes might look like this:

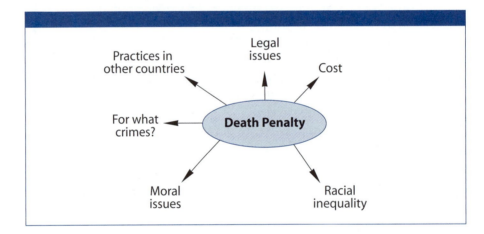

Initial Research   Once you have identified and narrowed your topic, it is time to do your initial research. The amount of research you need to do for a writing project will vary greatly depending on the type of assignment. A reaction paper requires little research; other writing assignments require you to interact broadly with the thinking of others before you write. Your goal for this stage of the research is not to go into detail on every facet of your topic but to get a general overview. What are the main points? What are the basic issues and arguments? Who are the major representatives of the various positions? Although you clearly need to research in tools other than an encyclopedia, an up-to-date encyclopedia article (particularly in a subject-specific encyclopedia) can be a good starting point for getting a general overview of the topic.

Thesis Statement   Once you have narrowed your topic and done the initial research, it is time to take a stand. Your topic needs to become a thesis statement. Write one sentence that captures the particular point of view that you will argue in the paper. For example, let us say you have been assigned a research paper related to World War II. After brainstorming, you decide you want to focus on the role of women during the war effort. After doing your initial research, you elect to focus on the topic of the Women Airforce Service Pilots (WASP). That topic becomes a thesis statement when you take a point of view on it. "The development of the Women Airforce Service Pilots (WASP) was critical to the success of the U.S. Air Force during World War II." Note that a thesis statement is more than a topic. A thesis statement assumes a position that you are willing to defend.

Working Outline   Creating an outline helps you organize all of the information you have gathered so far. Start with the main points you wish to cover in your paper. What background does your reader need to know? What evidence will you use to persuade your reader that your thesis is correct? How will you counter the opposing arguments? Then add the subpoints that further explain and support your main ideas. This is a working outline, so expect that some of the structure or certain components may change as you write. As you grow with your thesis, your working outline grows with you.

Additional Research   Once you create an outline, you may discover that you need to strengthen your own understanding with a return to the library. This is where the working outline plays such an important role. It focuses your additional research and reading very specifically to the needs that you have. With this step complete, you are ready to write.

Writing the First Draft

When you follow the preceding ideas and steps, writing the first draft does not seem like such a daunting task. You have done a great deal of work already. Simply follow your outline and refer to your research notes as you write each section. Above all, write the first draft knowing you will revise it later. This takes the pressure off because you do not need to labor over writing the perfect paragraph. As you write, keep the following tips in mind:

- Do not criticize your work or linger over one sentence with which you are struggling. Save the final polish for later.
- Although the introduction contains the first words your reader will read, it may not be the first words you write. If you do not have a clear introduction in mind, let it go. As you write the paper, ideas for the introduction will come to you.
- If you have used the work of others, be sure to cite the sources in your paper. Any words or ideas that are not your own need to be credited to the original author. Be sure to find out what citation style your instructor prefers (e.g., American Psychological Association, Modern Language Association, or Turabian). Check your library, learning center, or bookstore for the most recent edition of the style manual you will use. Examples of the various styles are also available on the Internet.
- Do not let your conclusion fizzle. This is a crucial part of the paper. Give yourself time to really work on this section. This is the last thing your instructor reads before assigning a grade, so end the paper with a strong conclusion that revisits and confirms your thesis.

Jennifer Brantsen

Major: Athletic Training/Physical Therapy
Hometown: Muskegon, Michigan
School: Trinity College

Revising a research paper consists of searching for grammar and editorial corrections but also evaluating content readability and relevance. As I read through my paper, I circle grammatical errors and substitute possible rearrangements for unclear sentences. I use a grammar book to check for difficult comma usage and for proper citation methods. After following these steps, I like to reread the paper out loud to check my revisions.

Revising the First Draft

After your first draft is complete, take a short break from the material. Put it away for a day or two. When you return to the paper to revise it, you will be able to look at it with a fresh perspective. The key to effective writing is revision. The more time you spend revising your papers, the better your writing becomes. Toward that end, use the following suggestions to revise your initial draft.

Be a Critical Reader As you wrote your first draft, you were concerned with getting all the necessary information on paper. Now it is time to put yourself in the shoes of your reader by critically reviewing your paper.

- Do the sections flow logically, or do you need to rearrange the material?
- Do you have transitions between the main points of the paper so the reader can easily comprehend the organization?
- Can you rewrite sentences using the active voice rather than passive voice?
- Have you varied the length of the sentences and grammatical patterns within them?
- Do the quotations fit smoothly into the text of the paper?
- Are your arguments well supported by your research?
- Are you using gender-neutral language?

Read It Out Loud One of the best revising techniques is to read your paper out loud. You will be able to identify awkward phrases and sentences much more easily. If you stumble over an odd choice of words or problematic sentence structure, your reader will too.

Check for Grammar and Spelling Errors Because you want your reader to focus on your ideas, you do not want to distract your reader with spelling and grammatical errors. Proofread your paper with a dictionary and grammar rulebook by your side. Use the spell checker on your computer, but remember that it will not catch every spelling error. For example, it will not indicate a spelling error in the phrase "Form 1950 too 1960 the United States. . . ." If you tend to make these kinds of mistakes, ask a friend to proofread your paper too. But remember, you are ultimately responsible for cleaning up the spelling and grammatical errors.

Go to the Writing Center If your campus has a center where students can get feedback about their papers, take advantage of this opportunity. You will receive valuable advice from students who have refined the art of evaluating their own writing.

Revise Again Once you have revised the first draft, revise it again in a few days. Your writing will continue to improve through each draft. And before it leaves your hands, make sure that you have met each of the criteria in the following checklist.

❏ I have an introduction that catches my reader's attention and previews the main points of my paper.
❏ I have logically organized the main points of my paper.
❏ I have appropriate transitions between paragraphs.
❏ I have supported my arguments with convincing evidence.
❏ I have appropriately cited any outside material I have used.
❏ I have correctly used the appropriate citation format.
❏ I have written a conclusion that summarizes the main points.
❏ I have checked for spelling and grammatical mistakes.
❏ I have taken my paper to the writing center for feedback.

High-quality papers require careful research, writing, and revision. Understand the assignment and create a writing plan. Know what you want to say and how you want to say it before writing the first draft. And when your first draft is complete, revise, revise, and revise again.

What Grade Did You Get on Your Paper?

Many of your instructors will return papers to you with more than just a grade. They will also write comments about the quality of the paper. If your pride has prevented you from hearing that critique or if you have been in the habit of ignoring these comments, it is time for a change. The comments written on your paper tell you not only why you received the grade but also how to improve your writing.

For example, they may indicate poor organization, grammar problems, or a weakness in citing resources. Look for patterns in the comments that you receive on returned papers. They signal ways to improve your writing. If the comments are not clear, ask your instructor to clarify them so that you can apply them in your next writing assignment.

Improve Your Speaking Skills

Public speaking enjoys a rich heritage in the Bible. Consider the powerful speeches delivered by Jeremiah and Peter (Jer 7; Acts 2). Although the advent of the computer and other technology allows us to connect with people through teleconferences, there is still no substitute for the interaction between a speaker and the audience during a public speaking engagement.

Understand the Assignment

Your public speaking opportunities will vary in nature and purpose, much like the various writing assignments you will have. But as with your writing assignments, you must understand the objective of your presentation. Speakers have various goals when they present a speech. Think of a graduation ceremony you attended during which you heard a speaker deliver the graduation address. This type of speech, called ceremonial speaking, honors and celebrates the graduates. It is a well-known form of address, but it is not the type of speaking you will be asked to do in college. Your speaking tasks typically aim to inform or persuade an audience.

Speaking to Inform Consider this type of speech an opportunity to expand your audience's understanding of a topic. Your task is to present information in a way that is interesting and understandable. Gather information from a variety of sources. Even if you do not use all the information you gather, you will become familiar with the material and more at ease discussing it in front of an audience. As with your research papers, you must orally cite your sources within your speech. You dare not claim an idea as your own when it is not. Giving credit to the authorities you consulted adds to your credibility as a speaker as well. Because the task of informative speaking is to create an interesting and understandable presentation, consider using visual aids to enhance your speech.

Speaking to Persuade On the other hand, you may be asked to deliver a persuasive speech. Here, your goal is to encourage your audience to change their opinions or motivate them to action. As with speaking to inform, you should gather a variety of resources in order to be familiar with a subject. However, your task is not simply to present interesting material; you need to advocate a position and support it with evidence. Again, you must cite your sources within your speech, not only because it is required and adds to your own credibility, but also because it creates a persuasive impact.

Basic Structure of a Speech

The old public speaking adage "Tell them what you are going to say, tell them, and tell them what you said" is still true today. Clear organization is critical during a presentation. Your audience has one chance to hear your message, so you must be clear the first time. In general, you should have an introduction, the main body of the speech, and a conclusion.

Introduction In order to inform or persuade your audience, you need their attention. The introduction should gain the audience's attention and preview your main points. Do not start your presentation with the words, "Today I'm

Using Visual Aids in Your Speeches

Visual aids such as pictures, graphs, charts, and objects can give your speech a lot of impact. But it is important to use visual aids in a way that enhances your presentation rather than distracts from it. Before you spend time creating visual aids for a speech, make sure you have a clear purpose for them. Are you using a lot of statistics in your speech? A chart with all your statistics clearly written out will help your audience understand your argument. Is the speech topic complicated? A diagram of the different subpoints of the speech will help your audience remember them. Are you speaking about different styles of artistic expression? Pictures of different works of art will help your audience see the various styles. Once you have created your visual aids, keep the following guidelines in mind:

- Does it look good? Poorly drawn charts, graphs, or posters look as if you did not care enough to spend time on the assignment. Use available technology to create professional-looking visual aids. If you must write out a visual aid by hand, plan it carefully and make it as neat as possible.

- Will everyone be able to see it? Small-print charts and posters may be unreadable even in a small classroom. Test your visual aids by standing as far from them as the people in the room will be. Also, think about how you will display your visual aids while you are giving your speech. Is an easel available? Will you need to bring tape in order to secure your visual aid to the wall?

- When should I use it? Generally, visual aids should be covered or placed face down until they are needed during the speech. Do not let your visual aid distract from your message when you are not using it.

- What about media aids? Always cue video and audiotapes ahead of time. If you are using computer images such as a Power-Point presentation, be certain you know how to use the software and the computer. Come to the classroom before your speech and set up any media equipment you will be using. This will help you prepare for your presentation and ensure that all the equipment is working properly.

- Will the visual aids be cumbersome to use while speaking? Not if you practice your speech with your visual aids. The visual aids should fit smoothly into the flow of your speech; therefore, practice holding, manipulating, or referring to the visual aids just as you would normally practice your speech.

going to talk about. . . ." That statement is overused and unimaginative. Start your speech with a short story, a question, or a shocking statement. Once you have introduced your topic, preview the main points of your speech. For example, a statement such as "Nuclear, solar, and wind power are three sources of energy that our nation has yet to use to their fullest potential" outlines your three main points and the position you will be taking in your speech.

Main Body Here is the heart of your speech, where you offer the bulk of your research. Organization is critical if you want your listeners to follow you through your major points and supporting points. Toward that end, you may organize your material in a problem/solution format by first offering evidence of a problem and then advocating for a specific solution. Whatever method you use, make sure your listeners can clearly follow it.

Conclusion The final segment of your presentation should review your main points and provide a short but eloquent closing. Professional speakers know that the last words often make the most impact. Summarize the main points of your speech, then wrap up the speech with thoughtful closing lines or a call to action. Do not end your speech with the words "That's it" or "That's all." Leave your audience with a clear and memorable ending to your speech.

Delivery

Unfortunately, all of us can recall a presentation in which the impact of the message was diminished because the speaker had distracting physical or verbal mannerisms. Your delivery—that is, your physical and verbal presentation—must support your message. You do not need to be the most dynamic of speakers; the great public speakers who inspire us have spent years honing their delivery skills. Your delivery needs only to be confident and polished.

Your delivery will improve with experience, but you can keep some things in mind from the start. Direct eye contact with your audience is an important component of your delivery. You should know your material well enough that you can maintain eye contact with your audience for approximately 70 percent of your speech. If you were taught to "look over the heads of your audience," you were given poor advice. Speakers who do not maintain direct eye contact appear disconnected from the audience members.

When you begin practicing a speech, you may tend to stumble over your words or add sounds such as "ah" and "um" to your sentences. The more you practice, the better you will know your material and the less likely you will be to stumble on words or rely on word fillers. If word fillers such as "ah" and "um" are a problem for you, try to discover why. Is it just a habit? If so, you may not even hear yourself doing it. Have someone listen to your speech and signal you when you use a word filler. This may be disheartening at first, but it will help you become more aware of this distracting habit. Do not feel the need to completely eliminate sound fillers, because this is an unrealistic goal. An occasional "um" will not diminish your message.

In general, your vocal delivery should include the natural variations in pitch, rate, and volume that you normally use while conversing. Beginning public speakers typically speak quickly because they are nervous. If this is a problem, remind yourself to relax by writing cues such as "slow down" in the margins of your speaking notes. Again, your vocal delivery, like your physical delivery, will improve with practice.

Anxiety

Even seasoned public speakers feel nervous before giving a speech, so it is perfectly normal for you to experience anxiety before a class presentation. Your level of nervousness will vary with different situations, but learning how to respond to speech anxiety will help you cope with speaking situations that you face in college and in the workplace.

People react to fear with physiological and psychological responses. You may feel tension in your stomach, you may perspire more than normal, or your hands may shake. These are common physiological reactions of anxiety. If you experience them, try responding with physiological coping techniques. Breathe in deeply, hold your breath for a few seconds, and then slowly exhale. You can also try tightening and relaxing your muscles. Tighten the muscles in your legs, hold the tension for a few seconds, and then slowly release. Continue to do this with muscle groups in your arms, neck, and shoulders. You may not be able to completely stop your hands from shaking or perspiring, but keep in mind that the symptoms you are experiencing may not be very noticeable to your audience. Concentrate on your message, not your symptoms, and you should start to feel some of that anxiety decrease.

Psychological reactions to fear and anxiety are usually manifested in the desire to flee a situation or in negative self-talk. Skipping class to avoid your speech because you are too anxious is not a good idea. If your anxiety is so overwhelming that you skip class, go to the counseling center on your campus. A counselor can provide strategies to diminish more intense anxiety. You may also need to defeat the negative self-talk that can attend your anxiety. You may tell yourself you are a poor speaker or that you will perform badly on your speech. This kind of talk is exactly what you should not do when preparing to speak. Too often people focus on their nervousness and not on the task. Instead, focus on the goals of the speech and the learning experience. Yes, you may make some mistakes during your speech, but your goal is to learn while giving the speech, not to be perfect. Focus on the goals of your message and the interaction with the audience, not on your anxiety.

Practicing

You can also reduce your anxiety through practice. Practice makes the difference between mediocre public speakers and good ones. You cannot become a better speaker without practice. Perhaps you, like many other people, think that good public speakers were born with that ability. That is simply not true. Dynamic public speakers have achieved their success through practice. They prepare their speeches, and they practice those speeches before attempting to deliver them in front of an audience. You have spent time gathering your material, developing an outline, and writing speaking notes. But you are not finished. As with the final editing of a paper, you are not finished preparing for a speech until you have spent time practicing it.

Practice the speech in the same manner in which you will present it in class. If you will be part of a panel of presenters sitting at a table in the front of the classroom, then practice the speech sitting at a table with your notes spread in front of you. If you will be standing to deliver your speech, then practice your speech while standing holding your note cards or placing them on a podium. Whatever the environment, try to simulate it as much as possible when you practice. Not only will this improve your presentation, but simulating the actual environment as much as possible may also calm your nerves.

You may discover other creative methods for practicing and improving your speaking skills. We encourage you to experiment with the preceding techniques and to explore several practice methods. But most important, do it. Practicing is the only way to become a better public speaker.

The Thief in the Library

Plagiarism is stealing. When people use someone else's words or ideas as their own, they steal that person's "intellectual property." You use others' intellectual property all the time when you gather research for your papers and speeches. These sources help you understand facts and perspectives with which you yourself may not have a personal experience. During your speeches, you must give verbal credit to your sources. When you use material from other sources to write a paper, you should also cite those sources in the paper. If you pass off someone else's experiences or thoughts as your own, you steal their intellectual property just as taking someone's bicycle would be stealing their physical property. You must give credit for any words, phrases, sentences, or ideas that are not your own. Furthermore, just changing a few words from another author's work is not sufficient to avoid citation. It is still considered plagiarism because you are using the author's structure and most of the words. Most instructors and colleges have stiff penalties for plagiarism, so you must understand what it is and not risk it. Not only are you stealing another person's intellectual property, you also risk severe academic penalties or possible expulsion from your school.

Research Tools You Can Use

The library at your college will be different from the library at your high school or local community. High school and community libraries offer a variety of popular and academic material, but libraries on most college campuses are collections of scholarly books and articles. Here, well-educated people can access scholarly work for papers and speeches. If you are not familiar with the library at your college, we strongly suggest you take a library tour or attend an orientation. Becoming familiar with the variety of research materials in your library and their points of access in the library is essential to your success. In general, libraries have the following resources.

Reference Materials

You may recognize several basic encyclopedias, dictionaries, atlases, and other such materials that you have used in the past. General reference materials such as *Encyclopedia Americana* and *Webster's Dictionary* are probably in the holdings, but you will also find more focused subject-oriented reference materials as well. For example, *Black's Law Dictionary* and *The Encyclopedia of Religion* provide information in highly technical and specific subject areas.

Popular Magazines and Newspapers

You will be able to find information about current events from the popular press. These resources are helpful for locating basic information and are good sources for editorials and opinions on national issues. However, some publications openly advocate from a particular political position. This does not mean they are unworthy of your attention. It does mean that you should read with the knowledge of the publication's political preference in view. In addition, magazines and newspapers rarely offer the depth of analysis you will find in scholarly journals and books.

Scholarly Journals

Every academic discipline has journals in which experts and scholars publish their work. In most cases, the journal articles you gather have been thoroughly reviewed by editorial boards. Furthermore, not every article submitted to a journal is published, and no initial draft finds its way into print without revision. These resources report on the most current research being conducted and present critical reaction to that research. Journal articles can be accessed via electronic indexes and databases available through your library's computer system or by paper indexes such as the *Humanities Index* and the *Social Sciences Index*.

Books

Books are a critical source of in-depth information. Because of their length, they can provide a good synthesis of a topic along with a historical background that may be lacking in a journal article or brief overview in an encyclopedia. They usually have extensive bibliographies that identify resources you may not have discovered. However, because of the time involved in writing the material and producing the actual product, books do not always present the most current state of the discussion.

Internet Sources

The Internet has given people access to an enormous amount of information. Although some of this information is excellent, the mere presence of a Web site does not automatically imply that the author is an expert. When you use the Internet to search for supporting materials for your papers and speeches, you must learn to discriminate between Web sites that are credible and those that are not grounded in credible research. You should consider several questions when evaluating the credibility of Internet sources:

- Who is the author? As in any print publication, the author should be identified on the Web site. And as with other printed publications, the author should be qualified to write about the topic. If you cannot find out who wrote an article on the Internet, or doubt the author's credibility, disregard the source and continue searching.

- Does an organization serve as "author"? Although we just said you ought to disregard material that has no author, there is an exception. Some organizations create Web sites with helpful and reliable information. For example, if you are gathering information about heart disease in America, you may visit the American Heart Association Web site, which offers credible, up-to-date information. Although no specific author's name is noted on the Web site, the organization acts as the "author" in this case.

- Consider the source. The Internet is a great place to find a variety of viewpoints. As students honing their critical-thinking skills, you should realize that some information on the Internet is produced by people or groups who feel strongly about a cause. This may affect the reliability of the information you find on their Web site. It is always a good idea to gather information from a variety of sources. If you find information from a person or group that is particularly biased toward a political, social, or religious viewpoint, balance those sources with others that take a different view.

- When was it published? As in a book or magazine, information on a Web site should indicate the date of publication. Older information is not necessarily bad information. But beware of using outdated evidence to support your position.

These guidelines will help you use the Internet more wisely. But your use of the Internet should not stop at general searches from sites such as Google and Ask.com. Search engines such as Google gather Web resources broadly without sorting that information for its value and quality. By contrast, scholarly databases do exist. These databases are filtered by scholars who eliminate Web sites of questionable quality. Do you have to write a paper for your psychology class? Try PsychINFO. Do you need sources for a religion paper? Visit ATLA. And if you prefer to work with a more general index, see ProQuest or JSTOR.

Finally, any information you obtain from the Internet or an electronic database is just like a print source and must be cited within your paper or presentation. This information is not considered "public domain" simply because it was easy to access. Be sure to properly cite all information obtained electronically. Go to "On the Web" at the end of this chapter to find Internet sites specifically designed for academic research and for assistance in shaping electronic citations.

Reference Librarians

Reference librarians may be your most useful "tool" while researching a topic. Your reference librarians can guide you to resources that you did not know existed. They are trained to find information and can quickly access resources in many different venues. If you are unsuccessful in locating information on a topic, cannot find a resource, or need help getting started on a task, ask for help.

Communication skills are essential to your academic success. Your ability to locate information from various sources is critical to writing papers and presenting speeches. Remember, each time you write a paper and deliver a speech, not only are you learning more about a subject, you are also becoming a better communicator.

Exercises for **Success**

Review Questions

1. Compare and contrast three different types of college writing assignments.

2. Explain the difference between a topic and a thesis. Illustrate this difference with an example.

3. When you select a Web site for use in a research paper or speech, what criteria will direct you to a site that has earned the right to be used in this way?

Create a Writing Schedule

Choose a paper that is currently assigned for this term and experiment with creating a writing schedule like the one presented earlier in this chapter. The following worksheet will help you structure your writing plan. Edit it as necessary to meet your needs.

The Paper Plan

Class:

Paper:

Final Due Date:

Task	Date for Completion	Done
Know the purpose of the paper		
Select a topic		
Do initial research		
Create a thesis statement		
Create a working outline		
Complete additional research		
Complete the first draft		
Revise the first draft		
Revise the second draft		
Final draft		

Find the Writing Center

If your college has a writing center, go to the center and find out how to take advantage of the help it has to offer. When is it open? What types of services does it offer? What are the busiest times during the semester? In what stage can you bring in a writing project? In other words, do tutors prefer a final draft, or are they willing to assist you in the early stages of the writing process as well? Find out this information and write it in your day planner or keep it posted near your work area.

Study Speaking by Other People

Check your library's holdings of videotapes or DVDs for recordings of public speeches. These could be speeches by famous politicians, activists, or entertainers, but there may also be speeches by college students. If speeches are available for viewing, watch them and evaluate how other people present their ideas. How is their delivery? How is their organization? What do you like about a certain speech or speaker? What do you not like? What can you learn from these speeches in order to become a better public speaker?

What Is the Penalty for Plagiarism?

Within the college catalog or student conduct code of your school, you will find both a definition of plagiarism and the possible penalties for it. Consult the source recommended by your instructor and learn all you can about the definitions and consequences of this illegitimate borrowing.

Take a Library Tour

Your college library may offer guided tours or orientations to students during the semester. Go to your library and find out the dates and times when these tours are offered. More important, attend one or more of the orientations. If your library does not offer something like this, ask the reference librarians for any written material that explains basic library holdings and procedures. Also, check to see if there is an online computer tutorial that can take you through basic research skills. Your goal is to learn about the different types of sources in the library, their locations, and their access points.

Try Out Your Research Skills

Identify a topic that you will need to research in the near future. This may be for a paper or a speech, or it may simply be of interest to you. Your goal in this exercise is to find information on your topic from a variety of resources. Use what you learned from your library orientation to create a bibliography that includes categories of material such as these:

• Subject-oriented encyclopedia

• Book

• Magazine or newspaper article

• Journal article

• Internet site

SPIRITUAL REFLECTION JOURNAL

Read Matthew 28:18–20, Luke 1:1–4, and Acts 17:1–4. Think about how important written and verbal communication skills were to the spread of Christianity in the early church.

How important are these skills to Christians in this century? How important are these skills to your own future profession?

Time in Prayer

In your personal time in prayer or in connection with others in your class, take time to pray for the following people and needs:

• For friends whom you have not seen in a long time

• For the courage to speak your beliefs

• For the ability to cope with speech anxiety

• For the ability to organize your writing projects

• For the wisdom to receive criticism and use it to improve yourself

• For the motivation to start your writing projects when they are assigned

On the Web

The Internet can be a helpful resource as you look for ideas to make yourself a happier and more successful student. Visit the College Success page offered by Thomson Wadsworth for Web links that will help you grow further on this topic. Go to http://www.success.wadsworth.com/ and click on Resource Web Links.

Several Internet subject directories are useful Internet research tools. These directories and search engines access material that is more scholarly and therefore more credible sources for your research:

http://lii.org/

http://library.sau.edu/bestinfo/

http://infomine.ucr.edu/

For information on how to critically evaluate Web sites, check the following sources:

http://www.library.cornell.edu/okuref/webeval.html

We also recommend the following Web pages:

http://www.bedfordstmartins.com/online/cite5.html

http://www.bedfordstmartins.com/online/cite6.html

http://www.bedfordstmartins.com/online/cite7.html

http://www.bedfordstmartins.com/online/citex.html

http://webapps.calvin.edu/knightcite/index.php

http://owl.english.purdue.edu/owl/resource/589/01/

http://owl.english.purdue.edu/oldindex.html

Making the Tough Decisions: The Role of Christian Values 10

He has showed you . . . what is good. And what does the LORD require of you? To act justly, to love mercy, and to walk humbly with your God.

Micah 6:8

- **How can I be sure that I am making a good decision?**

- **What are personal values?**

- **What role does my Christianity play in making important decisions?**

What career should I pursue? Should I use alcohol when I am in college? Should I copy that paper off the Internet and turn it in as my own? Decisions, decisions, life is absolutely full of decisions. As a college student, important decisions such as these can consume vast amounts of time while generating significant amounts of anxiety. And once you have graduated from college, imposing new decisions replace the old ones you have already made. Should I think about getting married now or wait until my life is more settled? Can I afford the payments on that house or should I continue to pay rent to someone else? Should I take the new job I am being offered and move to the other side of the country or should I be content with a lower salary and stay where I am? Should I declare that income on my tax return or hide it?

Because important decisions such as these will continue to be part of your life, your time in college is a great opportunity to practice and refine your skills in making them. You will have plenty of practice during any week of college doing just that. Every week will bring decisions that require you to assemble options, weigh advantages and disadvantages, and come to conclusions. Through this repeated practice, you will hone the speed and accuracy of your decision making.

In this chapter, you will have the opportunity to reflect on the different types of decisions you make in life. You will see that a decision-making system is not necessary for many of the mundane choices you make every day. But for those really important decisions, this chapter will challenge you to design a decision-making process that honors the critical role Christian faith plays in making weighty decisions. Furthermore, this chapter invites you to reflect on your personal value system. It will help you clarify the foundation that lies beneath your view of life and it will challenge you to check the content of your value system against the one outlined in Micah 6:8. Decisions, decisions, life is full of decisions. After reading this chapter, you will feel more comfortable and confident in addressing them.

Not All Decisions Are the Same

All decisions are not created equal. Some decisions are vastly more important than others. For example, if you do a poor job of selecting a meal at a restaurant or if you do a poor job of harmonizing the color of the clothes you wear to school today, the consequences of those decisions are minimal and will fade quickly. On the other hand, some decisions have enduring power. Whom you choose to marry, what occupation you pursue, and how you manage your credit card debt are decisions that have the power to affect your well-being for a very long time. Clearly, decisions vary in terms of their weight and the consequences that attend them.

Christians and Decision Making

Additionally, simply being a Christian is no guarantee that you will always make the right decision. In the Bible, we see believers making a variety of important decisions with varying degrees of success. For example, when the sons of Jacob saw their younger brother Joseph approaching them, they immediately began to discuss how to handle their upstart brother. After carefully weighing their options, they elected to kill this man with the fancy coat and fancy dreams, to hide his body in a cistern, and to mislead their father into believing that a wild animal had killed him (Gen 37:17–20). Within a short time, the brothers changed their mind. Instead of killing Joseph, they conspired to sell him as a slave and pack him off for an unknown future in Egypt. This narrative clearly illustrates that believers can make very poor decisions when they do not follow a careful process that honors the influence of biblical principles.

By contrast, the Bible also contains stories about believers who make very good decisions. Consider the subsequent experience of Joseph. After he arrived in Egypt, Joseph became the slave of a ranking Egyptian official named

Potiphar. When Potiphar was away from the house, his wife came to Joseph demanding that he participate with her in a sexual affair (Gen 39). The biblical author celebrates the honorable decision that Joseph makes when he rejects the repeated advances of his master's wife and stands as an example of a believer making a very good decision, one that we will explore in greater detail shortly.

A Decision-Making Process

Although simply being a Christian is no guarantee that you will always make the right decision, careful application of Christian beliefs can go a long way toward improving the quality of the decisions you make. This portion of the chapter will present a process that may be used when you are confronted by a significant choice. This process lengthens the time required to make such a decision, but we believe that critical decisions are best made over an extended period of time. Although less important decisions may be made more quickly, relying on intuition and past experiences, more important and unique decisions require careful thought, time, and a process that honors one's status as a member of God's family.

Step One: Clarify the Circumstances and the Question You Need to Answer

The first step in the process requires you to come to greater clarity about the circumstances of your decision and exactly what question you are attempting to answer. Take a pen and paper in hand or sit down at your computer. Write down as much as you can about the circumstances surrounding the decision. Who is involved and affected? What has happened to bring this situation about? What do you control, and what lies outside your control? Where would you like to be at the end of this process? Once you have done that brainstorming, filter all that you have written into a single question. As you reflect and write, you will come to greater clarity about the circumstances that surround this decision, and you will focus on the core question that needs to be answered.

Consider how this might have looked if Joseph had used this technique in determining his course of action with Potiphar's wife. His time in reflection may have looked like this: My name is Joseph. I have been separated from my family and am living in a household with a cultural and spiritual orientation that is different from the one I have known. I am a slave in this house and so I am not free to pursue certain courses of action. Yet the senior member of this household, who is a high-ranking Egyptian official, has great confidence in my management style and abilities. Over time, I have been placed in a position of high personal responsibility overseeing everything my master owns. God is blessing everything that is happening in this household through my leadership. I am also a very good-looking man who has attracted the sexual interest of my master's wife. I have sexual desires of my own. How should I respond to the sexual advances made by my master's wife?

Step Two: Clarify the Options

The second step in making an important decision is thinking through the various ways in which the question you have raised may be answered. Again, writing down your options will help you see your thinking more clearly. Keep the notes you made earlier close at hand, for the brainstorming you did in connection with the first step will prove helpful to you here.

This is how the process could have looked for Joseph as he clarified his options. How should I respond to the sexual advances made by my master's wife?

> I could have sexual relations with her just once.
> I could have sexual relations with her as often as she would want and try to keep it a secret.
> I could ignore her repeated invitations and try to avoid her.
> I could run away from this household.
> I could refuse her advances and hope that she would respect my point of view.

Step Three: Identify the Pros and Cons of Each Option

Every option you list in the second step of this process will have its own advantages and disadvantages. In the third step of this decision-making process, it is time to honor that reality by formally listing the advantages and disadvantages of each option. This is clearly the time to pray for clarity of thought, to pursue God's Word for direction, and to consult with trusted Christian friends who may be able to see advantages and disadvantages to your proposed choices that are less clear or absent from your own thinking. The Bible may or may not speak directly to the options you have listed, but the Lord will speak to you when he is invited to be part of the process. Remember the promise that Jesus makes, "Ask and it will be given to you; seek and you will find; knock and the door will be opened to you." (Matt 7:7)

We can again explore how the process may have looked for the decision Joseph needed to make. We will look at just one of his options: "I could have sexual relations just once with Potiphar's wife." This option boasts several advantages:

> If I follow this course of action, I could gain favor with a very influential member of the household.
> I could have my own sexual experience.
> And by giving in just once, I could get past the distracting invitations that keep interrupting my day.

By contrast, there are some grave disadvantages to pursuing this option:

> If my master finds out, I am sure to lose the high rank I have in this household or be put in prison.
> I have no guarantee that she would leave me alone if I give in just once.
> Most important, having sexual relations with her would be a sinful act that my God has forbidden.

Watch Out for Dualism

Many students leave high school with a very dualistic way of looking at life. They see issues as having only two sides and statements as completely true or completely false. Most matters in life are much more complex than this. To be sure, we need to define some matters in clear terms of right and wrong. But most matters in life are not that clear-cut. For example, a proposed state law that would allow the carrying of concealed weapons defies dualistic thinking. The issue is complex, with persuasive arguments for each position. Dualism is an excuse to stop thinking about a topic before you have thought your way completely through it.

Step Four: Decide and Proceed in Confidence

Once the matter has been carefully brought to this point, through prayer and meditation on the Word, it is time to proceed confidently with the option that appears most reasonable and that honors God. That is precisely what we see Joseph doing in Genesis 39. In the end, Joseph refused the advances of his master's wife, hoping that she would respect his point of view. After he considered every option, this was clearly the best course of action, the one that allowed him to remain faithful to his earthly overseer and to his heavenly Father. Once he made the decision, Joseph proceeded with confidence and announced his decision to Potiphar's wife: "With me in charge my master does not concern himself with anything in the house; everything he owns he has entrusted to my care. No one is greater in this house than I am. My master has withheld nothing from me except you, because you are his wife. How then can I do such a wicked thing and sin against God?" (Gen 39:8–9) And when Potiphar's wife continued to pursue him, Joseph did not revisit the question. He remained firm in his decision, confident that he had been led to the best option, a decision that allowed him to retain his integrity as a careful thinker and as a member of God's family.

Not every decision you make requires the same amount of time and this very thoughtful approach. But if you are a Christian, decisions that directly affect your integrity as a member of Jesus' household and impact your future life in a dramatic way deserve no less. This four-step process challenges us to think through our decisions carefully. It calls on us to acknowledge all the details and circumstances that surround the decision. It requires us to carefully articulate the question we are trying to answer. It demands that we identify all of our options and weigh the pros and cons of each. And, most important, it calls us to think through the potential decisions in a way that honors our personal values grounded in the Bible.

My Aesthetic, Moral, and Personal Values

Behind the scenes of the process just described, our personal value system is at work shaping the response to the decisions we make. In reality, this system plays a much bigger role in our lives, shaping who we are and how we view the world. We will briefly discuss the nature of aesthetic and moral values before pursuing the larger and more critical discussion of personal values.

Aesthetic Values

Aesthetic values may best be defined as your personal taste, evident in the music, the art, or the food you enjoy. The fact that your roommate loves country music while you detest it or the fact that you love sushi while your friend abhors it is evidence that people have differing aesthetic values. These preferences find their source both within the uniqueness of our creation and in the fostering hand of our cultural experience. Because these values are, in part, shaped by our cultural experience, people typically find that their personal tastes migrate under the influence of new people and new circumstances in life. For example, you may have refused to eat vegetables as a child but find that you now cannot get enough of them.

Moral Values

By contrast, moral values are the part of our value system we use to make decisions about what is right or wrong, just or unjust in the world. When torn down to the foundation, a moral decision is principally built on one of three foundations: reason, emotion, or authority. Enlightenment rationalism has strongly influenced modern thinkers to equate what is right with what is most logical. The person whose moral judgment is guided by reason may well see the death penalty as immoral because no one has adequately proven that the death penalty is an effective deterrent to crime. By contrast, a moral decision may be founded on personal feelings or emotions. A couple may make the moral decision to have premarital sex based on the feelings of love they have for one another. Because the decision to have sex with one another feels right to them, they become confident that they are making the right decision. Third, a moral decision may find its foundation in the authority of a respected book, person, or deity. For example, a Christian student who is tempted to plagiarize a paper from the Internet steps away from that act because it would violate God's instructions given in his Word. Respect for this authority figure lies at the foundation of that moral choice. Thus moral values are used to make ethical choices, and they are based on one of three foundations: reason, emotion, and authority.

Personal Values

Our personal value system is influenced by our aesthetic values and moral values but has its own distinguishing characteristics. It is not just your personal taste in clothing and your perspective on the death penalty, but also the core beliefs you have about who you are, the world you live in, and the people who surround you. It is the part of us that shapes everything including how we vote in a presidential election, when we read our Bibles, and how we deal with the homeless person who asks us for money on a busy street corner.

It can be more difficult to define your personal value system in the abstract. Perhaps the best way to see it is in response to practical situations. Consider what you can learn about your personal value system by observing your reaction to the following statements:

- The Democratic candidate for governor is speaking on your campus next week.
- Your roommate has just revealed to you that her uncle is gay.
- Your brother has not gone to church for one year.
- You just found a purse with $ 1,000 cash inside it.
- Your friend is planning to sleep overnight with her boyfriend in the residence hall.
- You have been invited to spend this weekend at your friend's house but have learned that his mother is an alcoholic.
- Your boyfriend cheated on his final exam in chemistry.
- Several of your friends invite you to hand out leaflets opposing abortion at a medical clinic.

Your reaction to each of these statements reveals the content of your personal value system. As difficult as it can be to get a handle on that value system, well-educated people consciously try to understand the personal value system that motivates their thoughts and actions in life. This is important for two reasons. First, it is important to have a sense of your personal value system so that you can understand and appreciate the thinking of those who do not agree with you. For example, your view of abortion may be radically different from the view held by your co-workers at your part-time job. Their arguments and their methods of arguing their point of view will make no sense to you unless you understand the personal value system that lies beneath their statements. You may be arguing your case from the foundation of the Bible's

Watch Out for Intolerance

College students, by design, encounter new ideas and interact with people who challenge their traditional point of view. In order for that experience to be a meaningful one, you must develop a tolerance that allows you to fully hear an alternate point of view before dismissing it out of hand. When you hear someone express a view that you have not traditionally owned, listen carefully. Try to understand the arguments being made and the foundation on which those arguments have been built. Although they may make you uncomfortable, it is unwise to flee from such forms of interaction or isolate yourself from them. Tolerance is not the same as acceptance. You can be a tolerant listener, grow in your understanding of a position, and still leave the conversation without accepting the alternative point of view.

authority, while the other person may see the Bible as just another book whose authority they do not respect. Perhaps they are using the foundation of reason, claiming that the fetus is not really a person who benefits from protection of the law until it is viable on its own. It is very easy for two people to simply talk past one another about a topic unless they clarify the foundation from which each of them is arguing their case.

Second, it is important to understand your personal value system to be aware of the vulnerability of your point of view. If you support the death penalty and base your position on a logical argument, your argument is most vulnerable if your logic is not sound. If you take a stand against abortion and base it on the authority of the Bible, your argument is vulnerable if you have misunderstood the teaching of the Bible or if you have overestimated the expertise of your authority. Careful thinkers must know and acknowledge where their position is most vulnerable. This does not prevent educated people from taking positions, but it means taking a position fully aware of its vulnerabilities.

Rethinking My Personal Values

Now that you have had a chance to think about your personal value system, it is time to rethink that system under the influence of the Bible's teaching. Christians acknowledge the authority of the Bible in their lives and seek to align their personal value system as closely as possible with the guidance and direction offered in God's Word. One could argue that the entire Bible is designed to shape and edit your view of yourself, of your relationship to God, and of your relationship to others you meet in life. But one Bible passage in particular challenges us to rethink our personal value system. That passage is Micah 6:8.

STUDENT VOICE

Eric Mallet

Major: Communication/Christian Ministry
Hometown: St. Louis, Missouri
School: Abilene Christian University

As a resident assistant, I live in the residence hall and am responsible for helping the students who live there. I often find myself in situations in which I really need the direction and power of the Holy Spirit. I use God's guidance to discipline, to encourage, and to teach my residents what it means to be a servantlike student. In all things, my faith serves as my foundation.

Micah 6:8

In this book of the Bible, Micah criticizes those who claim to be believers but whose personal value system is far from what God intended it to be. In particular, he reproves the wealthy and the political power brokers who use their wealth and power to exploit others. For example, in Chapter Two he says, "Woe to those who plan iniquity, to those who plot evil on their beds! At morning's light they carry it out because it is in their power to do it. They covet fields and seize them, and houses, and take them. They defraud a man of his home, a fellowman of his inheritance." (Micah 2:1–2) Micah criticizes the citizens of this state for seizing property that does not belong to them (2:2), for taking clothes off people's backs (2:8), and for bringing physical harm to others in the process (3:2–3). Given these kinds of social injustice, it is no surprise to read page after page of criticism in the Book of Micah announcing God's displeasure with this behavior and the coming of divine judgment against those who practiced it. But in contrast to the lengthy criticisms found in the book, we find a positive verse that calls attention to itself by virtue of its brevity. Micah poses the critical question and then answers it with a striking trilogy: "And what does the LORD require of you? To act justly, to love mercy, and to walk humbly with your God." (Micah 6:8) Here in three brief phrases, Micah provides the outline for a personal value system. This is a clear call to rethink your personal value system and to see if the outline Micah describes is operative there.

To Act Justly

The first charge Micah gives is to act justly. This, of course, implies that a standard exists against which our actions may be judged. In many situations, God has not given humans the authority to make up the rules for living or to change the rules when it suits them. Rather the Word of God is filled with volitional clauses that direct the actions and attitudes of humankind. In Deuteronomy 5, God articulates the Ten Commandments, which summarize how he expects human beings to act justly. This summary is enhanced throughout the rest of the Bible where God speaks about life and living. Because this blueprint that directs moral behavior comes directly from God, it cannot be improved. That is why God further states, "Do not add to what I command you and do not subtract from it, but keep the commands of the LORD your God." (Deut 4:2)

As we review those guidelines for just living, we find that some are widely accepted by society. For example, "you shall not murder" is a directive that controls daily life in most civilized societies. But other directives from God seem to fly in the face of common sense and certainly in the face of common practice. Consider the directions of Jesus to "Love your enemies, do good to those who hate you, bless those who curse you, pray for those who mistreat you." (Luke 6:27–28) Whether biblical directives are commonly held or contradict the social norm, Micah challenges us to use them as a standard to measure whether we are acting justly.

To Love Mercy

Secondly, Micah challenges his readers to check their personal value system and see if it celebrates and encourages the merciful treatment of others, "to love mercy." The Hebrew term that stands behind the English translation,

Watch Out for Relativism

Relativism is a very powerful force in our culture, driven by an existential world view that encourages the value-free acceptance of nearly all ideas. Although such relativism is certainly defendable in respect to aesthetic values, it runs into harsh opposition from the Bible when applied to moral issues. Although relativism plays down the possibility of much objective truth, the Bible makes it clear that there is such a thing as objective truth, particularly in regard to moral issues. Relativism may claim that each individual has his or her own right to define truth as he or she sees it, asserting that what is morally true for one person is not necessarily true for everyone. The Bible honors the fact that although aesthetic taste is relative, moral truth is not. Watch out for the form of relativism that removes the authority of God's Word from the stage.

"mercy," is somewhat more broad and powerful than this translation suggests. No single English word fully communicates the idea. We come as close as we can with the phrase "a loving-kindness that endures." People can act justly for a variety of reasons. People may act justly because they feel they will get something out of it if they do. Others may act justly because they feel you should just be good for goodness' sake. But the Bible challenges its adherents to live a life characterized by an enduring loving-kindness enacted in thanks for the greater mercy that has been shown to them. "This is how God showed his love among us: He sent his one and only Son into the world that we might live through him. This is love: not that we loved God, but that he loved us and sent his Son as an atoning sacrifice for our sins." (1 John 4:9–10) This Gospel message has so changed the life of believers that they are capable of loving even their enemies. "We love because he first loved us." (1 John 4:19)

To Walk Humbly with Your God

Finally, Micah challenges us "to walk humbly with your God." Considering all that God has done for the believer and all that believers are able to do through the power of God, they could easily become filled with an inappropriate pride. But the Lord cautions that this pride is out of place in the life of a Christian. In fact, the Apostle Paul warns that a person who feels prideful overconfidence is standing at the brink of failure: "So if you think you are standing firm, be careful that you don't fall!" (1 Cor 10:12) By contrast, Paul holds up the example of Jesus: "Your attitude should be the same as that of Christ Jesus: Who, being in very nature God, did not consider equality with God something to be grasped, but made himself nothing, taking the very nature of a servant being made in human likeness. And being found in appearance as a man, he humbled himself and became obedient to death—even death on a cross!" (Phil 2:5–8)

Our personal value system lies at the core of who we are. It impacts the way we make our decisions. It impacts the way we live our life in relationship to God and the way we treat others around us. Well-educated people know something about their personal value system and edit it as necessary. Micah challenges those honored by God's forgiveness to walk justly, to love mercy, and to walk humbly with their God.

Exercises for **Success**

Review Questions

1. Identify the four-step process suggested in this chapter for making important decisions. Summarize the purpose of each step.

2. Compare and contrast the various types of values: aesthetic, moral, and personal.

3. Define *intolerance* and describe the potential harm it can do as you advance your education.

It Is Decision Time

In this chapter, you encountered a decision-making process that you can use when making an important decision in your life. Now it is your turn to practice with that process by addressing a decision you are facing at the moment. Either sit down at your computer or take paper and pencil in hand and work through the following steps:

Step One:　Clarify the circumstances and the question you need to answer.

Step Two:　Clarify your options.

Step Three: Identify the pros and cons of each option.

Step Four:　Decide and proceed with confidence.

At the conclusion of this process, you will have positioned yourself to make a decision. But, more important, the experience will help you determine what portions of the process you will edit to fit your needs.

Identifying My Personal Values

To learn more about your personal values, place a check next to each of the following statements that you feel strongly about. Then go back and pick out the top eight and list them in order of importance to you.

_____ I want to be very well educated.

_____ I want to bring someone to know Christ.

_____ I want to be a community leader.

_____ I want to make a lot of money.

_____ I want to have a healthy spiritual life.

_____ I want to enjoy good relationships.

_____ I want to have as much personal freedom as I can find.

_____ I want to be happy.

_____ I want to make other people happy.

_____ I want to enjoy my work more than my leisure time.

_____ I want to be known as a person of integrity.

_____ I want to be known for my creativity.

_____ I want to be known for my athleticism.

_____ I want to eliminate racial prejudice from the world.

_____ I want to become famous.

_____ I want to be married and have a family.

_____ I want to become involved in politics.

_____ I want my children to grow up as Christians.

_____ I want there to be a cure for cancer.

_____ I want to be known for my good looks.

_____ I want to know my Bible better than my peers do.

_____ I want to be a leader in my church.

_____ I want to live a healthy lifestyle.

_____ I want to feed hungry children.

_____ I want to enjoy my leisure time more than my work.

Personal Values and a Moral Dilemma

Susan came from a small town where her widowed father was a Christian minister. He raised her very strictly, and only with great reluctance did he allow her to go to the state university. He feared that the big city and secular professors in college would corrupt her morals. After the initial college orientation, his final words to her were a warning: "If I ever find out that you have been fooling around with boys or using alcohol or drugs, I'll cut you off from all financial support and never let you enter our home again."

Susan had always obeyed her father and intended to do so at college. Her professors did challenge her value system and at times seemed to make fun of the Christian views she expressed. Nevertheless, she honored her father's request and stayed away from drugs and alcohol. But in November, she began dating Larry, a student in her history class. Eventually Larry invited her to parties where alcohol flowed freely. He said to her, "I know that you don't want to have anything to drink. I respect that decision; just come and have fun with me and my friends." At first, she refused the drinks offered to her at the party, but eventually her friend Alison persuaded her that "one drink won't hurt." Consuming alcohol was new for Susan. It made her feel free and liberated. Finally, she felt that she was doing something that she wanted to do.

Susan began to attend parties more regularly and kept experimenting with more and more alcohol. One night when she had become very drunk, Larry persuaded her to have sexual relations with him. Susan hardly remembered what had happened, but the physical evidence told her that she had gone to a place she had never intended to go. Susan felt guilty and devastated. She wanted to talk to Larry about what had happened, but he refused to speak to her about it. In the end, Larry told her that he did not want to see her any more. Alison saw how devastated Susan was and felt that she needed to get out and meet new people. She told Susan that the best way to get over this loss in her life was to find someone new. Alison was dating Jim, and his fraternity was having a party that night. Susan agreed to go. Once there, Susan began to drink more heavily than she ever had before. She drank so much that she became very sleepy. Susan went to a back bedroom in the house to lie down and passed out on the bed. While lying unconscious on her back, she choked to death on her own vomit.

List the characters in this story and rank them from the person you see as most responsible for Susan's death to the one least responsible for Susan's death. Compare your conclusions with those of others. Where do you agree and where do you disagree? How did your personal value system impact the way you organized your list?

Micah 6:8 and My Personal Values

Earlier in this chapter we saw how Micah 6:8 challenges us to demonstrate three qualities in our personal value system. The following is a list of statements to which you may apply your personal value system. Select three of the statements that are of greatest interest to you. Pretend that a friend of yours has made the statement. Write your response to your friend and demonstrate through your response that your value system lives up to the one outlined in Micah 6:8. Demonstrate that you act justly, love mercy, and walk humbly with your God.

War is a necessary evil.

Abortion is an appropriate method of contraception.

We must support our political leaders no matter what.

No church leader should be a practicing homosexual.

Honesty is always the best policy.

People who do not work for a living should not be given public financial support.

Cheating is only wrong if you get caught.

Love will always find a way.

Treat others as you would like to be treated yourself.

SPIRITUAL REFLECTION JOURNAL

Read the story of Abram in Genesis 12:10–20. Write about your reaction to the decision that Abram made about Sarai and the method he used to make the decision. Do you feel the decision was an honorable one? What was missing from the decision-making process reported by the author in this story? What meaningful application do you find for your own life in this story?

Time in Prayer

In your personal time in prayer or in connection with others in your class, take time to pray for the following people and needs:

- For the person you know who is in the midst of making a difficult decision

- For your church and government leaders who are making difficult decisions

- For your parents and family members in the midst of critical decisions

- That God may help you carefully think through your value system in light of Micah 6:8

- That God may give you the strength to live out your personal values in the midst of the challenges you face

On the Web

The Internet can be a helpful resource as you look for ideas to make yourself a happier and more successful student. Visit the College Success page offered by Thomson Wadsworth for Web links that will help you grow further on this topic. Go to http://www.success .wadsworth.com/ and click on Resource Web Links.

In particular, we recommend the following:

http://www.growingchristians.org/dfgc/seven2.htm

http://www.maristseminary.org.nz/discernment3 .htm

http://www.virtualsalt.com/crebook5.htm

http://www.me.uvic.ca/~suleman/Mech350/Presen tations/Lecture-4/index.htm

http://www.twopaths.com/faq_ChristianValues.htm

Seeking and Maintaining Healthy Relationships 11

Dear friends, since God so loved us, we also ought to love one another.

1 John 4:11

• What kinds of relationships will I have in college?

• How will those relationships influence my pursuit of success?

• How will diversity enhance my education?

• How can I keep my relationships healthy?

• How can I manage conflict in my relationships?

From the beginning, God designed human beings to be connected to one another in close, meaningful relationships (Gen 2:18). Those relationships are not merely tangential to our happiness and satisfaction, they are fundamental to our well-being. In a perfect world, we would always feel happy and satisfied with our relationships. But in a world that has been ruined by sin, we find ourselves depending on and managing relationships that are far from perfect. We need to turn no further in our Bible than the pages of Genesis to find such troubled relationships: a husband turns on his wife (Gen 3:12), a brother's jealous rage leads him to commit the first murder (Gen 4), a young woman is sexually assaulted (Gen 34), and a brother is sold as a slave (Gen 37). Consequently, the deep need we have for meaningful relationships lives in constant tension with the potential harm that those same relationships may bring into our lives. This chapter is about managing the relationships that live in that tension.

We will begin with an overview of the various types of people who affect you as a college student: old and new friends, romantic partners, spouses, parents, roommates, and faculty. Among those relationships, you will interact with people who are different from you, so we will also explore the nature and importance of diversity on a college campus. And because relationships can help or harm your pursuit of success, we will examine the qualities of healthy relationships and offer advice on managing the conflict that is bound to surface within those relationships. One thing is clear: the relationships you have as a college student will affect both your chances for success and your well-being. As you work to improve your relationships, we pray that the love of God may guide you in the process so that we may truly love one another in the same way that he has loved us.

Types of Relationships

Most people are surprised when they stop to count all the different kinds of personal relationships that affect their lives. If you make such a list, you too will find yourself connected to many different people and supported in many different relationships during your time in college. Consider the following list as a starting point for your own thinking:

- Parents
- Siblings
- Spouse
- Friends
- Roommates
- Romantic partners
- Stepparents
- Faculty
- Children
- Grandparents

The relationships that you enjoyed before going to college will likely change if for no other reason than that you will be changing as a result of your advanced education. You will become a better thinker, you will become more informed about the world, and your personal views about life may be edited. As you bring the "new you" to your old relationships, be patient with your parents, siblings, friends, and others who may need time to adjust to the person you have become. Healthy relationships go through such adjustments and become stronger as a result of them.

New Friendships and Old Friendships

From the moment you stepped onto campus, you were surrounded by a sea of new faces. Remember those first orientation sessions and classes? Some of you celebrate the opportunity to meet new people, while others may feel uncomfortable with the thought of making new friends. In either case, we hope that you have been getting away from the computer and spending time in the student union, at athletic events, and at parties. Attending college is an excit-

Alexis Glover

Major: Biochemistry/Molecular Biology
Hometown: Baltimore, Maryland
School: Liberty University

My fiancé fell asleep and all of a sudden stopped breathing. I thought he was just playing . . . but he was not. As an EMT I knew that even after I had given him mouth-to-mouth for almost a minute, he was slipping away. Why was the ambulance taking so long to arrive? Suddenly a peace came over me. Something told me to place my hands on his chest and to begin to pray. I said, *please God please help him, help me, tell me what else to do, bring him back to me, please have mercy.* Before the second tear could stream down my face, he began to gasp for air. At that moment I truly knew the mercy of God and realized that he had a plan for our lives.

ing time in your life, and one of the powerful commodities you will take with you when you leave is those new friendships. Seize the opportunity. Now is the time in your life to meet people with different interests and backgrounds. Make a point of breaking out of the old crowd and getting to know someone who is from a different country or of a different race. You will grow in ways that you cannot imagine.

But not everyone finds it easy to meet new people. If you have difficulty making new friends, consider the following suggestions. Make yourself available. If you have been in the habit of sitting in your room with the door closed, others may assume you want to be left alone. Open your door and leave your room behind for places on campus where the students go to have fun. It also helps to participate in activities beyond the classroom. Your school likely has a variety of clubs, teams, and organizations that allow people of similar interests to get together. Joining such a team, club, or organization will not only foster your mutual interests but help you find new friends.

Then there is the question of what to do with your friends back at home. You may feel a strong desire to keep in touch with old friends, particularly in your first semester of college. The familiar voice of an old friend can be very comforting as you adjust to your new surroundings. This kind of exchange has become so much easier and less expensive with the dawn of electronic mail and messaging. The use of this technology is an excellent way to maintain those older relationships, but beware of how much time you invest in it. Too much time spent nurturing old relationships may come at the expense of making new friends.

Finally, not every relationship you have had in the past will make the transition with you to college life. Honor the fact that although you have changed, others may not have changed or they may have changed in ways that are not

Are Your Friends Helping You Succeed?

How are your friends influencing you? Not everyone will be as committed or concerned about your success as you are. If your friends interrupt your study time, encourage you to skip class, or keep you up all night, you need to stand up for your best interests. Your friends may not be aware of the impact they are having on you. Speak to them. If they do not listen, take action and do what you need to do in order to be successful.

compatible with the way you have changed. This means some relationships will never be what they were before. Some old friendships will survive the challenge of distance and change. But expect that some of your past relationships will best be retired to happy memories as you move forward with your life.

Romance in College

College can also be a time when romance blooms in your life. Romantic relationships are important because they fulfill our need for companionship and intimacy. Both of these needs are natural and may be filled in a variety of ways. This requires us to make decisions in our romantic relationship about the level of intimacy we will pursue and where we will draw the line. Poor decision making in this arena can result in low self-esteem, feelings of guilt, a broken relationship, pregnancy, or even a sexually transmitted disease. That is why God has provided us with directions and limitations when exploring sexual intimacy with others. In his Word, he challenges us to flee from sexual immorality, for he has chosen our bodies to be his temple (1 Cor 6:19–20).

As you consider the level of intimacy in your romantic relationships and where you choose to demonstrate that intimacy, consider God's message to you in passages such as Hebrews 13:4, 1 Corinthians 13:1–13, and 1 Corinthians 6:12–20. After you read these passages, discuss them with your partner, your Christian friends, or your pastor. Through your reading and these conversations, the Holy Spirit will lead you to clarity on appropriate ways to express your intimacy with a romantic partner and what kinds of intimacy are best left for a later time. One thing is clear. The time to make a decision about the level of intimacy in your romantic relationships is before you find yourself physically aroused by your partner in a setting where temptation is harder to resist.

College and the Married Student

Being married while you attend college has its own unique rewards, but also presents some unique challenges. Your spouse can be an invaluable source of support and encouragement. So it is important to keep him or her involved in your campus life to the degree that this is practical. Attend guest lectures, drama productions, or sporting events as a couple. Invite classmates to your

Should I Become Exclusive?

A decision that needs to be weighed very carefully is the one to become exclusive—that is, dating just one person. Although we can become very comfortable with and even dependent on just one person, common wisdom recommends a different course. Date a variety of people during your college years so that you might further discover what you find most and least desirable in a romantic relationship.

home for dinner. And if your university allows people to audit classes, ask your spouse to join one of your classes for fun.

If you have children while you are in college, you will need to be strategic when planning your study time. Your children certainly deserve and need good quality time with you. But that does not mean giving them attention whenever and wherever they demand it. Some parents choose to do all their homework after their children are asleep. This is an option, but not always the most productive one. One alternative to consider is waking up earlier in the morning before your family wakes up and spending thirty to sixty minutes studying. If you attend classes on campus during the day, be strategic with your schedule. Time scheduled between class sessions may be time that you can spend in the library on research projects or doing homework. If not the library, find a place on campus that is quiet and free from distractions.

Spending time with your family is necessary for your relationship and enjoyable for all involved, but some parents feel guilty if they study during times that used to be strictly family time. Honor the fact that you are in a new situation that is temporary, requiring everyone to make adjustments for a time. Find a balance between time spent with children and study time. If you study at home in the evening, and it is very likely you will need to do so, establish some boundaries. When you are in your office or at the kitchen table with books in front of you, let everyone know that this is study time and interruptions should be kept to a minimum. Be sure to let your children know that you will spend time playing with them before bedtime. Your children can adapt to that kind of schedule, and you will be modeling excellent studying habits and time management behaviors.

Parents

The transition from adolescence to young adulthood typically brings a change in your relationship with your parents. Young adults who go to college often experience greater freedom in how they organize their time and more responsibility in making their own decisions. You are changing and growing as an independent person. Although most parents want to see their children grow to become responsible adults capable of being on their own, it may be difficult for your parents to see this change in you. Be patient with them. Talk with them and get their perspective on the changes they see in you. God calls for us to honor our parents for the unique contribution they make to our lives (Exod 20:12). It will be easier to do that at some times rather than others, but love, patience, and honest communication will help everyone make the necessary adjustments.

As you learn more about life, grow, and change, remember that your parents have walked the same road you are now walking. They have the advantage of experience and can offer you a wealth of advice and direction. Stay in contact with them, seek their advice, and let them know that you love them. They may well be missing you more than you realize.

Unfortunately, not everyone has an ideal relationship with their parents. If your relationship with a parent or parents is strained, seek support from other adults who have a concern for you. It could be grandparents, an aunt or uncle, a stepparent, or another adult on campus such as a counselor or advisor. But do not dismiss your parents. Do what you can to stay in contact and pray for the strength and guidance necessary to mend that broken relationship.

Living with Roommates

If you live on campus, you will probably have one or more roommates. Perhaps you were able to choose your roommate, or the university may have placed you with someone you had not met before. Regardless of your situation, new students who live on campus will at some point have a conflict with their roommate. Later in this chapter we will discuss conflict management, as using good conflict strategies is essential when living with a roommate. But even before a conflict arises, you can be proactive in addressing problems before they occur. First of all, give your perspective a quick check. Many students have an overly romanticized idea that their roommate will be their best friend and confidant. This could happen, but it puts a tremendous amount of pressure on everyone involved in the roommate relationship.

First and foremost, your roommate is your living partner for a relatively short time. A friendship may or may not develop between you. But even before a friendship can develop, basic living guidelines must be discussed, adopted, and honored. Will we share the right to use personal items we have brought to campus? How will we share responsibility for cleaning the room? When will we have quiet study time in the room? And when will we turn out the lights and go to bed? Those topics are best discussed before they become issues of discontent. If you follow the guidelines you've set, you can have an excellent relationship with your roommate, even if you are not best friends. Because you will be managing a living arrangement with this person, focus on the keys to successful living and let the friendship develop as it may. If you and your roommate are simply unable to negotiate basic living arrangements, it is perfectly acceptable to change roommates at the appropriate time designated by your residence director.

The Risk in Electronic Relationships

Although you may approach your Internet contacts with pure motives, not everyone in the electronic world can be trusted. Some take advantage of the anonymity offered by the Internet to try to harm you. Their goal may be to hijack your computer, steal your identity, or worse. Not everyone is who they claim to be in this electronic world. Be cautious about sharing personal information of any kind with someone you do not personally know.

Faculty Connections

The professionals who have been given the greatest responsibility for your intellectual growth are the faculty members who teach your classes. College teachers are different from other teachers you have had, both in their professional life and in the way they present their classes. They have advanced academic degrees in specialties such as history, business, or biology. Not only do they teach, but many write books and articles as well as speaking publicly on their area of expertise. Most college faculty members also advise students and serve on committees that are vital to the function of the university.

By their very nature, the classes they conduct ask more of you. Professors assign more reading over less time and give you exams on that reading even if they have not discussed that material in class. They expect you to bear the responsibility for keeping up with the class requirements. Therefore, they may not remind you to read assignments or pester you about the due dates for research papers. They are less likely to check up on your class attendance or note taking. Because they have advanced their thinking skills to a high degree through their own advanced education, they are less tolerant of simple answers to complex questions. And they are interested in maturing your thinking as they engage you in conversations that require you to express and defend your own views.

The differences between college teachers and other teachers you have had may lead you to conclude that they assign too much work or are treating you unfairly. In time, you will come to appreciate them for the professional work they do. And as you adjust to this new teaching style, give your college teachers the respect and patience they deserve. Jesus may serve as something of a model for us here. When he was a young man, he traveled to the Temple and sat among the teachers. Jesus first listened to those teachers and asked questions (Luke 2:46) before criticizing some of their conclusions later on in his life. This is a model worth considering and emulating.

As you are thinking about your college teachers, they are also forming opinions about you. That makes it critical to show your instructors that you are a serious student who has a passion to succeed. You can send that message in a variety of ways:

- *Attend class and be on time.* You cannot make an impression if you are not present. Students who regularly attend class not only benefit from the consistent learning, but also show that they are serious about their studies. Similarly, we know of no faculty who are favorably impressed with late students. If you are consistently late for class, apologize to the instructor and be on time in the future.

- *Know the syllabus.* If you have a question regarding attendance policies, grading, scheduling, or other course expectations, always check the syllabus first before questioning the instructor.

- *Sit near the front of the classroom.* You will find it easier to listen to the lecture and involve yourself in class discussions.

- *Participate in class.* If you find this difficult on the fly, try developing several questions from the assigned readings so you can ask them during appropriate moments. If you disagree with something said during class, do not be afraid to say so. However, be ready to defend your position. The professor is there to help you become a better thinker, and participating in class discussions is one way of doing that.
- *See your instructors during office hours.* Generally, instructors indicate their office hours on the class syllabus. Call for an appointment to discuss assignments and exams or get feedback on papers. And while you are in their office, take note of how it is decorated. You can learn a great deal about a faculty member from the pictures and artifacts on display.

Living with Difference and Celebrating Diversity

The world we live in is a mosaic of people all uniquely created to be who they are by the hand of God. The study of those differences and the construction of a society that benefits from that diversity lies at the heart of the university experience. As you travel about the campus, you will meet faculty, staff, and students who are both visibly and invisibly different from one another. The campus community is intentionally designed this way. When we live and work around people who are just like us, we learn less than when we live and work with people who are different from us. This diverse community challenges us to see the world and its issues through various perspectives as we confront new ideas, people, and cultural practices.

Take a walk through the hallways and down the sidewalks of your school, and pay attention to the differences of those you meet. Your walk may bring you into contact with people of a different gender, race, age, religious affiliation, or political ideology. You may meet someone who has a disability, is from a different culture, or has a different marital status from yours. These are just a few of the differences that exist on a university campus. This diversity is designed to enhance your learning experience. But that diversity can produce discomfort, tension, and even fear. When we are confronted with people who are different from us, we may retreat to old stereotypes.

Stereotypes

Stereotyping is a way of thinking about other people who are different from us. We tend to place people in categories and assign certain traits and qualities to all the people in the category. Some experts argue that stereotypes serve as "mental maps."[1] These maps may contain reliable information based on firsthand experience. However, that is rarely the case. Most often our stereotypes represent very little firsthand experience with that group of people. As a result, our beliefs are subject to error. These beliefs can range from the mundane to the serious. For example, if your mental map of African American women says they are all great cooks, that belief will not harm the relationship you have with members of that group. However, if your stereotyping leads you to believe that African American women are spiteful and untrustworthy, that will definitely harm your relationship with members of that group. You may even refrain from interacting with African American women based on this inappropriate generalization. When stereotypes become negative, rigid, and irrational, they will likely lead to prejudice.[2]

Prejudice

Whereas stereotypes have the potential for negative outcomes, prejudicial thinking is negative by definition. Prejudice is a negative feeling, attitude, or generalization about a group of people that leads someone to prejudge an individual based on these inaccurate beliefs and stereotypes. The stereotype about African American women being spiteful and untrustworthy creates the prejudgment that your African American history teacher will be unfair when she grades your papers and tests. Your stereotype of an entire group has resulted in prejudicial thinking and expectations about your history teacher. Entering a class with such a prejudiced view is bound to negatively influence your experience in that class and your interaction with that teacher.

You and Diversity

We often fear the unknown. Have you been reluctant to seek help from a professor because you felt uncomfortable with his or her religious affiliation or cultural background? Has your relationship with your roommate been strained because you felt uncomfortable with her or his disability or body weight? Our discomfort with people who are different from us may create barriers that block our association with others. If that has happened to you, try the following:

- See your level of comfort with others as a habit and realize that habits can be changed. You were not born with prejudicial attitudes.
- Try to become aware of when you make assumptions about people based on external characteristics such as age, skin color, gender, or disability.
- Read about different cultures. Knowledge is a powerful opponent to prejudice.
- Read about the psychological and sociological effects of stereotypes, prejudice, and discrimination.
- Begin changing that habit by stepping out of your comfort zone and intentionally building relationships with people who are different from you. Join a study group or campus organization. Sit near someone in your class and strike up a casual conversation.
- Before you explore the differences, see the common ground that all humans share. We all need to eat, sleep, love, be loved, and find hope in life. Seek common ground with personal preferences such as music, sports, hobbies, or art. These similarities can increase your comfort with those who are different from you in other ways.

Fear and prejudice hurt not only the targets; they hurt you too. Open yourself to God's glorious and diverse creation. And in doing so, let your curiosity lead you to appreciate the unique perspectives and insights others have to offer.

Maintaining Healthy Relationships

The relationships we have with faculty, family, friends, and mates need care and attention. You can reflect on the quality of your relationships in many different ways. Your local bookstore has shelves full of books dedicated to the study of healthy relationships. So what is offered in this section is only a starting point for reflecting on our key relationships. Here we will explore the general qualities of a healthy relationship and discuss strategies for managing conflict that develops within a relationship.

The Qualities of Healthy Relationships

All relationships vary in the level of their health. The best personal relationships are built on qualities such as the ones listed here. Are your current relationships built on these healthy attitudes and behaviors?

Mutual trust	*Forgiveness*
Mutual respect	*Mutual support*
Effective communication	*Shared interests*
Kindness	*Similar values*
Patience	

Conflict Is Natural and Inevitable

Even the healthiest relationships experience conflict. The inspired author of Proverbs implies that when he says, "The kisses of an enemy may be profuse, but faithful are the wounds of a friend." (Prov 27:6) Those wounds can occur in any number of settings. You and your roommate may have had words over the time the lights get turned out at night. You and your parents may have quarreled over your choice of major. Perhaps you and your spouse disagreed about household duties.

You may think that having an argument will hurt the relationship or that it signals that the relationship itself is bad. You may even fear conflict because you think it may expose some undesirable qualities such as pettiness or a need to control. But having such an argument does not automatically hurt the relationship, nor does it mean the relationship is bad. Conflict is an inevitable part of any relationship. It is a product of our being different from one another and not always seeing the world in the same way. The goal is not to avoid conflict, but to maintain a healthy relationship even in the midst of conflict.

Managing Conflict in Relationships

The first step in managing a conflict involves understanding the nature of the conflict. The clash may center on either the *content of your conversation* or the *nature of the relationship* itself. For example, suppose you and your significant other are arguing about the amount of time you spend together. If that conflict centers on the content, it may be a disagreement about the number of days and hours you spend together each week. On the other hand, if the conflict is generated by the nature of your relationship, then you may be disagreeing about who is really committed to the relationship or who is not. Successful conflict management begins with addressing the true causes of the conflict. Does it lie in the content of the conversation or in the nature of the relationship?

The second step in managing a conflict is to look carefully at the communication habits of the participants. "Reckless words pierce like a sword, but the tongue of the wise brings healing." (Prov 12:18) Maybe you never thought that your method of handling conflict can greatly influence the health of the relationship, but it can. Some habits help facilitate effective communication behaviors. Some habits harm the process of conflict management.

Poor communication habits obstruct the open and honest sharing that people can have in a relationship. Instead of communicating directly, people who engage in the following behaviors often do not get to the real issue and so prolong the relational tension. Over time, the relationship can suffer great harm if these become the primary tools of managing conflict.[3]

Avoiding This is the unwise avoiding of a conflict. It could be either a physical or mental retreat from the scene or topic, such as walking out of the room or ignoring the other person while watching TV. Time apart may be necessary to collect yourself before managing a conflict, but prolonged avoidance will only lead to more harm. Note that this advice does not apply if you are in a relationship in which you are being physically or verbally threatened. In such a case, physical separation from your partner is an absolute necessity to avoid further harm.

Blaming Conflict in a relationship almost always has more than one contributor. When we blame our partner, we make accusations and place all the responsibility for the conflict on the other person rather than carefully noting our own contribution to the disturbance in the relationship.

Uncontrolled Anger It is not wrong to be angry at someone, because anger can stem from righteous motives. Remember that God describes himself as being angry at times. However, anger is a vice when it springs from sinful motives or when that anger results in the physical or emotional harm of another. James says, "Everyone should be quick to listen, slow to speak, and slow to become angry." (James 1:19)

Dumping Some people do not confront the issues as they arise. Instead they keep long lists of past grievances. When they become involved in a personal conflict, they may not focus on the most recent problem but dump all the stored-up grievances on their partner.

Hitting below the Belt We are all more sensitive to some issues than others. And the closer we are to someone, the more we know what pushes his or her buttons. Someone who hits below the belt is not trying to manage the current conflict, but is using their personal knowledge of their partner's sensitive spots to lash out and harm him or her.

Withholding Sometimes people hope to be victorious in a conflict by withdrawing their love, affection, or civility from their partner. They may give others the "silent treatment" in hopes that this will so hurt their partner that he or she will give in.

Inappropriate Joking Humor can be very helpful in defusing a tense moment. However, inappropriate humor is a form of avoiding that blocks the open exchange of thoughts and feelings. When people joke inappropriately, they may also be sending the message that they do not take the conflict seriously.

Did you see yourself in any of these descriptions? All of us occasionally engage in obstructing communication habits. What is important is that you recognize your habit and try to replace your obstructing behavior with communication that facilitates an open and honest exchange. Instead of relying on poor communication habits, try to use the following when you are having a conflict.

Engage in the Conflict Although you may need a "cooling-off" period during a conflict, most issues do not improve with age. Confront the issues sooner rather than later.

Use "I" Messages An "I" message expresses your personal feelings without accusing the other person. For example, saying, "You never let me make my own decisions," will probably put the other person in defensive mode. Instead, an "I" message would sound like this: "I feel that I need to make my own decision about my major."

Stay Focused Focus on the issues within the present conflict, as opposed to bringing up past grievances. Stay focused by seeking clarification from your partner. Are you really listening to what your partner is saying? Is your partner hearing what you are saying? From time to time it is helpful to tell your partner what you are hearing him or her say. "If I am hearing you correctly, you are saying that we need to spend more time together." It is critical not to talk past one another. Be sure to ask questions in order to understand the other person's perspective.

Apologize If you have intentionally or unintentionally harmed someone, say you are sorry. Remember that you only need to apologize for your actions, not your feelings. Say that you are sorry for slamming the door when you left the room, but do not apologize for being upset. Sincere apologies show that you are taking responsibility for your part of the problem and usually help defuse some of the tension that may exist.

Be Truthful Although the truth may hurt, it deserves to be heard. You may be afraid of hurting someone else by telling the truth. You can still be sensitive to the other person's feelings by stating the truth with kindness. Speak the truth, but always do it in love (Eph 4:15).

Finding healthy ways to deal with relationship problems is important. The next time you are involved in a conflict, reflect on whether the conflict centers on the content of the conversation or is about the relationship itself. Then look carefully at the habits you typically use to manage a conflict. Do you need to eliminate obstructing behaviors? Do you need to foster facilitating behaviors? For some, it is hard to concentrate on anything else when relationship problems arise. If you find that relationship conflict is seriously affecting your well-being or day-to-day functioning, you may want to seek advice from a counselor or pastor.

God's Love Empowers Our Relationships

Finally, remember that the love of God in our lives gives us the ability to treat even those who have sought to harm us with love and respect. After Samuel had identified David as the next king of ancient Israel, King Saul aggressively sought to end the life of his royal rival. But again and again, David spared Saul's life (1 Sam 24, 26). The power of David to forgive and respect even a man who had attempted to kill him is a power that lives within every Christian. Jesus himself challenges us to love even those who seek to harm us. "Love your enemies and pray for those who persecute you." (Matt 5:44) And this same Jesus models that love on the cross, forgiving even those who encouraged his execution (Luke 23:34). Because he shows the way and empowers Christians, they are able to love in this way too. "We love because he first loved us." (1 John 4:19)

College life is full of relationships. Everyone needs to feel connected to other people. You have had the opportunity in this chapter to reflect on the relationships in your life and on the quality of those relationships. If you find weak spots in your key relationships, strengthen them. If you have discovered a severe shortage of people with whom you have healthy relationships, then it is time to pursue new relationships that provide the support you need.

Exercises for **Success**

Review Questions

1. What can you do to keep your need for intimacy in step with God's plan for your life?

2. Identify three things you can do to create a positive impression of you as a person and as a student.

3. Respond to the following statement: "The best way to maintain a healthy relationship is to avoid conflict."

Examine Your Critical Relationships

In order to be successful, you need to be connected to several people with whom you share a healthy relationship. This exercise allows you to put several of your close relationships to the test and see if they are dominated by the qualities of healthy relationships. Pick three relationships that you would like to evaluate. Write each person's name after each of the following statements if it accurately describes your relationship with him or her.

I enjoy spending time with him/her. _____

I trust him/her with personal information. _____

I can turn to him/her during a difficult time. He/she respects me and my needs. _____

I can talk easily and openly with him/her. He/she is kind to me. _____

We do not hold grudges. _____

We bolster each other's self-worth. _____

We share similar interests and values. _____

As you reflect on your responses, answer the following questions. Are your relationships filled with healthy qualities? What quality that is important to you is not being met in any of the relationships you have evaluated? If one of your important relationships has few or none of the qualities listed, can it be nurtured to greater health?

How to Say "I Love You" without Having Sex

We can express our love for one another in ways that do not violate God's direction. Ask your partner to join you in this exercise. Think creatively about all the ways you can express love without engaging in sexual intimacy that God has forbidden. For example, you can make hot chocolate on a cold night, send a funny note or card, cook your partner's favorite meal, or take a drive through the country. Join with the other members of your class to create an even longer list. See if you can find one hundred ways to say "I love you" without having sex.

Interview Your Instructors

Getting to know your instructors is well worth the effort. Pick out one or two instructors whom you would like to get to know and arrange for an informal interview. They could be potential advisors or mentors or people who simply seem interesting to you. Here are some possible questions:

1. Where did you go to college? Why?

2. What was the most significant event in your first year of college?

3. What advice would you give first-year students?

4. When did you decide to become a college teacher?

5. How can students be successful in your class?

6. What are your research interests?

7. What are your outside interests or hobbies?

My Favorite Kind of Professor

College teachers are different from other teachers you have had, but that does not mean they are all the same. If you visited a number of classes being taught on your campus, you would find faculty with a variety of personalities and presentation styles. Because not everyone likes the same kind of teacher, this exercise will help you find the qualities that are important to you. It will create a picture of your favorite teacher.

Pick a favorite teacher from the present or recent past. Assess that instructor according to the following criteria. Put an X on the continuum to indicate the relative strength or weakness of that teacher related to each teaching quality. The last two lines are blank so that you can add important qualities we may have missed.

	Knows the subject well	
Weak		Strong
	Keeps my attention	
Weak		Strong
	Is organized	
Weak		Strong
	Stops and starts class on time	
Weak		Strong
	Is approachable	
Weak		Strong
	Has a sense of humor	
Weak		Strong

	Grades fairly	
Weak		Strong

	Is available for meetings	
Weak		Strong

Weak		Strong

Weak		Strong

Using the information from the list, answer the following questions.

1. What qualities does this teacher have that helped you learn more easily?

2. Because you may have the option of choosing from several instructors who are teaching the same college class, what three qualities will be most important to you in making that choice?

Expand the Diversity in Your Relationships

Membership in a wide array of relationships helps you grow as a person. Review the following list. Write down the names of at least five people whom you know in each category.

Someone . . .

. . . of a different gender. _____

. . . from a different cultural background. _____

. . . from a different ethnic group. _____

. . . who has a different political ideology. _____

. . . who is ten years older than you. _____

. . . of a different socioeconomic status. _____

. . . from a different religious background. _____

. . . who has a disability. _____

Now think about the results of this exercise. Where was it easiest for you to list names? Where was it more difficult or impossible for you to come up with just one name? As you think about the latter question, what keeps you from engaging in relationships with people in those categories? Where would you like to change your habits to improve the diversity in your relationships? Write a two-page paper exploring the answers to these questions.

SPIRITUAL REFLECTION JOURNAL

Love lies at the foundation of all our relationships. Read 1 Corinthians 13, where Paul provides a definition of love from God's perspective. Write about ways in which you can put this definition to work in the relationships in your life.

Time in Prayer

In your personal time in prayer or in connection with others in your class, take time to pray for the following people and needs:

- For family and friends

- For the wisdom to handle conflicts effectively

- For the courage to confront your stereotypes and prejudices

- For the strength to remain pure in the face of temptation

- For opportunities to develop meaningful relationships with people who are different from you

- For helpful relationships with faculty members

- For the ability to use your relationships with others to win them for Christ

On the Web

The Internet can be a helpful resource as you look for ideas to make yourself a happier and more successful student. Visit the College Success page offered by Thomson Wadsworth for Web links that will help you grow further on this topic. Go to http://www.success.wadsworth.com/ and click on Resource Web Links.

We also recommend the following:

http://discoveryhealth.queendom.com/communication_short_access.html

http://www.highgain.com/SELF/index.php

http://peace.mennolink.org/cgi-bin/conflictstyle/inventory.cgi

http://www.tolerance.org/

http://www.diversityweb.org/

Endnotes

1. Gregory Sawin, "How Stereotypes Influence Opinions about Individuals," in *Understanding and Managing Diversity: Readings, Cases, and Exercises*, eds. C. Harvey & M. J. Allard (Reading, MA: Addison Wesley Longman, 1995).

2. Norma Carr-Ruffino, *Managing Diversity* (Boston, MA: Pearson, 2002).

3. Ronald B. Adler and Neil Towne, *Looking Out, Looking In*, 10th ed. (Belmont, CA: Wadsworth, 2003).

Maintaining the Temple: Physical and Mental Wellness 12

Do you not know that your body is a temple of the Holy Spirit . . . ? Therefore honor God with your body.

1 Corinthians 6:19–20

- **What can I do when I am unable to fall asleep?**

- **How can I eat in order to sustain my energy level and alertness?**

- **How often should I exercise and what forms of exercise are beneficial?**

- **What can I do when stress overwhelms me?**

- **What can I do when the world crashes down around me?**

We have been carefully designed by the divine hand so that there is an intimate link between our ability to think and the health of our body. Mind and body are so closely linked that neither survives very long without the life-giving support of the other. When both mind and body are healthy, they produce a wonderful symphony of thought and actions. But if the health of either deteriorates, the health of its partner is also compromised. This book has paid a great deal of attention to developing your mind as a college student. It is now time to give the body its due. The Apostle Paul calls on the family of God to take special care of the bodies we have been given. For although we may grasp the wonderful promises of God with our mind, it is the body that Paul calls the "temple of the Holy Spirit," a place worthy of respect, care, and attention. If we fail to maintain this temple, then we face both physical and mental consequences of that inattention. Our bodies break down and our ability to grow as thinkers is compromised.

Consequently, the role of this chapter is to visit the physical and mental health habits that have a powerful effect on your success as a student. If you have been living on food that comes from vending machines, sleeping poorly, and worrying incessantly, now is the time to commit to a course correction. Getting physically and mentally healthy is too important to put off for another day. Now is the time to develop healthy habits that not only will propel you to greater success as a college student but also will enhance the quality of your future life. To that end, this chapter will lead you to think about both your physical and mental health habits, discussing the topics of sleep, diet, exercise, alcohol, stress, worry, suicide, and responding to personal tragedy.

Physical Health Habits

Sleep

Good physical health starts with careful consideration of our sleep habits. Restorative sleep can easily elude us when we sleep in an unfamiliar place, when we attempt to sleep at the wrong time of the day, or when nagging events from the day keep us from relaxing. But we need a sustained period of deep sleep in order for our bodies to function at their peak. To help you achieve the benefits of such sleep we will address the following topics: how much sleep we need, when it is best to sleep, and what to do when we have difficulty sleeping.

How much sleep do I need? Although the amount of sleep needed varies greatly from one person to the next, the average person requires eight hours of sleep every night to fully recharge.[1] When college students compare their sleep habits to that standard, many find that they are getting one to two hours less sleep per night than their bodies may require. But perhaps the best way to determine whether you are getting enough sleep is to check for the physical and emotional symptoms associated with too little sleep, which include the following:

Inability to concentrate	*Poor emotional control*
Falling asleep during classes	*Headaches*
General feeling of exhaustion	*Impaired memory*

Although these symptoms may have other causes, one or more may combine to indicate that you are getting too little sleep.

Another way to measure whether your current sleep habits are giving you enough down time is to note the way you wake up. If you wake up on your own without an alarm clock and feel alert shortly after getting up, you are likely getting enough sleep. However, if you require an alarm to rouse you from sleep or if you feel groggy well into the morning, these are signs that you are getting less sleep than your body requires.[2]

When is it best to sleep? As you consider how much you sleep, give thought to when you sleep. Our bodies appear to respond to a certain circadian rhythm that seeks to align our sleep time with darkness and our wakeful time with daylight. If you have traveled quickly across the globe or even between the coasts of the United States, you may have experienced *jet lag*—the confusion that results as our bodies work to adjust our sleep time and wakeful time to the new darkness and daylight cycles of our destination. We can force our bodies to stay awake late into the night and sleep during the day, but this often

Lauren Burge

Major: Biology
Hometown: Amarillo, Texas
School: Abilene Christian University

My mood is better, my health is better, and my grades are better when I get enough sleep. The most important thing I do to preserve my sleep time is to watch carefully how I use my time. When some of my friends drag into class after staying up until 3:00 am and say they did not have enough time to finish a project, study for an exam, or complete an assignment, the truth is they did not manage their time well.

results in less than satisfactory results. If you feel the need to sleep more effectively, check out the time during the day when you sleep and remember that the more consistent your bedtime and rising time, the more restful your sleep patterns are likely to be. Sleeping in on the two days when you have a later class may not be as helpful as keeping your rising time consistent.

This, of course, also leads to the question of taking a nap during the day. There is some debate on the value of such naps, with advantages and disadvantages cited for each perspective. Begin by considering the relationship of a nap to your time management plan. Is the time you are napping giving you a greater benefit than if you had employed that time in some other way? From the physiological perspective, a couple of things seem certain. It is unwise to sleep during the daylight hours as a substitute for sleeping during the nighttime hours. This daytime sleep has less restorative power than nighttime sleep. Second, if you are going to take a nap, be sure that it does not last too long (twenty minutes is often recommended). A nap that takes you into the deepest sleep modes causes you to awaken groggy rather than feeling refreshed and may make it difficult for you to get to sleep that night.

What can I do when I cannot sleep? The inability to fall asleep at night can be caused by either physical or mental discomfort. For example, if things on your mind are causing you stress, your body produces adrenaline that jolts you into a greater state of alertness rather than into the relaxed state required for sleep. Alternatively, if you are in the habit of using some form of stimulant (such as coffee or a soft drink with caffeine in it), this chemical culprit may be keeping you awake.

If you are having difficulty falling asleep for any reason, consider changing your lifestyle in one of the following ways. Because we are all creatures of habit, it is wise to reserve your bed for sleeping rather than other daily activities such as studying for exams, which may cause you stress. Then when you climb into bed, your body will unconsciously associate this environment with relaxation and sleep rather than with an activity that demands alertness and action. If you are in the habit of napping during the day, try to either shorten or eliminate those naps and do your sleeping at night. And as your day comes to a close, plan the hour before going to bed carefully. Give yourself time to disengage from the daily activities that are part of your work life. Instead, read for pleasure, watch television, exercise, or take a warm shower as a way of creating a transition between your work life and your sleep time. If you are in the habit of using some form of caffeine or other stimulant during the day, restrict the use of that beverage to the morning or noon hour so that your body has a chance to eliminate the stimulant before bedtime. If your brain clicks on just when you are trying to shut down for the night, keep paper and pencil near your bed so that you can write down the thoughts that circle through your mind again and again. By doing so, you can give yourself permission to set them aside for the night and take them up again in the morning rather than rehearsing them over and over again at night. You may also find it helpful to distract your mind by refocusing your attention using the relaxation techniques described later in this chapter.

Diet

Going to college is hard work. Just as our bodies require rest and sleep to function at their peak, they also need appropriate fuel. God designed us with this need and has provided nutritional resources for us to use in this world. As the provider, he has invited us to pray for those daily needs in the Lord's Prayer: "Give us today our daily bread" (Matt 6:11), and he has promised to provide the raw materials for our nourishment (Ps 136:25). Here we will explore how the use of this food contributes to your success as a college student.

What should I eat? God has permitted us to find nourishment from both the plant and animal kingdoms (Gen 1:29, 9:3). In this way, he has provided us with the critical vitamins, minerals, fiber, protein, fat, and carbohydrates that maintain and strengthen our muscles and bones, give us energy, aid digestion, and create immunity from disease. Diet plans that emphasize one type of food over another come and go. But as a starting point, it is safe to assume the value of the basic food pyramid that you learned about when you were in grade school.

This basic pyramid has been edited for people of differing sex, age, and activity level. Check out the suggestions that more closely match you at http://www.mypyramid.gov/, or visit the National Agricultural Library at http://www.nal.usda.gov/fnic/index.html.

What are the danger signs of unhealthy eating? Because we live in a world ruined by sin, even food can bring us harm when it is misused. Check your lifestyle for any of these signs that you may be eating in an unhealthy way:

Excessive weight gain
Intense fear of gaining weight
Substituting soft drinks for water
Relying on vending machines and fast food for your meals
Excessive weight loss
Not eating as a way of gaining a feeling of control in life
Eating excessively as a form of comfort
Designing a diet from the top of the food pyramid down rather than from the bottom up

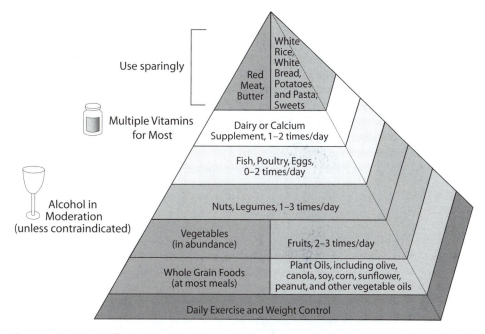

White Rice, White Bread, Potatoes and Pasta, Sweets

Red Meat, Butter

Use sparingly

Multiple Vitamins for Most

Dairy or Calcium Supplement, 1–2 times/day

Fish, Poultry, Eggs, 0–2 times/day

Alcohol in Moderation (unless contraindicated)

Nuts, Legumes, 1–3 times/day

Vegetables (in abundance)

Fruits, 2–3 times/day

Whole Grain Foods (at most meals)

Plant Oils, including olive, canola, soy, corn, sunflower, peanut, and other vegetable oils

Daily Exercise and Weight Control

Source: From Your College Experience: Strategies for Success *7th Edition by Gardner/Jewler/Barefoot, 2007. Reprinted with permission of Wadsworth, a division of Thomson Learning.*

Eating Disorders

As new college students go through the stress of adjusting to college life, a form of eating disorder may become evident. Each one is treatable, but if left untreated they can cause significant emotional and physical harm.

Anorexia nervosa is the unnatural fear of becoming fat that is not diminished with weight loss. People with this disorder have a distorted self-image that does not improve even in the face of continued self-starvation.

Bulimia nervosa is a disorder that is an inappropriate method for dealing with stress. People with this disorder overeat to compensate for their feelings of stress but then are overwhelmed with a concern for gaining weight. After eating, they purge the food from their system through either forced vomiting or the use of laxatives.

If you or someone close to you suffers from an eating disorder like these, you can learn more about the disorder and how to help by visiting the counseling offices on your campus or visiting one of the following sites:

National Association of Anorexia Nervosa and Associated Disorders—http://www.anad.org/

Anorexia Nervosa and Related Eating Disorders, Inc.—http://www.anred.com/

Mental Health America—http://www.nmha.org/

Exercise

As first-year college students get busy with the demanding academic and social life of college, it is easy to give exercise a backseat to other activities. But a strong exercise plan is just as critical to maintaining your physical health as healthy eating and sleeping. If you are already involved in a weekly exercise regimen, you are on the right track and may find ways to improve it in the following paragraphs. If you are not currently involved in such an exercise program, now is a good time to start and make it as much of a habit as going to class or brushing your teeth. However, one word of caution is in order. If you are over thirty-five and have not exercised regularly for several years or if you have a physical condition such as high blood pressure, heart trouble, arthritis, or excessive weight, please seek the advice of a medical professional before starting an exercise program.

What kind of exercise is right for me? A complete exercise program consists of activities that address four different components of our physical health: cardiorespiratory endurance, muscle strength, muscle endurance, and flexibility. Let's consider each.

The ability to sustain a physical activity over an extended period of time is directly related to the effectiveness of our lungs in providing oxygen to the bloodstream and the effectiveness of our heart and circulatory system in delivering that blood to our muscles. Cardiorespiratory exercise is designed to improve our endurance by improving those systems. To stay fit, we further need to address muscle strength and muscle endurance. Muscle strength is the ability of our muscles to contract and sustain a force for a brief period of time. By contrast, muscle endurance is the ability to use a muscle or a group of muscles for a sustained period of time. Finally, flexibility is the ability to move our joints and our muscles easily through the full range of motion. This has been given increasing attention in the design of exercise programs and deserves a place in our workout schedule as well.

Each exercise session should begin and close with a five-to-ten minute warm-up and cooldown period no matter what types of exercise are included in the session. Within your weekly routine, consider following a regimen that resembles this model. Start with three twenty-minute sessions during the

Hitting the Target Zone

Hitting the target zone during aerobic exercise means elevating your heart rate to the range suggested by the following formula. Subtract your age from 220 and multiply the result by 0.60. Subtract your age from 220 again and this time multiply the result by 0.75. The two resulting numbers represent the heart rate target zone in which aerobic exercise is most beneficial for you. For example, if you are 20 years old, your minimum rate would be 120 beats per minute ($220 \times 20 = 200 \times .60 = 120$) and your maximum target rate would be 150 beats per minute ($220 - 20 = 200 \times .75 = 150$).

week in which you focus on *aerobic exercises*, which are designed to address the health of your heart and lungs. Examples of aerobic exercise include walking, jogging, biking, swimming, cross-country skiing, dancing, handball, volleyball, basketball, cycling, and in-line skating. In order for these activities to be effective, they must be done so as to elevate your respiration and heart rate.

When you engage in aerobic exercise, you also address strength and endurance of the muscle groups you use. You can further address muscle development by lifting weights and doing calisthenics, push-ups, sit-ups, and pull-ups. In addition to your aerobic exercise sessions, consider adding two to three twenty-minute sessions per week targeted at muscle strength and endurance.

Finally, include a time of daily stretching (ten to twelve minutes) to elongate muscles and create greater flexibility in the joints. These stretching exercises can be included in the cooldown at the end of your workout.

What about exercise and weight loss? Many people who begin an exercise program also intend to lose weight. The exercise program just outlined above will do just that as long as you do not increase your caloric intake when beginning such a program. If you expend more energy than you take in, you burn up stored fat reserves. Consider the following: a medium-sized college student who wants to burn off five pounds of fat needs to walk 150 miles! That may be too discouraging to contemplate. But if you set up a program that would challenge you to walk 2½ miles per day for sixty days, you would have achieved your goal in two months. Exercise goals are great. Set them and design a plan of action to achieve them. But remember that goals must be realistic if they are going to be accomplished.

Alcohol and Drug Use

The college experience and experimentation with alcohol are closely linked in American culture. The Core Institute at Southern Illinois University (http://www.siu.edu/departments/coreinst/public_html/) closely studies patterns of alcohol use on the college campuses of America. In a 2005 survey, it found that 72.8 percent of college students interviewed had consumed alcohol within the last thirty days. Given the pervasive presence of alcohol in the life of the average college student, one thing is clear: you will be invited to use alcohol. The time to decide whether to accept that invitation is long before it comes, certainly before you take your first drink. From the moment you begin

Fighting the Freshman Fifteen

As first-year students experience all the changes that college has to offer as well as the changes that are occurring in their own body chemistry, they often gain weight, the so-called freshman fifteen. The addition of this weight can lower your self-esteem and make you feel less energized for the work ahead. If you find yourself gaining weight, intervene with changes in diet and exercise that keep you physically fit and mentally alert.

to consume alcohol, your ability to make an effective decision is impaired. As you make that early decision, consider a number of important matters: the teachings of the Bible, the laws of your state, the student conduct code at your school, and what we know about the impact of alcohol and drug use on college success.

Alcohol Use and the Bible The first place to begin is in reading Bible passages that take up the matter of chemical use, such as Proverbs 20:1, Proverbs 23:29–35, and Ephesians 5:18. These passages speak directly to the misuse of alcohol but also apply to the way we use other drugs. It is also critical to consider Bible passages that speak about the sturdy Christian character and the witness we bring to others about Jesus. In reading these passages, some churches have concluded that it would be wrong for a Christian to ever consume an alcoholic beverage. If that is the position of your church, it deserves to be honored. Other Christians have concluded that occasional use of alcohol is not a sin, but that the Bible clearly forbids the loss of control that comes with becoming drunk.

Alcohol Use and the Law God directs our lives not only through his Word but also through the institutions and laws of our state and rules of our school. He makes it clear that disobeying those authorities is as much of a sin as disobeying him (Rom 13:1–7). Consequently, you should know the state laws that govern your campus and the penalties associated with violating them. In most states, if you have not reached age twenty-one, it is illegal for you to purchase or to consume an alcoholic beverage. And because the misuse of alcohol has very negative implications for college success, colleges and universities have their own alcohol policies, articulated in places such as the student conduct code, that may further limit the use of alcohol even beyond the state's legislation. Given the importance of this topic, violations of state law or the student conduct code typically have very strong penalties associated with them.

Alcohol Use and College Success As a college student who is passionate about success, you also need to be aware of how alcohol can affect your plans to graduate with high grades from college. The same Core Institute study noted at the beginning of this section asked students to report on the consequences of their use of alcohol as a college student. Among the things they reported were poor test performance, getting into more fights and arguments, becoming physically ill, missing classes, and memory loss. The study clearly indicates that the more alcohol a college student uses, the less effective he or she is as a college student, a pattern that leads to lower grades and less overall success. As you consider your views of God's instruction about alcohol and drug use, the state and college regulations that govern their use, and the potential impact on your grades, you will be empowered to design a habit that keeps you in a healthy place, a place that honors God's temple.

What are the warning signs? If you have been using alcohol and exhibit any of the following warning signs, seek help immediately.

You drink just because your friends think you should.
You drink to avoid feeling bad.
You drink to cope with life.
You have tried to stop using alcohol but could not.

Alcohol and Blood Alcohol Content

The introduction of alcohol into our bodies has an effect on both our mood and our physical systems. Because two people of different sizes will respond differently to the same amount of alcohol, the best way to know the impact of alcohol is by measuring the blood alcohol content (BAC, stated as a percentage) in the system.

0.025 to 0.050 BAC	Feeling of animation and energy
0.050 to 0.080 BAC	Slowed reflexes and impaired thinking
Above 0.080 BAC	Significantly impaired coordination, speech, and compromised values
Above 0.20 BAC	Vomiting, memory loss, passing out
Above 0.45	Death is increasingly certain

If you find someone who is unresponsive, vomiting, and/or breathing unnaturally and has pale or bluish skin, lay the person on his or her side, do all you can to keep the airway clear, and get medical help immediately. One or more of these conditions in someone who has been drinking heavily constitutes a medical emergency. Act quickly—you may be the one person who stands between them and death.

You believe that your use of alcohol has no ability to harm you.
You regularly consume more than five drinks at one sitting.
You have experienced blackouts while drinking when you cannot recall what happened.

For help or more information, please contact a campus counselor or one of the following organizations:

Alcoholics Anonymous—http://www.alcoholics-anonymous.org/
National Institute on Drug Abuse—http://www.nida.nih.gov/

Mental Health Habits

A part of caring for your body also includes the strategic way you manage your stress, deal with worry and discouragement, address suicidal tendencies, and respond to personal tragedies in your life. This portion of the chapter will speak to each of these topics to help you think of ways to keep yourself mentally healthy.

Stress

Because new challenges cause us stress, stress and starting college go hand in hand. Feeling stress for shorter periods of time in lower doses is a natural part of being human and can actually improve your academic performance. During periods of stress your breathing and heart rate may increase, your muscles may begin to tighten, and you may experience "butterflies" in your stomach. None of these symptoms is inherently harmful in the short run. But this good form of stress can quickly degenerate into a bad form of stress that lasts for much longer periods of time and comes on with increased ferocity. This negative form of stress can cause us to lose sleep, become more irritable, be plagued by headaches, and have a variety of stomach complications including nausea, diarrhea, and even ulcers. This type of stress clearly compromises your quest for success.

Life Change Events Miller and Rahe have explored the relationship between significant events in life (called *life change events*) and the risk of serious health problems. Their study found that certain events are more harmful than others. For example, the death of a parent or the loss of a job are much more harmful than buying a car or leaving for college. However, even minor events that are less threatening by themselves can combine to create potential health problems. To determine whether you are experiencing life change events that may compromise your health, see the study by Miller and Rahe titled "Life Changes Scaling for the 1990s."[3]

If your stress level is so significant that it interferes with your ability to sleep or live life the way you would like to live it, then it is time to intervene. Masking the symptoms of stress through the use of tobacco or alcohol or through excessive sleep are not solutions. But by combining physical, mental, and spiritual interventions, you can find ways to help you put stress in its place. Once again, the techniques described here are not meant to be a substitute for the professional counseling you may require.

Relaxing Your Body When we experience heightened levels of stress, we respond physically by increasing our breathing rate and tightening our muscles. We are preparing ourselves physically to either flee or fight the perceived enemy before us. Thus one way to reduce our stress level is to reverse that process by doing things that slow our breathing and relax the tension from our muscles. Exercise is a wonderful way to turn tension into a helpful activity. When we go for a long walk, play a game of basketball, or dance with a friend, we put that muscle tension to good use and signal the body to release the endorphins that lead to greater feelings of happiness and contentment. Couple exercise with a massage and you are on the road to significant stress reduction.

But going for a run or getting a massage may not be the answer if you feel high stress levels during an exam or are lying in bed trying to sleep. In those cases, you can try an alternative form of physical intervention. Close your eyes or focus on something in the room. Observe your breathing rate and breathe more slowly and more deeply using the full volume of your abdomen. Then begin to progressively tighten muscle groups in your body and release that muscular pressure in the following way. Start with your feet. Curl your toes toward your heels and hold the muscle pressure for a count of five. Then slowly but steadily release that pressure over the next twenty to thirty seconds until you have completely relaxed the tension you introduced into that muscle group. Then move up to your calves and repeat the same procedure, tightening your muscles as much as possible for five seconds and then slowly releasing that tension. Continue up your body through every muscle group. You will feel a significant reduction in stress as you tell your body that it is all right to relax.

Considering What You Can Control In connection with the physical interventions just described, adjust your psychological focus. Consider what is causing your stress to surge. Then ask yourself what you can control and what you cannot control about the situation. For example, if your boyfriend or girlfriend back home has not responded to your most recent letter or phone call, your stress level may rise because you are wondering why he or she seems less interested in your relationship. What do you control in this situation? You certainly cannot control the feelings or actions of your partner. Attempting to do so will only make you more frustrated and stressed. What you can control is your own reaction to your friend's perceived lack of interest. You can phone your friend and articulate your concerns about the relationship. That is empowering because it allows you to clarify the reasons for his or her lack of communication. If your partner is no longer interested in pursuing a close relationship with you, you do not have the power to change that, but you do have the power to identify and date another person and so meet the relationship needs you have. In the same way, you cannot control the fact that your grandfather has been diagnosed with cancer. But you can control your reaction to the news by seeking the support of others, reading your Bible, and praying for the medical team that is caring for him. It may sound too simple to be valuable. But one of the best places to begin when you are feeling stressed is to identify what you control and what you do not control about a situation. Then limit your thinking and actions to the things you can control.

Seeking Distractions Stress can be debilitating when we must manage it constantly. When a particularly stressful event occurs, we tend to narrow our focus to that event, ignoring all the other places of greater peace where we might focus our attention. We all deserve a break, and we have many ways to refocus our attention on something else for a time. One way to distract yourself is via leisure activities such as listening to music, exercising, playing a musical instrument, or enjoying a favorite hobby. Laughter is also wonderful medicine that can be amplified by enjoying a funny movie or just spending time with a friend who makes you laugh.

And if you are alone and feel the need to take a break, why not make it a thought vacation? Close your eyes or focus on something in the room and create an image of the thing that is causing you stress. Now remove that image from the stage and instead take a mini-vacation to one of your favorite physical settings. Whether it is standing at the base of the Rocky Mountains or idling on a sunny beach in Florida, go there mentally and get into the moment. Smell the smells you remember, feel the temperature, and recall the sounds of that place. A thought vacation may not be as good as being there, but it can recreate the feelings of contentment and peace when we vividly recall that favorite vacation spot.

Finding Forgiveness Because we are sinful people living in a sin-damaged world, we may worry about our own relationship with God or feel that God is unable to help us in the days that lie ahead. There is no pain like the pain of feeling unforgiven. God does not want us to live in that guilty place, and so he has sent various messages of comfort and assurance in his Word that address our spiritual concerns and our anxiety. As we live out our lives, we can become very aware of our own failings. The knowledge that we have violated God's law leads to feelings of guilt and unworthiness before the holy God. Although God detests the sin that so infects our actions and thoughts, he does not want us to live with feelings of guilt or unworthiness. Read Luke 15:11–32. In the Parable of the Lost Son, a young person drifted away from his father's home and lived a life that was completely violated all his father wanted. When he had ruined his life, he returned to his father's home expecting nothing more than to become a hired worker for his father. But as this young person came into sight, his father began a celebration because the young person whom the father thought he had lost was found again. If you have wandered away from your Heavenly Father, he is anxiously waiting at home for your return to him.

Taking God's Perspective Even people who have a personal relationship with Jesus and know they are forgiven can still struggle with the challenge of living in a sin-ruined world. Jesus himself said, "In this world, you will have trouble." However, he quickly added the next two sentences: "But take heart! I have overcome the world." (John 16:33) Because of who Jesus is and his power, he can share that victory over the sinful world with us. In Matthew 6:25–34, we find the discourse on worry that may be the most powerful sermon ever given on the topic. For people who are prone to worry about the essentials of life over which they have little control, Jesus challenges us to think about the way God takes care of birds and flowers, assuring us that he will do even more in caring for our needs.

In the end, we are empowered to do two things when confronted by a challenge in life that threatens our sense of well-being. First, we can change our perspective. When confronted by a problem that seems too large to handle, we often focus on our own inabilities rather than on God's presence and power. The psalmist offers a fresh perspective: "God is our refuge and strength, an ever present help in trouble." (Ps 46:1; see also Ps 73:25–26 and Ps 121:1–2) Second, we can put into practice the powerful tool of prayer. The invitation from the Lord is clear: "Call upon me in the day of trouble; I will deliver you, and you will honor me." (Ps 50:15) Jesus invites weary and worn people to come to him and find such rest (Matt 11:28–30).

Suicide

Discouragement and depression that is left untreated can lead to thoughts of suicide and even attempts to commit suicide. Those who have a relationship with the Lord are not exempt from such thoughts or actions. Consider the stories of Saul (1 Sam 31), Elijah (1 Kings 19:4), and Judas (Matt 27:5). Although the Bible records these suicidal thoughts and acts, it absolutely does not condone such actions as the answer. Nevertheless, Christian college students are not immune from the risk of suicide, so the more we know about it and how to prevent it, the better off we are. Satan has a way of causing us to spiral down, losing hope in God's interest in us or his ability to help us despite the clear words of the Bible to the contrary.

Intervention A person who is going to attempt suicide typically gives off early warning signs that he or she is thinking seriously about this drastic measure. Watch for one or more of these indications in yourself or others close to you:

Change in eating habits
Change in sleeping habits
Loss of interest in school, friends, or activities
Expressions of hopelessness
Talking about "ending it all" or "just wanting out of life"
A passion for engaging in risky, life-threatening actions
Giving away personal possessions

Do not assume that someone is not serious when speaking about attempting suicide or that he or she is just trying to get more attention. Engage your friend by being open and confrontational about the topic: "Are you thinking about taking your own life?" "Do you intend to harm yourself today?" Listen to what the suicidal person is saying and do not leave him or her alone. Rather, assure your friend that he or she can come to a better place. Pray for your friend, pray with your friend, and take him or her to a mental health professional who will know what to do next.

For more information on this important topic, speak to the mental health counselors on your campus or check out the following sites:

Mental Health America—http://www.nmha.org/
National Institute of Mental Health—http://www.nimh.nih.gov/
American Foundation for Suicide Prevention—http://www.afsp.org/

Responding to Personal Tragedy

College students are not immune from experiencing significant personal tragedies, including divorce in the family, significant medical problems, or the death of a loved one. When such personal tragedies occur, they strike the new college student with even greater ferocity because he or she may be some distance from supportive family members and in a new place with a growing but limited support group. Personal tragedies are so invasive that they can completely disrupt a student's already busy schedule, causing him or her to miss classes and get behind on assignments, adding to the stress the event has caused. For all of these reasons, you should prepare yourself as a college student for the way in which you will deal with personal tragedy should it come knocking at your college door.

Learning from Job The book of the Bible that takes this issue on more directly than any other is the Book of Job, which asks and attempts to answer the tough questions that we all ask when we are devastated by such events. Job faced an incredible series of personal tragedies. In a short amount of time, this wealthy man experienced the loss of his personal wealth, his children, his health, and the support of his marriage partner. "If only my anguish could be weighed and all my misery be placed on the scales! It would surely outweigh the sand of the seas. . . ." (Job 6:2–3)

Dazed by this series of events, Job tried to make sense of it all. He asked the very questions we ask when personal tragedy visits our lives: Have I committed some sin for which God is punishing me? Is God simply unaware of what has happened? Is God so powerless that he knows but cannot act? Or is

God so uncaring that he knows but elects not to act? Through long, painstaking dialogue with a series of "friends," Job articulated and sought answers to these questions. In the end it was clear that God was not seeking personal revenge on Job for a particular sin he committed, that God was aware of what is happening, that he had the power to intervene, and that he cared. But the one question that was not answered was the one that may have been most vexing: why did Job have to suffer in the way he did?

Why, God? The answer to this question eluded Job, as it eludes the reader. As no mortal speaker adequately dealt with this issue in the book, the Lord appeared in a storm. "Who is this that darkens my counsel with words without knowledge? Brace yourself like a man; I will question you, and you shall answer me." (Job 38:2–3) In the verses that follow, God asked Job one challenging question after another, questions that were impossible for any mortal to answer. In doing so, God brought Job to confess his own limitations. "Surely I spoke of things I did not understand, things too wonderful for me to know." (Job 42:3)

The answer to why Job suffered was not revealed to him, and it may remain hidden from us in our tragedy. But as God quiets this question, he respond to the frustration of not receiving an answer by confirming his loving intervention even in the midst of personal tragedies. In Romans 8:28, Paul says that all things, even tragedies, will work out for our own personal benefit even if we do not know what that benefit will be. At minimum, these tragedies will carry us through a process that will deepen our faith in the Lord and strengthen our relationship with him. That is Paul's message in Romans 5:1–5, where he challenges us to rejoice in suffering, knowing that this suffering leads to greater perseverance, to a tested character, and to a deeper hope. We may not know why God has allowed a tragedy to come our way, but he does tell us that he will remain at our side during this difficult time and engineer life so that the challenge we face draws us closer to him.

Success as a college student is much more than just studying effectively and developing our intellect. It is also about managing our physical and mental health. Our body is the temple of the Holy Spirit and so deserves thoughtful attention. Consider all that you have read and take steps to improve your physical and mental health where it needs such attention. In so doing, we are involved in an act of worship using our body as the place of worship.

Exercises for **Success**

Review Questions

1. What signals will make it clear to you that you are getting insufficient sleep?

2. Outline an effective exercise program and explain the role of each component in improving your total health.

3. Explain how controlling your breathing rate can lower the physical stress you may feel.

Create a Sleep Diary

For the next week, record how long you sleep each day of the week and at what times of the day you are sleeping. Compare the results of your sleep habits to the suggested habits in this chapter and write down any specific changes you plan to make.

Keep a Diet Diary

Because we are what we eat, it is helpful to think through your weekly eating habits. For the next week, record the times that you eat, the type of food you eat, and the amounts of each kind of food you eat. Compare your habits with the suggestions in this chapter and write down any specific changes you plan to make.

Design a Weekly Exercise Plan

With all the activities competing for your time as a college student, it is easy to get less exercise than you need. Consider again the four types of fitness that are important: cardiorespiratory, muscle strength, muscle endurance, and flexibility. After reviewing your current habits, design an exercise program that you can fit into your weekly schedule and that will help you remain physically fit.

Alcohol and the Law

Consult the statutes that govern the use of alcohol in the state where you attend school as well as the university conduct code. Write a summary of what you find that includes the penalties for violating those laws.

Design a Stress Management Plan

Identify the top five sources of significant stress in your life and when they cause the greatest disruption to your life during the week. Then, using the ideas from this chapter and those suggested at http://www.managingstress.com/, design a plan to diminish the negative effects of stress in your life. Write a two-page report that details both the causes of your stress and the plan you will use to combat it.

Prevent the Suicide of a Friend

You may meet someone during your college years who is deeply depressed and is showing signs of considering harming himself or herself. Visit one of the Internet sites that discusses suicide and deepen your understanding of this important topic so that you will have the correct words to say and will be prepared to help. Prepare a two-page report that identifies the Internet source you used and briefly summarize what you learned about this important topic.

Personal Tragedy Preparation List

Some families have constructed emergency shelters in their homes that are stocked with the basics for life, including food and water. You too can prepare for personal tragedies that may touch your life or the life of someone close to you by assembling a set of Bible passages that you find most comforting in times of trouble. Build or expand that spiritual "emergency kit" and share the passages most meaningful to you with your class.

SPIRITUAL REFLECTION JOURNAL

Read Job 1–2 and 42. Considering the experience of Job, write about a personal tragedy that you have experienced and compare your personal tragedy to that of Job. What questions did Job ask that you yourself have asked or are asking? What insights did Job gain from his experience that help you? What passages from Scripture help you the most when you are handling a personal tragedy?

Time in Prayer

In your personal time in prayer or in connection with others in your class, take time to pray for the following people and needs:

- That you may honor your body as the temple of the Holy Spirit by caring for it

- That you may develop a sleep schedule that gives your body adequate rest

- That you may be more conscious and careful about the kind of food you eat

- That you may avoid the temptation to misuse alcohol

- That you may discover and employ techniques to diminish the harmful stress in your life

- That you may prepare yourself to handle personal tragedy well

- For the person in your school who today is thinking about harming himself or herself

- For the person in your school who needs to be assured that his or her sins are forgiven

On the Web

The Internet can be a helpful resource as you look for ideas to make yourself a happier and more successful student. Visit the College Success page offered by Thomson Wadsworth for Web links that will help you grow further on this topic. Go to http://www.success.wadsworth.com/ and click on Resource Web Links.

In particular, we recommend the following:

http://www.mayoclinic.com/health/stress/sr99999/

http://www.mayoclinic.com/health/fitness/sm99999/

http://www.mayoclinic.com/health/sleep/sl99999/

http://www.nutrimundo.com/test_your_nutrition_knowlege.html

http://www.eatbetteramerica.com/

http://www.healthyeating.net/he_1.htm

Endnotes

1. Michael Breus, "How Much Sleep Do You Really Need," September 10, 2004, http://my.webmd.com/content/article/62/71838.htm.

2. Ibid.

3. M. A. Miller and R. H. Rahe, "Life Changes Scaling for the 1990s," *Journal of Psychosomatic Research*, Sept. 1977, Vol. 43, pp. 279–292.

Seeking Satisfaction in My Career 13

A person can do nothing better than to eat and drink and find satisfaction in their work. This too I see is from the hand of God, for without him who can eat or find enjoyment?

Ecclesiastes 2:24–25 (author's translation)

- **What will the work world be like in my future?**

- **What can I do to discover, confirm, or change my vocational goal?**

- **How does my status as a Christian influence my career planning?**

- **What can I do now, as a college student, to prepare for the day I look for a professional position?**

God created humans with both the capacity and the passion for work. On a bad day, work itself may seem inherently evil, but the Bible portrays work as part of God's perfect creation. Early in the Book of Genesis, the inspired author describes a wonderful world without the presence of sin. In that perfect world, God gave Adam and Eve the responsibility of working in and caring for the Garden of Eden (Gen 2:15). But once that perfect world became contaminated by sin, even the work of caring for the Garden of Eden became a tiresome burden. The workday was no longer filled with joy and satisfaction but rather marred by literal and figurative "thorns, thistles, and sweat." (Gen 3:17–20) Any professional will tell you that some days his or her work seems unsatisfying, frustrating, and emotionally draining. Fortunately, not every workday is like that. As the writer of Ecclesiastes states, we can still find satisfaction and enjoyment in our professional work when we pursue it in connection with God's plan for us. "A person can do nothing better than to eat and drink and find satisfaction in their work. This too I see is from the hand of God, for without him who can eat or find enjoyment?" (Eccl 2:24–25, author's translation)

Finding a Career Takes Work

From the start, let us acknowledge that the selection of a career path and major is both complex and time consuming. Many schools do not give students academic credit for the time and energy they invest in this process. Nevertheless, this critical part of your college life deserves an appropriate amount of your time, attention, and energy. Toward that end, this chapter will guide you through the process of preparing for your career as a college student, which includes learning more about the work world in your future. It will offer suggestions on how to discover, confirm, or change your career plans. And it will suggest specific tasks that will prepare you for the first step into your professional world. At each step along the way, we will offer suggestions on how a member of God's family may investigate and pursue these very important plans.

The World of Work in Your Future

You may be returning to school after having spent time in the work world, or your work experience may be limited to part-time summer jobs. In either case, the work world you will enter and experience in the first ten years of your career will be different from the one you have experienced in the past. For that reason, you need to learn as much as you can about the world of work in your future.

General Predictions

A good place to begin looking for the picture of that world is within the general forecast articles available from the Bureau of Labor Statistics (http://www.bls.gov/). The current postings on this site discuss the work world from the present to 2014. Here you may read projections about both the general work environment and specific career fields. For example, the BLS predicts that your future workplace and its employees will increasingly be influenced by a global rather than a local economy. Despite this increase in the playing field, the speed of all sectors in the work world will need to become faster and more efficient to remain competitive. Finding a job will increasingly depend on personal introductions by members of the organization rather than through anonymous applications. And once positioned, the future employee can expect to work more frequently in a team on which effective communication and problem-solving skills are strongly valued. Because the knowledge and skills required for a position will continue to evolve, all professionals will need to improve their knowledge and skills through continuing education (home-study courses, seminars, and conferences). One thing that seems to be guaranteed is change. Have you considered that the job you will hold in the future may not even exist at the moment? This fact favors college graduates who have learned to educate themselves and adapt to new challenges.

Career Field Predictions

Apart from these general descriptions of the work world, the Bureau of Labor Statistics also offers predictions on specific career fields. For example, it predicts that the need for registered nurses will increase 29.4 percent by 2014.

Similarly, the need for postsecondary teachers will increase 32.2 percent, and the call for accountants will increase 22.4 percent. By 2014, the computing demands of our society will increase the need for software engineers 48.4 percent. Are you curious about the forecast for one or more career fields of interest to you? If you are, visit the BLS Web site to learn more. And whether you are pursuing general trends or specific predictions, spend time now learning as much as you can about the work world of tomorrow, because it will make a difference in how you prepare yourself today.

Discovering, Confirming, and Changing Your Choice

The process of making a career choice calls for discovery, confirmation, and change. Although it is important to keep moving forward toward a final career choice, it is unwise to rush the process. The typical college student experiences and even re-experiences all three stages of making a career decision en route to a final choice. This takes time, but the key is to invest that time of reflection wisely. Toward that end, this portion of the chapter will raise questions you will wish to consider as well as suggest tools and techniques you may use in answering them. What does your work personality look like? What personal values will influence your decision? How can you identify career options that lend themselves to someone with your personality and values? What individuals and tools can be resources for this investigation? Finally, how does your status as a Christian affect this planning process?

What Is My Work Personality?

God has created each of us and shaped us through our experiences in life. As a result, we all bring a unique personality to the career search. The more we know about that personality, the easier it is to pick careers that are commensurate with who we are. As a starting point, consider the following list of adjectives that may describe a person's personality. Where do you find yourself on this list?

Logical	*Outgoing*	*Modest*
Intellectual	*Shy*	*Fiery*
Cooperative	*Energetic*	*Curious*
Adventurous	*Forceful*	*Emotional*
Aggressive	*Calm*	

Dr. John Holland, a psychologist at Johns Hopkins University, has studied the people employed in various career fields and observed a connection between the types of careers people enjoyed and their personality. This led Holland to separate people into six general personality types: realistic, investigative, artistic, social, enterprising, and conventional. He further identified the careers that tended to attract people of one type rather than another. Using this research, individuals can measure their personality and then learn what careers attract people of their personality type.[1]

Realistic people prefer careers in science or mechanical areas that require fine motor coordination and physical strength. They see themselves as practical people who prefer to invest themselves in tasks that produce concrete results. Realistic personalities are attracted to careers such as agricultural engineer, electrical contractor, electronics technician, or computer graphics designer.

Investigative people like intellectual stimulation. They would rather work on an abstract project that requires thought and organizational skills than a project that requires them to work manually on a concrete task. These are the analytical, rational problem solvers. Investigative personalities are attracted to careers such as urban planner, chemical engineer, flight engineer, quality control technician, computer programmer, physician, and college professor.

Artistic people also enjoy the abstract world but prefer the aesthetic to the scientific. They prefer to work independently and without a lot of structure on creative projects that give voice to their own self-expression. Artistic personalities are attracted to careers such as architect, actor, interior decorator, journalist, sculptor, librarian, and public relations specialist.

Social people value interpersonal relationships that allow them to express kindness, care, and understanding to others. They enjoy speaking with others one-to-one or in small groups with the goal of providing help and support. Social personalities are attracted to careers such as nurse, teacher, social worker, counselor, minister, travel agent, and convention planner.

Enterprising people are interested in people and carrying forward the mission of their organization. They are risk-taking and assertive, working as leaders directing and persuading others in their course of action. Enterprising personalities are attracted to careers such as banker, health administrator, judge, lawyer, sales representative, and city manager.

Finally, conventional people are detail-oriented people who like to plan and organize. They are self-controlled and structured individuals who enjoy following clear guidelines in their work life. They finish what they start and value that quality in others. Conventional personalities are attracted to careers such as accountant, data processor, hospital administrator, insurance administrator, office manager, auditor, and statistician.

It is clear from this small sample of John Holland's work that a career choice may be greatly influenced by our personality. As part of your career investigation process, you may complete the John Holland Self-Directed Search online (http://www.self-directed-search.com/index.html).

What Are My Work Values?

In addition to your personality, your personal values can play a key role in the selection of a career. These values are related to your personality but deal more generally with your perspective on the work world. In order to get a clearer picture of your work values, consider how you would answer the following questions:

Do you see your career as primarily a way to make money or primarily as a way of helping others?
Is it important that your work be an extension of your Christianity?
Are you willing to work weekends and holidays?

Do you wish to travel extensively or remain close to home?

Do you wish to dress up for work or dress down for work?

Are you willing to take work home at night or not?

Would you prefer fewer hours at a less satisfying task or more hours at a more satisfying task?

How does work time relate to family time?

What income and benefit package will give you the lifestyle you desire?

How much vacation time do you need each year?

The answer to these and other questions like them will give you a perspective on the general work values you currently hold.

Because others can help us see ourselves for who we are, it is wise to use the services of the career center on your campus when investigating both your work personality and work values. There you will find professionals who are eager to help you in this process. They will provide you with instruments that allow you to investigate both your personality and your work values; these instruments may include the Keirsey Temperament Sorter, the Strong Campbell Interest Inventory (SCII), SIGI Plus, Focus II, and the John Holland inventory just mentioned. Conclusions drawn from one assessment tool alone are not as meaningful as conclusions drawn from several assessment tools. That is why your career counselor will likely suggest that you complete more than one vocational inventory. Then personal time spent with a career counselor can help you interpret the results of those inventories and build the bridge between where you are now and where you would like to be with your career planning.

How Do I Personalize My Career Choice?

Once you have come to a better understanding of your work personality and work values, it is time to personalize your career choice. There are two approaches to personalizing your career choice, each with its own advantages and disadvantages. You can decide to pursue a specific career and then select a major that will lead to it, or you can select a major first and then determine which career you will pursue later. In either case, first-year students need to do some research.

The Call to Ministry

As Jesus prepared to send out seventy-two of his followers to announce the coming of his kingdom, he noted that the "harvest was plentiful but the workers were few." (Luke 10:2) Today there are still thousands of people who need to hear about Jesus and who need to grow their faith. Thus a need remains for pastors, teachers, missionaries, and evangelists (Eph 4:11–13). Listen carefully for the Lord's voice. Perhaps he is calling you to such service.

Career Directed If you have already selected a career toward which you are working, it would be wise to pause and broaden the scope of your search. The first-semester college students we have met can name about fifty specific occupations when they are asked to create a list. By contrast, *The Dictionary of Occupational Titles* published by the U.S. Department of Labor lists some 20,000 occupations. That means many college students are making an initial career choice knowing less than 1 percent of the available options. A little research can open your eyes to occupations previously unknown to you but that may fit very well with your personality and work values. Because the average college student changes his or her major three times, you should not feel that this kind of change indicates any kind of weakness. It is a natural part of getting to know yourself and the work world better.

Major Directed If you have selected a major but are uncertain about which career to pursue, it will help to know how graduates in your major from your school are currently employed. Your career center may have collected this type of data. If not, visit the site maintained by Dickinson College at http://www. dickinson.edu/career/student/majorcareerindex.html. This archive lists all of the major courses of study offered by the college as well as the occupations in which the graduates of their majors have found placement.

Career Investigation Once you have settled on a possible career or (even better) careers, it is time to investigate those occupations more completely. You will want to know answers to questions like the following.

> What would I be doing on a weekly basis if I took this job?
> What working conditions are associated with this job?
> What education, training, or experience is necessary to enter this occupation?
> What are the prospects of my finding a job like this when I graduate?
> What income and benefits would I enjoy in this occupation?

The career center on your campus will be an important ally to you in answering these kinds of questions. Those professionals have access to a number of resources and will likely encourage you to consult with your academic advisor, attend job fairs, join the campus association or club associated with your major, and speak with recruiters. You may also wish to pursue the answers to these questions online. One of the most productive online sites you can visit for this information is the one maintained by the U.S. Department of Labor, Bureau of Labor and Statistics at http://www.bls.gov/oco/home.htm. Each year, the BLS provides visitors to the site with an updated *Occupational Outlook Handbook* in which each of the preceding questions is answered for the occupations it has researched. In certain cases, your career path requires a graduate school degree. If that is the case, consider visiting http://www.gradschools.com/ for a detailed listing of graduate schools that have an academic program tailored to meet your needs. For additional Web sites that will support your career investigation, see the list provided under "On the Web" at the end of the chapter.

How Does My Christianity Affect My Career Choice?

As you face a critical decision about your major and career choice, you need to learn about the future work world, the projections for various careers, your own personality, and your work values. But the career choice of a Christian is

Danger Zone

As you personalize your career choice, be aware of falling into the "danger zone"—harboring attitudes or behaviors that will make your search less productive:

- Making your choice without knowing all the options available

- Focusing on just one factor when making your decision (e.g., salary)

- Ignoring the potential impact on your family life

- Making a decision without speaking to someone who is working in that career

- Rushing your decision and not allowing time for extended reflection

- Limiting yourself to just one career option without an alternate plan

- Taking a major because it is supposed to be "easy"

- Believing that you will have only one career during your lifetime

- Pursuing a career only because someone else thinks it is a good idea

Undecided or Underdecided

In some ways, schools are designed for people who have already made a decision about their major. That can make it uncomfortable for students who either are undecided about their major or have significant reservations about their current choice. If you are undecided or underdecided, realize that you have a great advantage over students "who know for sure" what they want to do. You can approach the career investigation phase of your college life in a less biased way, allowing you to see options that a decided student may miss. Your academic advisor, academic advising center, or career center can be a wonderful aid as you work toward clarity. Just keep moving forward. There is nothing wrong with being undecided as long as you are doing things that help you move forward toward a decision.

also affected by his or her relationship with the Lord. As the inspired author says, "Commit to the LORD whatever you do, and your plans will succeed." (Prov 16:3) That commitment includes our willingness both to pray for direction and to weigh any option with our Christian values in plain sight.

Prayer The question of how to pray about such a matter depends on how you read and understand the Bible when it speaks about God and your future. Has God already determined the specific career you will have in life, or has he allowed you to make a free choice in this matter? Bible-believing Christians have looked at the evidence and come to both conclusions. On the one hand, the Bible gives very clear examples that illustrate God's selection of specific vocations for certain people. In the case of Jeremiah and even before his birth, the Lord predetermined that Jeremiah would be a prophet of God who would speak to the nations (Jer 1:4). Based on texts like these, some Christians presume that God predetermines the vocation of all believers. If that is your belief, then pray to the Lord so that he may reveal to you what he has planned your life to be.

By contrast, other Christians have been reluctant to generalize such Bible passages to all believers. They believe that the Lord gives Christians the free will to select from any number of vocational paths although he knows the subsequent outcome of any choice they might make.

If this is your belief, then pray for insight from the one who knows the advantages and disadvantages of your options so that he may lead you to the path that will be best for you. In either case, avoid the error of the Israelites who were taken in by the Gibeonite deception when they sampled the provisions but failed to consult the Lord.

Christian Values   Furthermore, the process of selecting a career path and a future employer will also be influenced by your Christian values. Clearly one of the advantages of graduating from college and pursuing a career is that it will produce an income for you and for your family. Unfortunately, the blessing of an income can turn into an obsession. As the author of Ecclesiastes looks for meaning in life, he considers whether meaning may be found in accumulating more and more wealth. His conclusion is clear: "Whoever loves money never has money enough; whoever loves wealth is never satisfied with his income. This too is meaningless." (Eccl 5:10) This same caution comes to us in the New Testament as well. Jesus told the story of a rich man who became completely obsessed with his growing wealth. He was determined to build more and more storage barns for his grain and his goods, presuming that this would create a life of happiness and ease for him. But Jesus noted that in the midst of his celebration, he failed to take into account his own spiritual health. The very night he was planning his earthly life of leisure, he died and his property became the property of another. "This is how it will be for anyone who stores up things for himself but is not rich toward God." (Luke 12:21) Christians certainly take income into account as they select a vocation, but they carefully guard against an obsession with financial matters that distorts reality.

The Bible also affirms the importance of time off from work and time in God's Word. Among the Ten Commandments is a clear directive to set aside time each week to rest physically and to spend time in worship and meditation on God's Word. "Remember the Sabbath day by keeping it holy. Six days you shall labor and do all your work, but the seventh day is a Sabbath to the LORD your God." (Exod 20:8–10a) As you do your vocational planning, ask whether the career you are considering will allow you time both to rest physically and to grow spiritually during the week.

Finally, the Bible challenges us to see our career not merely as a means of generating income for our family, but also as a tool that glorifies God and advances the cause of his church on earth. This perspective is more and more difficult to maintain in a world that bombards us with the message that we are the center of life's stage. That is not the view encouraged in God's Word. When

STUDENT VOICE

Peter Beck

Major: Art Education
Hometown: Lake Mills, Wisconsin
School: Concordia University

I did not enter college knowing what I wanted to do with my life, but my experience in the last four years has filled me with a passion for teaching. Before my senior year, I spent several months working in Nepal with orphaned children. This powerfully shaped my understanding of the world's need for teachers, particularly teachers who split their energies between self-improvement and improving the lives of those around them. This kind of sacrifice is the fuel for social change.

Jesus wished to summarize all of the law, he offered the following encouragement. First of all love the Lord with all your heart, soul, and mind. Secondly, love those with whom you share this world as you would love yourself (Matt 22:34–40). These words challenge us to think of our career in a way that the world does not. And that teaching challenges us to consider ways in which the career we select may glorify God and help others.

Living College Life to Get an Interview

All the advice and direction that you have read so far suggests that you can be doing important things now to select a career. Once you have made that career choice, you can do other things during your college years to position yourself for that first job interview. These include gaining personal experience in the career you have chosen, gathering the evidence that you will use to make your case, and organizing your résumé.

Get Personal Experience

You can read about it, but nothing is like being there. So it makes sense to use every opportunity to make personal contact with someone in the career you have selected, or even better, the organization you hope will employ you when you graduate. This personal contact can take a number of forms. You can interview several people holding the career that is interesting to you. Find out what they enjoy and what they find less enjoyable about their work. One or more of those individuals may also be willing to let you shadow them as they go about their work. This "job shadowing" may lead to a part-time job, a

Transferable Skills

Although each career position is unique, certain transferable skills apply in many employment settings. Be ready to showcase the transferable skills you have developed:

Public speaking	Commitment
Integrity	Teamwork
Writing	Critical thinking
Leadership	Interpersonal communication

summer job, an internship, or a volunteer opportunity that allows you to have more sustained contact with this career or organization. This personal experience will help you confirm your career choice as well as build a network of people who can help you in the future.

Gather Your Evidence and Support Team

In almost all career fields, you will compete with other applicants for the position you desire. Therefore, you need to know what makes you look like a desirable hire and how to begin collecting that evidence even as a first-year student in college. It is unwise to assume you will know the type of evidence your future employer is seeking without investigation. When you interview people who hold the type of position you would like to have and when you work part-time or volunteer at that organization, find out all you can about the qualities of a desirable applicant. Each career and even each organization may have unique qualities they find desirable. For example, is a minimum college GPA required for application? What is the GPA of those who are subsequently granted interviews? Is membership in or leadership of a campus organization viewed favorably during the hiring process? What type of volunteer work will make my application stand out from others? The answer to these and other questions will help you identify the evidence that will help your cause.

Furthermore, as you work, intern, or volunteer in the career field that interests you, you will network with individuals who may help you get your first career placement. An employer that posts an opening in the organization is likely to receive dozens if not hundreds of applications. One way to make your application stand out is to have a personal recommendation from a current employee. Even if you have worked at a lower-level position in that organization, personal knowledge of your work ethic, your honesty, and your intellect can give you an advantage that other applicants do not have. It is well worth the time and effort you spend building a strong professional network.

Prepare Your Résumé

Typically, prospective employers ask to see your résumé as part of the application process. A résumé is a summary of your qualifications and is intended to convince your prospective employer that you are worthy of an interview. It is your first opportunity to sell yourself, so you will want to make it as effective and convincing as it can be. A typical recruiter spends only eight seconds scanning your résumé before deciding whether to interview you, so you will want your prospective employer to see accessible and convincing evidence within those eight seconds.

The format of the résumé depends on the type of career path you chose. To determine the general résumé format used by applicants in your career field, visit your academic advisor or the career center. Generally, a résumé is one page long, providing the reader with a summary of your qualifications under several standard headings. At the top of the page you will place your full name and contact information, including current address, phone number, and e-mail address.

Beneath this contact information the reader expects to encounter several standard categories that summarize your desires, experience, and strengths. The first is *OBJECTIVE*. Under this heading, identify the specific position that you wish to have within the organization. Keep the language simple and clear, using terminology that is unique to the organization with whom you are seeking employment.

EDUCATION is the next category. Provide the names of all the schools you have attended since graduating from high school, beginning with your most recent graduation. Identify the institution(s) from which you have graduated, the degree you received, your major and minor, any academic honors you received, and your GPA as long as it is greater than 3.00 on a 4-point scale.

The third category is *EMPLOYMENT HISTORY*. Again, beginning with your most recent employment, identify the jobs you have had that promote your ability to do the job you seek. Provide the name of the organization or company, your title (if applicable), and a summary of your responsibilities. Do all you can to showcase the skills your future employer would find desirable, particularly those that demonstrate the level of responsibility you carried.

The fourth category is the *ACTIVITIES* in which you have participated that were not directly connected to past employment. Once again, provide the names of the organizations, positions you held, and any relevant accomplishments that suggest your desirability as an employee.

Under the fifth category, *INTERESTS*, list any unique hobbies or passions you enjoy. Here you might communicate your interest in building your own airplane, reading mystery novels, acting in a local theater troupe, or driving a stock car. This information will not play a larger role than your education or work experience in convincing your reader to give you an interview, but your unique interests may make your name stand out on the list of prospective candidates in ways that are difficult to predict.

The last item on your résumé is *REFERENCES*. References are people who either have volunteered to write letters of recommendation on your behalf or are willing to give an oral summary of your value as a potential employee. Select two to four people who will give you the strongest recommendation, and always get their permission to offer their names as potential references. Your future employer will let you know if they would like to contact these references. So rather than consuming page space with a list of potential references and their contact information, simply state on your résumé that references are "available upon request."

Given the important impression that the résumé gives, have others read it and check for typographical and grammatical errors. You do not want an error in spelling, grammar, punctuation, or spacing to give the impression that you are careless and less than thoughtful in your work. Because larger employers use computer technology to scan hundreds of résumés and sort them for their value, speak with your career center about selecting words for your résumé that not only are persuasive to the human eye but also will be detected by the electronic eye.

The presentation of your résumé may seem too remote for consideration when research papers and lab reports demand your time and attention. But now is the time to begin. Create a file titled "Professional Résumé" and begin to enter evidence under each of the categories. This file will remind you of things you can do now to enhance your employability and store evidence that you may otherwise forget.

The process of coming to clarity on your career choice can be both complex and time consuming. But the strategic investment of time and energy as directed in this chapter will pay off in the long run for you. And as you think, also take time to pray that the Lord may guide you to a satisfactory career.

Exercises for **Success**

Review Questions

1. Describe three general trends in the work world that may affect your search for employment.

2. Explain how Christian values will affect how you think about career selection and job satisfaction.

3. List three attitudes or behaviors that diminish the effectiveness of your career search.

Developing a Mission Statement

Effective career planning requires a vision of where you would like to be at the close of your career planning. Franklin Covey has helped thousands of people come to greater clarity on this topic through workshops and published material. Visit http://www.franklincovey.com/mission-builder/index.html, where you will be led through an exercise that helps you produce your own personal mission statement.

Exploring Your Career Personality and Values

Visit the career center on your campus and find out which tools you might use to explore your career personality and values. The advisors may point you to the Keirsey Temperament Sorter, the Strong Campbell Interest Inventory (SCII), SIGI Plus, or Focus II. Many students have also used the John Holland Self-Directed Search to learn more about their vocational personality and values.

This inventory, available online at http://www.self-directed-search.com/index.html, takes about fifteen minutes to complete and results in an eight- to sixteen-page personalized report that not only summarizes your personality and values but also provides a list of occupations that most closely match your interests. A fee is charged for this service.

Vocational Interview

Pick three careers that interest you. Identify people who are employed in each career and interview them for at least fifteen minutes. Find out all you can about what they do every day at work, what they like most about their workweek, and what they like the least. Condense the product of your interviews into a two-page summary report.

Career Evaluation

Pick one of the careers that you are most closely drawn to at this time and complete the following evaluation form. Behind each statement place a "+" if it is true of you, a "−" if it is not true about you, and a "?" if you are not sure. Write any thoughts you have about that statement in the box at the right.

Statement	+−?	Additional Thoughts
My personality and values are in harmony with my choice.		
I have visited the career center to learn more about myself.		
I know what the entry-level requirements are for this career.		
I can afford the time and money necessary to prepare for this career.		
I have personally visited with someone who works in this career.		
I know both the advantages and disadvantages of this career.		
My teachers, friends, and relatives think I would be happy in this career.		
My weaknesses will not be a problem in this career.		
I am aware of the salary and benefits offered in this career.		
I know the future outlook for this career.		
I have spent personal time working or volunteering in this career area.		

Writing Your Résumé

Visit your career center to learn all you can about the type of résumé applicants use for the career that most interests you. Prepare a blank copy of that résumé with its major headings and then fill in as much information as you can. Keep this initial résumé in a file folder so that you can add to it throughout your time in college.

SPIRITUAL REFLECTION JOURNAL

Work has been part of the life of human beings since the Garden of Eden. Through such work we can purchase the basics of life such as food, clothing, and shelter. But the money from work can also be used for "luxury" items that can appear to be necessities. Read the words of Jesus in Matthew 6:19–24. In your own words, explain what that portion of Scripture means to you as you think about your future career.

Time in Prayer

In your personal time in prayer or in connection with others in your class, take time to pray for the following people and needs:

- For the Lord's guidance during your time of career investigation

- That the Lord may lead you to clarity about the career you will pursue

- That the Lord may encourage the person in your class who is struggling with this decision

- That the Lord may lead you to full-time church work if that is his will for you

- That the Lord may encourage those called to mission fields

On the Web

The Internet can be a helpful resource as you look for ideas to make yourself a happier and more successful student. Visit the College Success page offered by Thomson Wadsworth for Web links that will help you grow further on this topic. Go to http://www.success.wadsworth.com/ and click on Resource Web Links.

In particular, we recommend the following:

http://www.bls.gov/

http://www.rileyguide.com/

http://www.monster.com/

http://www.ajb.dni.us/

http://www.jobweb.com/

http://www.careerpath.com/

http://www.salary.com/

http://www.internships.com/

http://www.jobhuntersbible.com/

http://keirsey.com/

Endnote

1. John L. Holland, *Self-Directed Search Manual* (Odessa, FL: Psychological Assessment Resources, 1994).

Epilogue

How is it possible that this semester is almost done? It seems like just yesterday that you were unpacking your car and purchasing your textbooks. With all the papers and exams of the last weeks, there has not been time to reflect on and to celebrate just how much you have changed. You were once the least experienced person on campus, searching the hallways for your English composition class and feeling overwhelmed by the details of the class syllabus. Now you know more than anyone else about what it takes to make it as a college freshman. Old time management habits have given way to new ways of organizing and prioritizing your week. You have modified old habits of reading and writing to meet the demands of the college experience. And you have come to see that healthy relationships can be as important to your college success as going to class.

While some of you may wish to postpone the celebration of your growth until you graduate, we want to celebrate the success of this semester now. You made it! We congratulate you on your accomplishment and give thanks that God has answered our prayers for your success. We know that your achievements are no accident but have an intimate connection to his presence in your life. You have found success because the Lord was with you, illuminating your path with the light of his Word.

But now what? What are you going to do with everything you have learned? We have two suggestions. First, realize that by reading this book, you have been studying not just a success plan for college but a success plan for living. Success and happiness have eluded the grasp of many people because they have missed or ignored the basic advice given here. As you take the next steps in your college education and into the world beyond, export what you have learned here into that life. We promise that it will not disappoint you.

The second encouragement we offer is on behalf of the next group of first-year students who are waiting to take your place. They are facing the same challenges you faced only a few months ago. To become successful college students, they need to know what you know and do what you have done. Toward that end, we know that they will benefit immensely from the insights and support that you can share with them. Recognize that God has been a blessing to you so that you might now be a blessing to others. That is how his light on the path grows brighter.

Index

Index